SOME HEROES
OF THE
AMERICAN REVOLUTION

BY
REV. J. D. BAILEY

1924
BAND & WHITE, PRINTERS
SPARTANBURG, S. C.

CONTENTS

	PAGE
FOREWORD	7
GENERAL DANIEL MORGAN	9
GENERAL ANDREW PICKENS	24
LIEUTENANT-COLONEL JOHN EAGER HOWARD	38
LIEUTENANT-COLONEL WILLIAM WASHINGTON	44
COLONEL JOHN THOMAS, SR	57
COLONEL JAMES WILLIAMS	70
COLONEL SAMUEL HAMMOND	116
LIEUTENANT-COLONEL BENJAMIN ROEBUCK	132
COLONEL THOMAS BRANDON	141
COLONEL ELIJAH CLARKE	153
LIEUTENANT-COLONEL WILLIAM FARR	185
COLONEL JOSEPH HUGHES	195
MAJOR JOSEPH MCJUNKIN	216
MAJOR THOMAS YOUNG	250

SOME OTHER HEROIC PERSONAGES AND THRILLING INCIDENTS—

Anne Kennedy	267
Dicey Langston	270
A Remarkable Adventure of Samuel Clowney	274
William Sharp's Adventures at Grindal's and Love's Ford	276
Major Samuel Otterson	278
The Narrow Escape of Captain James Caldwell	279
The Rugged Honesty of Adam Skain	280
"Long Sam" Abney	280
"Old" Arthur Patterson	281
The Goforth Brothers	282
Another Whig Soldier Kills His Brother	283
The Four Logan Brothers	283
The Affair at Graham's Fort	284
A Tory's Sad Experience at Kings Mountain	285
The Origin of the Name Fairforest	286

Foreword

UT FEW, if any sections in the Southland, are richer in Revolutionary history than that of upper South Carolina. Yonder in the extreme northern part of the State stands Kings Mountain like a mighty sentinel, rearing its head heavenward, forming the pivot on which the tide turned in favor of the liberty of the American Colonies. A few miles to the westward, near the base of Thickety Mountain, lies the elevated plain of The Cowpens, where the "Bloody" and seemingly unconquerable Tarleton met his Waterloo. These two mighty victories, won in the darkest days of the war, did more to hearten the lovers of freedom and hasten the culmination of full liberty than any other. Then, there was Musgrove's Mill, Blackstocks, Fishdam, Thickety Fort, Prince's Fort, First and Second Cedar Spring, to say nothing of the many daring and heroic achievements of a lesser nature. There are but few square acres together in all our territory that did not at some time drink the blood of friend or foe and witnessed more or less suffering endured by the heroes and heroines of Independence Unfortunately for us, no early chronicler arose to record their names and deeds, as was done in other sections.

Though a Wisconsin man, no one ever did more to rescue our local history from oblivion than Lyman C. Draper, as his "Kings Mountain and Its Heroes" will verify. The one among us that did most was the Rev. James H. Saye, a noted Presbyterian divine, who more than eighty years ago wrote a "Memoir of Major Joseph McJunkin," and gathered many recollections from the Revolutionary survivors whom he knew, and committed them to manuscript form The "Memoir of McJunkin" came perilously near being lost, it being published as a serial in a Richmond, Va., paper in the forties; but, fortunately, we rescued it, and a part of the manuscript in the nick of time. These have been an invaluable source from which to draw in compiling the following articles.

From early life, having the most profound admiration and veneration for those who participated in the mighty struggle for independence, during the past forty years as we have itinerated among the Baptist churches in Union, Spartanburg and Cherokee counties, we have left no stone unturned, as far as we were able, to secure any and everything bearing on local Revolutionary history. In the following narratives, naturally we have drawn freely on these, but are indebted to Saye's "Memoir of McJunkin" and Draper's "Kings Mountain and Its Heroes" more than all.

Several months ago Charles O. Hearon, editor of *The Spartanburg Hearld,* repeatedly urged us to put our collections in a more durable and tangible form, by writing them up for his paper. His request was granted, and we chose to write the lives of the leaders who figured most prominently in our section, recording their names and achievements, rather than one straight narrative. Writing in that manner, naturally there will be repetitions. Where different ones took part in the same contest, while we have tried to emphasize the part each one took, yet many took part in the same acts, and therefore some repetitions are unavoidable.

The narratives published in *The Spartanburg Herald* have been slightly changed and re-arranged, but the bulk of the matter is just as it was published in *The Herald,* and because of the generosity and patriotism of Horace L. Bomar they are now presented to the public in book form, trusting that it will be a small addition to our local history.

J. D. BAILEY.

Cowpens, S. C., June, 1924.

The Life of General Daniel Morgan

HE PARENTS of Daniel Morgan were said to be of Welsh extraction, but little is known of them or of his early childhood. Authorities differ as to the date and place of his birth. One says that it was in 1736, another in 1737, but General Wade Hampton, the Cowpens Centennial orator, fixed it in Huntington County, New Jersey, in 1735. When about seventeen years of age, he removed to Jefferson County, Virginia, where he labored on a farm.

When war broke out between France and England in 1755, he began his military career as a teamster in Braddock's army. This, and subsequent team work, gave him the sobriquet of "The Old Wagoner." After Braddock's disastrous defeat, Morgan did good service in bringing off the wounded. It was at this time that he became acquainted with George Washington. A little later he was attached to the quartermaster department, and his duty was to haul supplies to the military posts along the frontier.

Beginning of Military Career

In 1757 a British lieutenant struck Morgan with the flat side of his sword, whereupon Morgan knocked him down, and it is said that his punishment for this offense was five hundred lashes. The officer, being afterwards convinced of his cruel error, made every amend in his power to the maltreated Morgan, who, satisfied with the contrition evinced by the officer, magnanimously forgave him. Nor did the recollection of this personal outrage operate in the least to prejudice him against British officers in the Revolution, for it is well known that those who fell into Morgan's hands received only kind treatment. Soon after that affair, at the head of a few backwoodsmen, he defeated a small force of French and Indians and

DANIEL MORGAN

received from Governor Dinwiddie an ensign's commission. While on his way to Winchester with dispatches, he encountered a body of Indians and a fierce fight took place, in which nearly all of his comrades were killed and Morgan himself shot through the neck with a musket ball. Almost fainting because of his wound, which he thought at that time to be fatal, he resolved nevertheless not to leave his scalp in the hands of the Indians. Falling forward, with his arms tightly clasped around the neck of his stalwart horse, though the mists were gathering before his eyes, he spurred away through the forest paths until his foremost Indian pursuer, unable to come up with him, hurled his tomahawk after him, with a yell of baffled rage, and gave up the chase. This was the only wound he ever received.

About 1762, Morgan obtained a grant of land a few miles east from Winchester and there he devoted himself to farming and stockraising. He married Miss Abigail Bailey, the daughter of a farmer in that neighborhood, a woman of rare beauty and of loftiness of character. He named his home "Soldier's Rest," but he was not allowed to rest long, for he was soon called away by Pontiac's war, in which he served as a lieutenant. For eight or ten years following 1765 he prospered greatly as a farmer and acquired considerable property. In 1771 he was commissioned captain of the militia of Frederick County, and two years later served in Lord Dunmore's war on the frontier.

Lexington having been fought in April, 1775, in June Congress called for ten companies of riflemen from the colonies of Pennsyl-

His Answer to the Call of Independence vania, Maryland and Virginia to join the Continental Army in besieging Boston. Morgan responded to the call by raising a company of ninety-six Virginians, of which he was chosen captain. About the middle of July he reached Cambridge, and at the head of his company he reported to General Washington for duty.

A month later he was detached at the head of three companies to take part in Arnold's memorable march through the wilderness of Maine against Quebec. On November 13 he and his men were the first to cross the St. Lawrence and reconnoiter the approaches to Quebec, which were found to be too strongly defended to be attacked with any hope of success.

The great assault was delayed until January 1, 1776, when General Montgomery was killed and Arnold disabled. Morgan then stormed the battery opposed to him and fought his way far into the town, but having no adequate support, his success only isolated him from the main army and made him an easy prey for the enemy. He and his detachment were surrounded and captured. General Carleton, the British commander, so greatly admired his bravery that he treated him kindly.

While Morgan was in confinement at Quebec the following anecdote told by himself manifests the high opinion entertained by the enemy of his military talent, as shown by his conduct in the assault. He was visited occasionally by a British officer, to him unknown, but from his uniform he appeared to belong to the navy, and an officer of distinction. During one of his visits, after conversing upon many topics, he asked Morgan if he did not begin to be convinced that the resistance of America was visionary; and he endeavored to impress him with the disastrous consequences which must follow if the idle attempt was persevered in, and very kindly exhorted him to renounce the ill-advised undertaking. He declared, with seeming sincerity and candor, his admiration of Morgan's spirit and enterprise, which, he said, were worthy of a better cause, and told him if he would agree to withdraw from the American and join the British standard, he was authorized to promise him the commission, rank and emoluments of a colonel of the Royal Army. Morgan rejected the proposition with disdain, and concluded his reply by saying "that he hoped he would never again insult him in his distressed and unfortunate situation by making him an offer which plainly implied that he thought him a rascal." The officer withdrew and the offer was never made again.

The following summer he was released on parole. When he arrived in New York, Morgan cast himself on his native soil as if to embrace it, and cried aloud, "O, my country." Reporting at once to General Washington, the commander-in-chief, he transmitted his views of the patriot soldier in the following letter:

"Harlem Heights,
"September 20th, 1776.
"To the President of Congress:
"Sir:—I would beg leave to recommend to the particular notice of Congress Captain Daniel Morgan, just returned among the pris-

oners from Canada. His conduct as an officer on the expedition with General Arnold last fall, his intrepid behaviour in the assault upon Quebec, when the brave Montgomery fell, the inflexible attachment he professed to our cause during his imprisonment, and which he perseveres in, all, in my opinion, entitle him to the favor of Congress, and leads one to believe that in his promotion the State will gain a good and valuable officer.

"I am, sir,

"Your very humble servant,

"GEORGE WASHINGTON."

About the beginning of 1777, having been duly exchanged and released from parole, Captain Morgan raised a regiment of rifles and joined the army at Morristown, N. J., late in March. In the meantime, Congress commissioned him as colonel. By an extremely skilful campaign the following June, Washington prevented General Howe from crossing into New Jersey. Morgan's services in reconnoitering were considered invaluable.

Burgoyne's descent into northern New Jersey made it desirable to effect as strong concentration as possible to oppose him. In August, Morgan was sent with his regiment to join the army near Stillwater, which was now under General Gates. "From this force of about five hundred picked riflemen," said Washington in a letter to Governor George Clinton, "I expect the most eminent services," and he was not disappointed.

In the bloody battle of Freeman's Farm, September 19th, in which Arnold frustrated Burgoyne's attempt to dislodge the American left wing from Bemis Heights, Morgan played a principal part, and in the final conflict of October 7th, in which the British Army was wrecked, his services were equally valuable. It is said that when Burgoyne was introduced to Morgan after the surrender at Saratoga, he seized him by the hand and exclaimed, "My dear sir, you command the finest regiment in the world."

After this great victory, Gates was unwilling that Morgan and his regiment should go back to Washington, and it was with difficulty that he obtained them. At length, on November 18, 1777, Morgan joined Washington at Whitemarsh, near Philadelphia, in time to take part in the affair at Chestnut Hill, December the 8th. He served in the campaigns around Philadelphia in 1778. A year later, June, 1779, owing to the dissatisfaction of many officers with the acts of Congress relative to promotions, and finding his health seriously impaired, Morgan resigned and returned to his home near Winchester.

When General Gates took command of the Southern army in June, 1780, Morgan was urged to enter the service again, but refused to serve as a colonel because he would be outranked by so many commanders of State militia that his movements would be seriously hampered and his usefulness greatly impaired. As Congress declined to promote him, he remained at home, but after the great disaster at Camden, he declared that it was no time to let personal considerations have any weight, and he immediately joined Gates at Hillsboro in September. On October 13, he was promoted brigadier-general, and it was not long before Congress had reasons to congratulate itself upon this tardy act of justice, which resulted in placing Morgan in a situation where his great powers could be made of the utmost service to the country. Gates being relieved of the command of the Southern army, General Nathaniel Greene assumed that position at Charlotte, N. C., December 4, 1780. He was pleased to find General Morgan with his forces, as he had served with him at the siege of Boston. As soon as he could reorganize his shattered army, Greene began the offensive. Morgan was ordered to cross the Catawba and threaten Cornwallis' position at Winnsboro. He was given entire command west of the Catawba, and all officers and soldiers engaged in the American cause were enjoined to obey him. Morgan's detachment consisted of three hundred and twenty Marylanders under Lieutenant-Colonel Howard, two hundred Virginia militia under Major Triplet, and eighty cavalrymen led by Lieutenant-Colonel William Washington.

On December 16, 1780, orders came for Morgan to march, and leaving Charlotte, he crossed the Catawba and Broad rivers and pitched his camp at the Grindal Shoals on the east bank of the Pacolet, on Christmas Day. Soon after his arrival at the Grindal Shoals, Morgan was joined by a body of North Carolina militia under the command of Major Joseph McDowell. The first and second Spartan regiments under Colonels John Thomas and Thomas Brandon took post close to Morgan. At the same time, McCall's regiment, which was a part of Pickens' brigade, joined his standard; and also a party of Georgians under Majors Jackson and Cunningham came up.

Having no supplies, Morgan's army must subsist by foraging, and, being in a section long overrun by Tories, his parties sent out for this purpose must need go long distances. A body of two hundred Tories, down in Laurens County, advanced as far as Fairforest Creek to embarrass their operations. Morgan immediately detached two hundred mounted militia and seventy-five calvarymen, under Colonels Washington and McCall, and falling on the Tories at a place called Hammond's Store, destroyed them.

These bold movements on the part of the Americans made Cornwallis fear for the safety of Ninety-Six, so on the 1st of January, 1781, he ordered Tarleton, who had already advanced as far as Brierley's Ferry, now Strother, on Broad River, to move toward Ninety-Six, with special instructions that he "push Morgan to the utmost." Tarleton's corps consisted of about eleven hundred men, five hundred of which belonged to his dreaded legion, which had carried desolation into every part of the State. After moving some twenty miles, Tarleton found that Ninety-Six was safe and Morgan quite a distance from that point. He then proposed to Cornwallis that they make a joint movement against Morgan, which was acceded to The plan was for Cornwallis to march up on the east side of Broad River in the vicinity of Kings Mountain, while Tarleton was to move up to the westward and head Morgan off. "When I advance," said Tarleton in his message to Cornwallis, "I must either destroy Morgan's corps or push it before me over Broad River toward Kings Mountain." Hence, on January 12, Tarleton resumed his march, moving in a westerly direction, and on the evening of the 15th he reached the valley of the Pacolet at Easterwood Ford, about two miles below the present Pacolet Mills.

The Battle of Cowpens

Soon after General Morgan reached the Grindal Shoals, Colonel Andrew Pickens, with his force, took post in the Plumber settlement between Tyger River and Fairforest Creek. About nightfall, on the 14th, he learned of Tarleton's advance on Morgan. He immediately dispatched a messenger to Morgan informing him that Tarleton was coming "to give him a blast." Colonel Washington was at Wofford Iron Works, now Glendale, having his horses shod.

A hurried order was sent for him to meet Morgan the next evening "at Gentleman Thompson's, on the east side of Thickety Creek." On the morning of the 15th Morgan began to march up the Green River road toward the place of juncture, where he encamped for the night. Here he was joined by Colonel Washington. The march was resumed the next morning and about sundown The Cowpens was reached, and the soldiers informed that it was here that they should meet the enemy.

About the same time that Morgan left his camp at Thickety, Tarleton was crossing the Pacolet at Easterwood Ford. Colonels Thomas Brandon and Benjamin Roebuck, with some others, sat on their horses and watched him cross, counted his men and sent their report to headquarters. Tarleton proceeded until he came to the camp that Morgan had deserted the morning before. Still watched by Brandon and Roebuck, he remained there until three o'clock on the morning of the 17th, when he renewed his march toward Cowpens.

Some time before day, Morgan's faithful scouts came running in and informed him that Tarleton was approaching and was not more than three miles away. Upon receipt of this intelligence, Morgan, accompanied by Pickens, began to go from mess to mess, saying: "Boys, get up, Benny is coming and you that have sweethearts, or wives, or children, or parents, must fight for them, and above all must fight for liberty and your country."

After thus speaking to both the militia and the regulars, the tattoo sounded and the lines of battle were formed. The first line was formed on the crest of the eminence, supposed to be just a little to the southeast of the monument. This line of four hundred and thirty guns consisted of the regulars under the command of Lieutenant-Colonel Howard. One hundred and fifty yards in front of Howard's line a second line was formed, consisting of about three hundred volunteer militia commanded by Colonel Andrew Pickens. One hundred and fifty yards in front of Pickens' line a third one was formed, consisting of sixty or seventy picked riflemen, commanded by Colonel Cunningham and Major McDowell. Some three or four hundred yards in the rear of the main line under Howard, Colonel Washington was posted behind an eminence with his cavalry as a reserve. Orders were then given that the front line should open fire and then fall back to the second line under Pickens, when this line should maintain its ground as long as possible and then fall back to the main line under Howard, where the final assault was to be made.

Everything being in readiness, General Morgan addressed his soldiers as follows: "My friends in arms, my dear boys, I request you to remember Saratoga, Monmouth, Peola, and Brandywine, and this day must play your parts for your honor and liberty's cause." Then turning to the great Sovereign of the Universe, he thus addressed Him: "Oh, Thou, the great disposer of all events, the battle is not to the strong nor the race to the swift. Our domineering enemy now being in sight, oh, leave us not or forsake us!"

When Tarleton arrived at The Cowpens shortly after sunrise, he found Morgan in perfect readiness to meet him. Hurriedly forming his lines, the British advanced in a sort of trot, uttering a loud halloo. Morgan was heard to say: "Boys, they give us the British halloo; boys, give them the Indian halloo," and galloping along the lines he cheered the men and told them not to fire until they could see the whites of their eyes. Every officer was crying, "Don't fire," for, says Major Thomas Young, of Union District, "it was a hard matter for us to keep from it." As the Redcoats streamed along, a column marched up in front of Colonel Brandon's men, led by a gaily-dressed officer on horseback. This fellow seemed to be rather busy and made himself obnoxiously conspicuous in the eyes of the patriotic Americans. Word passed along the line, "Who can bring him down?" John Savage, of the Brown's Creek section of Union District, looked Colonel Farr full in the face and read "yes" in his eyes. So Savage darted a few paces in front, laid his rifle against a sapling, a blue gas streamed above his head, a sharp crack of a rifle broke the solemn stillness of the moment, and the result was that a horse without a rider wheeled from the front of the advancing column. The next moment it was pop, pop, pop, and then a whole volley from the front line of picked riflemen. Their fire was unerring, and a number of saddles were empied, as they had been ordered to mark the "epaulet men." The British continued to steadily advance, and the front line fell back to the second line under Pickens. After delivering some murderous fires, this line was forced back and retreated toward Howard's flank, as they had been ordered to do. But before they could gain the cover of this line, the British cavalry on the right charged and drove them back towards the position held by Washington. That brave officer immediately met this bold dash by a counter charge, which scattered the British horsemen in the wildest confusion Pickens now promptly rallied and reformed his men, and passing around the ridge behind which Washington had been posted, he reached the right flank of Howard's line just as the enemy were about to turn it. When the militia by their retreat uncovered Howard's line, he poured a terrific fire into the columns of the advancing enemy. This was vigorously returned, and for fifteen or twenty minutes the ground was bitterly contested. Seeing that his advance was checked, Tarleton ordered his reserves into action; the infantry to take a position on his left, while the cavalry was to charge the American right. His object was to turn Howard's flank with the reserves, while those already engaged should entertain the main line. This was a dangerous move for the Americans, but Morgan was equal to the occasion He ordered Pickens to attack the enemy's left flank, and Washington to charge their right. Both orders were faultlessly executed.

Pickens struck the left flank of the reserves and Washington charged and broke through their cavalry just as they were about to swoop down on Howard's right. Before these movements were understood by Howard, and seeing the danger to which his right was exposed, he ordered the flank company to change their front. Just here a singular but very fortunate thing happened. Howard's order to change front was understood that they should retire to the eminence some distance in the rear; consequently they began to fall back in good order to that point. Howard, seeing this, supposed that Morgan had given the order, and Morgan supposed that Howard had given it. The enemy, seeing this movement, mistook it for a retreat, and somewhat confusedly dashed forward, yelling at the top of their voices, until they were within thirty yards of Howard's men.

Seeing the confusion of the enemy, Washington sent Morgan word "that they were coming on like a mob, and if he would give them one fire, the cavalry would charge them." Morgan instantly ordered the men to face about and fire, which was done with such deadly effect that the enemy gave way. Howard then ordered a bayonet charge, and Washington wheeled into the rear and was about to charge when they laid down their arms. The victors now concentrated their efforts against the forces of the enemy, who were still trying to maintain their ground, and they, too, were soon put to flight. At that late hour, Tarleton vainly hoped to reverse the fortunes of the day. He ordered his flying cavalry to halt and reform, and an effort was made to collect his straggling infantry, but all to no avail. To use Tarleton's own words, "Neither promises nor threats could gain their attention; they surrendered or dispersed."

The conflict was now over and one of the most brilliant and glorious victories that was ever achieved by any people perched on the American banners.

Morgan's forces at The Cowpens numbered about 850, while Tarleton's amounted to 1,150. The American losses were 12 killed and 62 wounded; the British losses were 80 killed, 150 wounded and 600 prisoners. Two small field guns, called grasshoppers, two stands of colors, 800 muskets, 100 horses, 35 wagons and all the enemy's music fell into the hands of the victors. When Tarleton was forced to see that all was lost, in company with some of his horsemen, he fled from the field in the direction of Hamilton's Ford, on Broad River, and never stopped until he reached Cornwallis' camp on Turkey Creek, in York District. For some unknown reason, Cornwallis had not co-operated in the movement against Morgan, as previously arranged.

Never in all his career did Morgan render more valuable and efficient service to the cause of independence than that at The Cowpens. In recognition of it Congress voted him a gold medal, the description of which is as follows: An Indian queen with a quiver on her back in the act of crowning an officer with a laurel wreath; his hand resting upon his sword; a cannon lying upon the ground; various military weapons and implements in the background. Legend: "Daniel Morgan Duci Exercitus Comitia, Americana. The American Congress to General Daniel Morgan." Reverse: An officer mounted at the head of his troops charging a flying enemy. A battle in the background. In front: a personal combat between a dragon unhorsed and a foot soldier. Legend: "Victoria Libertatis Vindex—Victory the Assertor of Liberty. Exergue: Fugatis, Captis, Aut Caesis Ad Cowpens Hostibus, 17th January, 1781. The foe put to flight, taken or slain, at The Cowpens, January 17, 1781."

Although the plan of the battle was masterful, its execution of the highest order, and the victory most complete, Morgan received much censure for his selection of ground. Johnson, in his "Life of Greene," says: "An open woodland, possessing nothing to recommend it but a trifling elevation, and a river winding around his left at a distance of six miles and extending parallel to his rear, so as to cut off all retreat in case of misfortune. It is obvious that the alternative exhibited is extraordinary indiscretion, or extraordinary boldness and originality of design. The well-read tactician, who squares his opinion by military dogmas, will not hesitate to decide against the prudence of leaving his wings in air exposed to a superior cavalry and a more numerous infantry, and a river in his rear, which cut off every hope of retreat."

In later years Morgan defended himself by saying: "I would not have had a swamp in the view of my militia on any consideration; they would have made for it, and nothing could have detained them from it. And as to covering my wings, I knew my adversary, and was perfectly sure I should have nothing but downright fighting. As to a retreat, it was the very thing I wished to cut off all hope of. I would have thanked Tarleton had he surrounded me with his cavalry. It would have been better than placing my own men in the rear to shoot down those who broke from the ranks. When men are forced to fight, they will sell their lives dearly, and I knew that the dread of Tarleton's cavalry would give due weight to the protection of my bayonets and keep my troops from breaking as Buford's regiment did. Had I crossed the river, one-half of the militia would immediately have abandoned me."

Such an expression of utter lack of confidence in the men who fought under him so heroically surely could not have come as a result of sober thought. Annoyed by frequent nagging, it must have been an outburst of irritation. To say the least of it, it was an undeserved censure, and not creditable to the great commander.

Notwithstanding the criticism of Morgan, and the criticism by Morgan, a writer has said: "In point of tactics it (Cowpens) was the most brilliant battle of the Revolutionary War, and it still appears brilliant when judged by the standards that we apply to the work of the greatest masters of the military art."

After the battle of Cowpens, the only road by which Morgan could rejoin Greene lay northward across the Broad and Catawba Rivers. He lost no time in moving this way, for Cornwallis was only twenty-five miles away, but by superb maneuvering and the aid of Divine Providence, he succeeded in rejoining Greene in North Carolina. Then came a series of masterly movements, which resulted in the battle of Guilford and Cornwallis' retreat into Virginia. But before the campaign was completed Morgan was attacked so severely by rheumatism that on February 10, 1781, he had to quit the field and go home. By June he had sufficiently recovered to command the troops that suppressed Claypool's insurrection in the Shenandoah Valley in Virginia. He then reported to General Lafayette, at his headquarters near Jamestown, and was put in command of all the light troops in the Marquis' army, but in August his malady again returned and he was obliged to go home. This ended his Revolutionary career.

For the next dozen years he spent a quiet life on his estate—Saratoga. He became quite wealthy, and his house became the rendezvous of many eminent guests. In 1795, with the rank of major-general, he commanded the large army that, by its mere presence, quelled the whiskey insurrection in Western Pennsylvania.

Life Subsequent to the Revolution

In 1796 he was elected to Congress by the Federalists, where he zealously supported the administration of President John Adams, but failing health called him home again before the expiration of his term, and from then until the time of his death he seldom left his fireside.

General Daniel Morgan 21

In early life Morgan was dissipated and was famous as a pugilist, yet the teaching of a pious mother always made him reverential when his thoughts turned towards the Deity. He was a fine specimen of physical manhood, was more than six feet high and weighed more than two hundred pounds. His strength and endurance were remarkable, and in beauty of feature and expression he was equaled by few men of his time. His manners were quiet and refined, his bearing was noble and his temper sweet, though easily aroused by the sight of injustice. He was noted for truthfulness and candor, and throughout life his conduct was regulated by the most rigid code of honor.

His Personal and Religious Character

In his latter years he professed religion and became a member of the Presbyterian Church in Winchester. "Ah," he would often say when talking of the past, "People said Old Morgan never feared, they thought Old Morgan never prayed—they did not know Old Morgan was often miserably afraid." He said he trembled at Quebec, and in the gloom of early morning, when approaching the battery at Cape Diamond, he knelt in the snow and prayed, and before the battle at The Cowpens he went into the woods, ascended a tree, and there poured out his soul in prayer for protection.

Morgan resided at "Saratoga" on his estate in Clark County, Virginia, a few miles from Winchester, until 1800, when he removed to Winchester, where he died on the 6th of July, 1802, in the sixty-seventh year of his age. The house in which he died stood in the northwest part of the town. He was buried in the Presbyterian cemetery at Winchester. In the procession that escorted his remains to the grave were seven members of the rifle company he had led to Boston in 1775. His grave is marked by a plain horizontal slab, raised a few feet from the ground, upon which is the following inscription:

His Death

"Major-General Daniel Morgan departed this life on July the 6th, 1802, in the sixty-seventh year of his age. Patriotism and valor were the prominent features of his character, and the honorable services rendered to his country during the Revolutionary War crowned him with glory, and will remain in the hearts of his countrymen a perpetual monument to his memory."

The beautiful monument standing in the Public Square in Spartanburg speaks for itself. The superb granite pedestal is twenty-

Monument Unveiled to Morgan in Spartanburg, May 11, 1881 one feet high and is crowned with a bronze statue of General Morgan, which is nine feet high and weighs two thousand pounds. The celebrated J. Q. A. Ward was nine months preparing it, and Congress voted an appropriation of twenty thousand dollars to defray the expenses.

The following inscriptions appear in the bronze panels on the North, South, East and West panels:

(EAST FACE)

To the American Soldiers who on the Field of Cowpens, January 17th, 1781, Fought Victoriously for the Right of Self-Government and Civil Liberty. We enjoy the result of their toil and sacrifice. Let us emulate their fortitude and virtue. This column is erected by the States of New Hampshire, Massachusetts, Connecticut, Rhode Island, New York, New Jersey, Pennsylvania, Delaware, Maryland, North Carolina, Virginia, Georgia, and South Carolina, the Old Thirteen States, and the State of Tennessee.

MORGAN.

(ON THE SUB-BASE THIS RECORD)

The unanimous resolve of the Congress of the United States crowns this Memorial Column with the form and face of General Daniel Morgan, the Hero of Cowpens, who on that Field was victorious in the great cause of American Independence.

(NORTH FACE)

(New England States)

New Hampshire, Massachusetts, Rhode Island, Connecticut, to Patriotism and the Brave Forever. In the past is sacrifice; in the future progress, liberty and union.

HOWARD.

(WEST FACE)

(Southern States)

One hundred years ago the Men of the North and the South fought together, and by their blood secured the

Independence and cemented the Union of the American States. The bond that then bound them together is the Bond of their Fellow Countrymen today. The common country they created is the heritage of all their sons. The perpetuation of the Republic of their fathers is the safety and honor of North and South. Alike the sentiment and duty of all the States—Esto Perpetua.

WILLIAM WASHINGTON.

(On the Sub-base This Record)

The Washington Light Infantry, to whose custody the widow of Colonel William Washington committed his crimson battle flag, projected this Memorial Column and participated in its dedication, again unfurling the glorious standard, which at Eutaw shone so bright, and as a dazzling meteor swept the Cowpens deadly fight.

(South Face)
(Middle States)
1781—One People—No North, no South, no East, no West. A common interest. One Country—One Destiny.
1881—As it was, so ever let it be.

PICKENS.

Owing to the severity of January weather and the inability of those having matters in charge to get ready, the Centennial was held May 11th instead of January 17th.

Never before, nor since, has Spartanburg witnessed such a day as this. The throngs were innumerable. For many hours previous, streams of passenger trains poured in from all directions, bringing troops, officials and visitors galore from every section east of the Mississippi. The pageantry was simply indescribable. The speakers' stand was in front of the old court house, now the Cudd-Huitt corner. Many officials and magnates were heard, but our own General Wade Hampton was the orator of the day.

It was the good pleasure of this scribe to see the drapery of the Stars and Stripes pulled from around Morgan's statue, hear General Hampton's oration, and witness all the ceremonies.

The Life of General Andrew Pickens

ANDREW PICKENS was of a lineage that could be traced back to the time of Louis XIV, when a half million of French Protestant refugees, exiles for liberty and religious opinions, crossed the guarded borders of France and found a temporary resting place in Scotland. Later another sojourn was made in the north of Ireland, where the parents of our hero were born. Still yearning for absolute liberty—"A State without a king, a church without a bishop,"—the Pickens family crossed the Atlantic and settled in Paxon Township, Bucks County, Pennsylvania, where, on the 19th of September, 1739, the subject of this sketch was born. In early childhood his family removed to Augusta County, Virginia. The news of rich lands to the southward being thrown open to white settlers, and a desire for a milder climate, caused the Pickens' to join the many long wagon trains from Pennsylvania, Maryland and Virginia, which were moving toward the upper section of South Carolina. The Pickens and Calhoun families, with some others, crossed the Upper Catawba and journeyed all the way across the State at its greatest width and settled on the western border of Long Cane, near the Savannah, in what is now Abbeville County. Andrew was then a boy of thirteen years of age, with no educational advantages. He engaged in farm work, hunting, and

ANDREW PICKENS

24

Indian warfare, which was the training received by all our pioneer citizens. Bred on an Indian frontier, a strong character with undaunted courage was developed, which made him a leader of men.

Maddened because of some murderous imprudence on the part of the English in 1761, the Cherokees fell on the frontiers of South Carolina with all their merciless fury. Death and destruction followed in their wake. Governor Bull sent Colonel James Grant into the Indian country to suppress the insurrection. On the 27th of May he arrived at Fort Prince George, on the Keowee River, in what is now Pickens County, with about 2,600 men. For thirty days Grant carried on such a vigorous campaign of warfare and destruction that the Indians were compelled to sue for peace. Andrew Pickens was a volunteer in Grant's army. Lossing says that he was made a colonel, being just twenty-one years of age.

Beginning of Military Career

The settlements on Long Cane were broken up by the murderous ravages of the Indians. Some families escaped and took refuge in the Waxhaw settlement, in what is now Lancaster County. Among these was that of Ezekiel Calhoun. Young Pickens found his way there and met Miss Rebecca Calhoun, whom he subsequently married.

When the Indian troubles were over, Ezekiel Calhoun returned to his home at Long Cane. Here, at the bride's residence, Andrew Pickens and Rebecca Calhoun were married March 19, 1765. Tradition says it was the largest wedding party that had ever assembled in upper South Carolina up to that time; the festivities lasted three days without intermission, and the beauty of the bride was the theme of all tongues, and the wedding was long talked of as the important event of the neighborhood in that decade.

When the Stamp Act troubles arose in 1765, Andrew Pickens was well known to be opposed to "taxation without representation." Hence, when the storm of war broke over the country in 1775, we find him on the Patriot side at the first fight at Ninety-Six Fort—an event, however, seldom mentioned by historians. This fight occurred just seven months after Lexington and Concord, and eight months before the Declaration of Independence.

His Activities in the Revolution

Neither Andrew Pickens, nor the prosperous region in which he lived, had any personal grievances, but the love of liberty caused him, at that critical moment, to throw all his power and influence into the American cause. At this we are not to be surprised, for it will be remembered that for two hundred years his ancestry wandered from place to place seeking a haven of liberty, both civil and religious.

He was widely known, and his piety and bravery had much to do with shaping public opinion in his section. The moment Andrew Pickens took the field in upper South Carolina against George III, many flocked to the Patriot standard. His decision cost him much—for seven long years hostile Indians were in his rear, and British and Loyalists in his front, his family and neighbors dangerously exposed at all times. However, he went boldly forward, the freedom of the Colonies being his highest aspiration.

What Marion was in the low country, Sumter in the middle, Pickens was in the upper. When the country, from the mountains to the sea, was overrun by the British, these three irrepressible champions of Independence, by their bold moves and great personal influence, kept the spirit of liberty alive; and their names should forever shine out in South Carolina history with an unfading brilliancy. Historians have been sadly negligent in giving Pickens full credit for his share in the cause of freedom.

In 1779 a party of Loyalists from North Carolina, under Colonel Boyd, tried to force their way into Georgia and form a junction with another Loyalist—Colonel Hamilton. Andrew Pickens now, for the first time, appeared as a leader. We have seen him as a lieutenant in the Cherokee War, and captain of the militia at Ninety-Six; but now he became a leader and commander. To oppose Hamilton and prevent Boyd's junction with him, Pickens assembled his militia, and with five hundred men from the Ninety-Six District, attacked Hamilton. Unable to make an impression on him, Pickens turned against Boyd and came up with him at Kettle Creek. After a hotly contested action for three-quarters of an hour, Boyd was killed and his force routed.

His First Appearance as a Leader

After the fall of Charleston in May, 1780, many loyal Patriots regarded the cause as lost, and quite a number took protection and received paroles from the British. The militia, to which Pickens belonged, were to be regarded as prisoners of war under parole, which parole, as

Pickens Ceases Activities For a While

long as it should be observed, would secure their property from being molested by British troops.

Colonel Pickens and other influential men in the Ninety-Six District were often urged to resume their arms in the American cause; but to these appeals and remonstrances Pickens would reply that his honor was pledged and that he was bound by the solemnity of an oath not to take up arms unless the conditions of his parole were violated by the British, or those who acted under the Royal government. It was not long, however, until all who refused to take up arms in support of the King were raided, and their homes plundered by the King's men.

Chief among these marauders was Major James Dunlap, who, with his own troops and parties of Loyalists, made a general sweep over the country, murdering and pillaging. Notwithstanding his promised protection, the house of Colonel Pickens was plundered and his property wantonly destroyed. The Colonel, who had so steadfastly observed his parole as involving his personal honor, now considered its conditions broken, and with many of his former officers and men determined to resume arms in defense of their country. But Pickens was not one, even under such circumstances, to steal away without openly avowing his purpose, for, says McCrady: "As soon as his determination was taken, he sought an interview with Captain Kerr, a British officer at White Hall, General Williamson's residence, with whom he had become very intimate, to whom he disclosed his intentions and assigned his reasons. Kerr earnestly advised him against the measure, assuring him that his execution was certain, in case he should thereafter fall into the hands of the British, and that he would literally fight with a halter around his neck; that though their countries were at war, he had given him proofs of personal friendship, and ardently hoped he might never fall into the power of the British government. To this Colonel Pickens replied that he had honorably and conscientiously adhered to the rules laid down in his protection, but that he now considered himself completely absolved from its obligations by the plunder and wanton waste which had been committed upon his plantation, and the insults and indignities which had been offered to his family. He requested Captain Kerr to communicate these remarks to Colonel Cruger, the commanding officer at Ninety-Six, and to thank him for his civilities while he was under the protection of the British government."

On the 7th of October, 1780, Patrick Ferguson and his army was practically annihilated at Kings Mountain. This brought great relief to the Patriot cause in this part of the State—in fact, it was the turning point of the Revolution. Soon after General Greene assumed command of the Southern army and reorganized its shattered forces, he sent a detachment into South Carolina under General Daniel Morgan. Morgan pitched his encampment on the east bank of the Pacolet River at Grindal Shoals, on Christmas Day. Colonel Pickens having again taken the field, in a short time he and Colonel McCall had enlisted one hundred men. Morgan needed reinforcements badly; for he was soon to meet the dreaded Tarleton, and his force was inadequate. Pickens, with his followers, moved toward Morgan's post, and early in January he was encamping in the Plumber settlement on Fairforest, in what is now Union County. Fully conscious of Morgan's peril, no one did more to obtain help than Pickens. He sent couriers in all directions for sixty miles around to summons men to the rescue. Colonel Howard, of the Maryland line, says: "Morgan did not decide on action until he was joined on the night of the 16th by Colonel Pickens and his followers."

Pickens Resumes Activities

When returning to Morgan's camp at Grindal Shoals from the affair at Hammond's Store, Colonel Washington passed near Pickens' camp on Fairforest. Major Joseph McJunkin obtained leave to stop there for a while. Just at this time Pickens heard of Tarleton's advance on Morgan. No time was to be lost. Feeling that it was unsafe to send a written message, Pickens chose Major McJunkin to bear the information verbally. In company with James Park, after a dark and perilous journey, Morgan's camp was reached and the message delivered. Morgan immediately dispatched a message to Colonel Washington, with orders that he meet him at Gentleman Thompson's, now Thickety Station, the next evening. Washington was at Wofford's Iron Work, now Glendale, having his horses shod. Consequently, on the next morning, which was January the 15th, Morgan left Grindal and the juncture was made with Washington at Thompson's, where they encamped for the night.

The next day Morgan continued to move until he arrived at The

Cowpens, where a halt was again made. No doubt Pickens made all possible haste to join Morgan, but as we have already seen, he did not overtake him until The Cowpens was reached.

During the night the officers outlined the plan of battle, and early the next morning every man was in line early, awaiting Tarleton's approach. This was not long, for shortly after sunrise Tarleton came in sight, and to his surprise found his enemy in readiness for him.

A full account of the battle will not be given here, but only such part as Pickens was most conspicuous in. Three lines of battle were formed. The first and main line consisted of four hundred and thirty guns, commanded by Lieutenant-Colonel Howard. One hundred and fifty yards in front of Howard's line a second one was formed, consisting of about three hundred and fifty militia, commanded by Colonel Pickens. One hundred and fifty yards in front of Pickens' line was a third, consisting of sixty or seventy picked riflemen, commanded by Colonel Cunningham and Major McDowell Colonel Washington, with his cavalry, was posted behind an eminence, some three hundred yards in the rear of Howard's line, as a reserve. Orders were given that the front line should open fire and then fall back to the second line under Pickens, where they should hold their ground as long as possible and then fall back to the first line under Howard, where the final assault should be made.

When Tarleton got near the American line his front was met by a well-directed fire from the picked riflemen, and a number of saddles were emptied. The British, however, continued to steadily advance, and the front line fell back to the second under Pickens. After delivering some murderous fire, this line was forced back and retreated toward Howard's line as they had been ordered to do, but before they could gain the cover of this line, the British cavalry charged them and drove them back in the direction of the position held by Washington. That brave officer immediately met this bold dash by a counter charge, which scattered the British horsemen in the wildest confusion. Pickens now promptly rallied and reformed his men, and passing around the ridge behind which Washington had been posted, reached the right flank of Howard's line just as the enemy were about to turn it. Pickens struck the left flank of Tarleton's reserves, and Washington charged and broke through their cavalry just as they were about to swoop down on Howard's right. Pickens and Howard, in person, advanced with their troops to finish the fight, and in twenty minutes the larger part of the British forces were in the hands of the Americans. The Seventy-First regiment held out a little longer, but when their cavalry was put to flight by Colonel Washington they soon laid down their arms, and Major McArthur, their commander, surrendered his sword, and it was received by Colonel Pickens in person.

We feel safe in saying that Pickens' greatest achievement in behalf of independence was wrought at The Cowpens. While not generally known, he was next to Morgan in rank and commanded in person more than half of the troops engaged in the action. General McCrady, the historian, pays him the following tribute:

"The distinguishing feature of the battle of Cowpens upon the American side was undoubtedly the effective work of Pickens' marksmen. It was this which in the very commencement of the action had carried terror into the hearts of Tarleton's dragoons, and it was this which disorganized the British line to such an extent

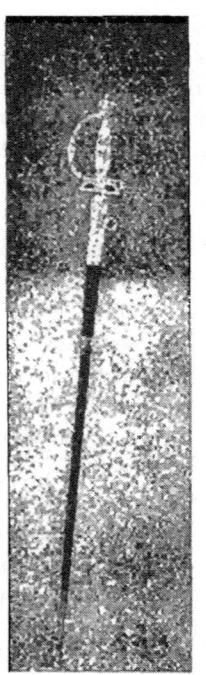

as to render it only a mob when the critical moment of the onslaught had arrived. It was Pickens himself who received the sword of the gallant commander of the Seventy-first Regiment."

For his heroism and gallantry, Congress voted him a sword with the following engraved upon it: "Congress to Colonel Pickens, March 9th, 1781-Cowpens January 17th." This sword is still in the hands of his descendants.

It was not yet noon when the battle of Cowpens ended. Being encumbered with so many prisoners and knowing the proximity of Cornwallis, Morgan remained on the battlefield only long enough to refresh his men and prisoners, and make such provisions as humanity required of him. He moved across Broad River that evening, leaving Colonel Pickens with a detachment of his partisans to bury the dead and to provide as far as possible for the needs of the wounded on both sides. After performing his duties, the wounded of both armies were placed under safeguard and a flag, and the next day Pickens rejoined his commander.

All the while that Morgan was pushing into North Carolina, Pickens was doing his part in looking after the safety of prisoners. At one time they were committed to his care entirely, but he was soon released for other duties.

The North Carolina militia had been deprived of their leader in the death of General Davidson. Morgan having come among them, they held a meeting and requested General Greene to assign him to their command, but Morgan, having become disabled on account of rheumatism, declined the command and retired from the field. Then, it appears, that Greene hoped that Sumter might be available, but he went in another direction. He now turned to Pickens. He accepted, and was made a brigadier-general by Governor Rutledge. Pickens' South Carolina followers had been reduced to a mere handful, but the gallant little band under McCall still stuck to him, and by the accession of volunteers from Virginia and North Carolina, the number was increased to three hundred and sixty. Forty-five of these were McCall's horsemen, and the rest well-mounted riflemen.

Pickens Made a Brigadier-General

The first move of General Pickens in the North Carolina war was an advance on Cornwallis in the direction of Hillsboro. McCall was sent forward, and surprised and destroyed a British picket. Colonel Lee, being in the same vicinity, formed a junction with Pickens. On the night of the 21st of February, General Greene, with a small escort, visited the camp of Pickens and spent the greater part of the night in his bush tent consulting with Pickens and Lee as to their future movements. As a result Greene combined the forces of the two leaders and gave Pickens the command of the whole. Tarleton being in striking distance, Pickens, with his combined force, set out immediately in pursuit of him, and came near surprising and bagging that gentleman while at dinner. A Tory party, under a Colonel Pyles, suddenly appeared between them. Quick work followed. One hundred men were left dead on the field and very few escaped being severely wounded. Pyles himself was badly mutilated, but recovered. This conflict with Pyles enabled Tarleton to get away.

Conditions in South Carolina were still very serious, hence Pickens was ordered to repair to the back part of the State to

Pickens Returns to South Carolina protect Whigs, suppress Loyalists, and co-operate with Sumter in active enterprises. On his return he was joined by Colonel Elijah Clarke. While on the march, Pickens heard that the notorious Dunlap had been sent out from Ninety-Six with seventy-five dragoons on a foraging expedition. He at once detached Clarke and McCall to attack him. On the 24th of March they came up on Dunlap encamped at Beattie's Mill on Little River, in what is now Abbeville County. Conscious of his atrocities and his great danger if he should fall into the hands of the Americans, Dunlap resolved to sell his life dearly. He resisted until thirty-four of his men were killed and himself and several wounded, when he held out a flag and surrendered. The prisoners taken were thirty-four, including the wounded. McCall, the historian, says that Dunlap died from his wounds the ensuing night, but there is little or no doubt that he was killed by his captors, for General Pickens offered a reward for the murderers. Thus ended the career of the blood-thirsty villain, whose tracks were followed by destruction and all manner of inhuman savagery—Major James Dunlap.

While Greene and his subordinates were busy in the eastern part of the State, Pickens was busily engaged in rousing the people in the Ninety-Six District. In this he was ably assisted by Colonels Samuel and Leroy Hammond. Having procured about four hundred men, he began a series of maneuvers between Ninety-Six and Augusta. The latter place was defended by two forts, viz.: Grierson and Cornwallis. On May 23rd a junction was formed by Pickens, Lee, and Clarke. After reconnoitering, it was determined to dislodge Colonel Grierson, who commanded the fort by his name. Grierson and practically his whole force were killed or captured. The American loss was slight. Pickens and Lee now pressed forward against Fort Cornwallis, which was commanded by the notorious Colonel Brown, and laid siege to it, which lasted about a week. On June 5th Brown surrendered. The British loss was fifty-two killed and three hundred and thirty-four prisoners. That of the Americans was sixteen killed, thirty-five wounded, seven of these mortally.

While Pickens and his associates were reducing the forts about Augusta, General Greene had avanced and laid siege to Ninety-Six, and ordered Pickens to join him, which he did. This was a severe defeat for the Americans.

In September, Greene determined again to give battle at Eutaw Springs. He ordered Pickens to join him and he was put in command of all the State troops. These troops composed the first line at Eutaw, and Pickens commanded the left wing in person. During the battle he was struck by a bullet, which, but for his sword buckle, would have inflicted a mortal wound. This was another serious affair for Greene, for surely he was ill-starred in his southern campaigns.

About the 1st of November, Pickens was dispatched to guard the frontiers against the Indians, who had been cited to insurrection. About the first of January, Pickens, with his own brigade, aided by Major Cunningham, of Georgia, made a rapid march into the eastern part of the Cherokee nation, in what is now Oconee County, and laid every town, village, and settlement east of the mountains in ashes. In this expedition, Pickens killed forty Indians, captured a great number of prisoners, and burned thirteen towns, with the loss of only two men wounded.

This, however, did not end the Indian troubles. By the encouragement and aid of British and Tories, they continued their pillaging depredations along the frontiers of South Carolina and Georgia. Wilkes County, Georgia, was the repository for their stolen negroes, horses, cattle, and other property. To break up this banditti, Pickens asked Governor Matthews to be allowed to carry out another expedition against the Cherokees. His scheme was approved, and he was joined by Colonel Elijah Clarke, making a total force of four hundred and fourteen men.

After a number of brilliant and successful achievements, the Indians sued for peace and asked for a set time and place for a treaty. It took place at Long Swamp on the 17th of October.

By the treaty all the lands claimed by the Cherokees south of the Savannah River and east of the Chattahoochee were to be surrendered to the State of Georgia as the price of peace. The articles of peace being signed by both parties, Pickens returned to his former position on Long Creek, where the troops were discharged on the 23rd day of October and returned to their homes, without the loss of a single man.

Not a tent or any other sort of camp equipment was carried by

Pickens and his command on this campaign. After the small portion of bread which they could carry in their saddle-bags was exhausted, the men lived on parched corn, potatoes, peas, and beef, which they gathered in the Indian towns. For this great work the State of Georgia ceded to General Pickens a large territory of lands.

With this successful expedition the Revolution virtually ended in South Carolina, and with it the end of General Pickens' military career. 'Tis true that he was made a major-general of militia in 1795, but it does not appear that he ever did any actual service.

The war over and the priceless boon of liberty having been won, General Pickens returned to his home, but he was by no means to be idle. The national government being fully established, he was called on to serve his country in various capacities. He held the first county court that sat under the new laws, near Abbeville Court House, and his son, afterwards Governor Andrew Pickens, then a boy five years old, drew the first jury. He ran the boundary line between North Carolina and Tennessee. He was appointed to make the treaty of Milledgeville, also at Natchez—in fact, almost all the treaties made with the Southern Indians. He was chosen a member of the legislature, and afterwards of the convention which formed the State Constitution. In 1794 he was elected to Congress, which at that time convened in Philadelphia. We quote the following: "At that time there were neither railroads nor stage coaches—all travel was done on horseback. Picture to yourself a man who was approaching his three-score years, of martial figure and dignified demeanor, mounted on a spirited milk-white Andalusian steed, whip in hand, and holsters filled with a brace of pistols, the silver mounting of which glittered in the sunlight; a three-cornered hat, from beneath which the silver-gray hair was put smoothly back and tied in a que, an undress military coat, ruffled shirt, fair-top boots, with handsome silver spurs. Following at a little distance, on a stout draft horse, is his African attendant—Pompey—in livery of blue, with scarlet facings, carrying a portmanteau, with a consequential and dignified air, showing in every movement the pride of a body servant to his revered master. Paint this in your mind's eye, and you have before you a gentleman of the Eighteenth Century, with his servant, on his way to Congress; such was General Andrew Pickens, as he passed through to Philadelphia in 1794."

Services Rendered After the War

He declined re-election to Congress, but was again returned to the legislature, where he remained a member until 1811. In 1779 Pickens fought the most desperate battle with the Cherokees at Tomassee that he ever did, but so completely did he subdue them that they were safely under his control. In fact, they became greatly devoted to him, so much so that they called him the "Great Sky Augusta," and adorned in the highest style of Indian costume, would bring their first offerings to him.

The home of General Pickens was in the beautiful mountain section of Tomassee, in what is now the old Pendleton District of Oconee County. To this place he retired to spend his last years in peace and tranquility, after having contributed such a vast amount of hard service in securing independence.

The second war with England coming on, he reviewed the causes of this struggle with great interest and was alive to its various incidents. In this hour of peril, the eyes of his fellowmen were again turned to their faithful and tried servant. Without his knowledge, he was again called into public service. He could not disregard their call and confidence. He accepted a seat in the legislature in 1812, and was pressed to serve as governor in that eventful crisis, but declined. He thought such high service should be left to more youthful hands.

He was from early life a firm believer in the Christian religion, and an influential memebr of the Presbyterian Church. On the 13th of October, 1789, "a people on Seneca" ap-

General Pickens' Religious Life plied to the Presbytery of South Carolina to be taken under its care for "supplies and preaching." Their request was granted, and Rev. John Simpson, a native of New Jersey, and a graduate of Princeton, was sent to these people, who soon organized as a congregation and took the name of Hopewell. This name was given in honor of the home of General Pickens on the Seneca River, near where the Blue Ridge Railway crosses that stream.

Andrew Pickens, Robert Anderson and Major Dickson, all officers of the Revolution, were chosen elders when the church was organized. The first building was of logs, and was put up in 1790. It was a mile or two from the present stone house. Tradition says that this house was burned, catching from a forest fire. In 1797, says one writer, in 1802, says another, the stone building was erected on lands belonging to John Miller—Printer John—who published the first newspaper in upper South Carolina, and the second in the State. The name of the paper was *Miller's Weekly Messenger,* later the *Pendleton Messenger,* and, so it is said, was printed on a press used by General Greene while in camp.

The first load of stone for the new building was hauled to the spot by a Mr. Robertson, and John Rusk, a veteran of the Revolution, was the builder. One of the most liberal contributors to this enterprise was Andrew Pickens. The pulpit and seats were given by him individually. This historic building is still standing and is only a short distance from the present Clemson College.

An incident illustrative of General Pickens' deep religious nature occurred at Kettle Creek. He attacked the Loyalist, Colonel Boyd, at that place and routed his party. Boyd fell mortally wounded and was taken prisoner. Seeing his critical condition, Pickens asked the dying man leave to pray for him. He, being an infidel, spurned the offer, saying, "I want none of a d—d Rebel's prayers." Pickens then asked if there was anything that he could do for him. He replied, "Keep my silver spurs and deliver them to my wife," which, it is said, he promised to do.

At his home in the lovely valley at the foot of the beautiful mountain peak Tomassee, on the 11th of August, 1817, in his eightieth year, the soldier, statesman, and Christian fell on sleep. He died suddenly, while sitting in his chair opening his mail, under a cedar tree.

The Death of General Pickens

He was buried in the Stone Church cemetery, and the plain tombstone marking the spot bears this simple inscription: "General Andrew Pickens was born 13th of September, 1739, and died 11th of August, 1817. He was a Christian, a patriot and soldier. His character and actions are incorporated with the history of his country. Filial affection and respect raises this stone to his memory."

As has already been said, General Pickens married Rebecca Calhoun, an aunt of the great statesman—John C. Calhoun. She was one of the most gifted and best educated women of her day. She was born November 18th, 1745, and died December 19th, 1814. Three sons and five daughters were born unto Andrew and Rebecca Pickens. At The Cowpens Centennial, held in Spartanburg, May, 1881, Colonel S. B. Pickens, a great-grandson of the General, while on the military parade, wore

Addendum

the sword that was voted by Congress to his great-grandfather. This sword is still in the possession of the Pickens family.

A most remarkable thing is that General Pickens never drew a cent of pay for his Revolutionary services, as the payrolls in the comptroller's office will show. The freedom of his country was reward enough for him.

The Life of Lieutenant-Colonel John Eager Howard

JOHN EAGER HOWARD was born in Baltimore County, Maryland, June 4, 1752. His grandfather, Joshua Howard, was an officer in the army of the Duke of York during the Monmouth rebellion. He was the first of the name of Howard that settled in this country. John's father was a wealthy planter and gave him an excellent education under tutors, but with no profession in view.

At the beginning of the Revolution, he joined the American army and was made captain of a company of militia, called the **His Military Career** Flying Camp, and fought under General Hugh Mercer at the battle of White Plains, New Jersey, October 28, 1776. His company being disbanded in December of that year, at the solicitation of his friends, he accepted a commission of major in one of the Continental battalions of Maryland. In the spring of 1777 he joined the army under Washington, in New Jersey, and remained with him until June, when he returned home on account of the death of his father. A few days after the battle of Brandywine, he rejoined the army and was distinguished for his cool courage in the battle of Germantown, of which he wrote an interesting account. In that engagement he was major of the Fourth Regiment, commanded by Colonel Hall, of Maryland. Major Howard was present at the battle of Monmouth in 1778. On the first of June, 1779, he received a commission of lieutenant-colonel of the Fifth Regiment, "to take rank from the 11th day of March, 1778"

In 1780 he went with the Maryland and Delaware troops to the South. Hence, when General Greene took charge of the Southern

JOHN EAGER HOWARD

army at Charlotte, North Carolina, December 4, 1780, he found Colonel Howard in his command. A few days after Greene assumed command, he detached a part of his forces under General Morgan and ordered him to march into South Carolina. A part of this detachment was three hundred and twenty Marylanders, under Lieutenant-Colonel Howard. After remaining at Grindal Shoals, on Pacolet River, about twenty days, Morgan heard of Tarleton's advance on him, when he fell back to The Cowpens, where the battle took place January 17, 1781. The main line at that place, consisting of four hundred and thirty guns, and from which Morgan expected more than any other, was commanded by Colonel Howard. Morgan was not disappointed. When the militia, under Pickens, gave way before Tarleton's cavalry charge, their retreat exposed Howard's line to the British assault. He met this onslaught by pouring a terrific fire into the advancing columns of the enemy. This was vigorously returned, and for fifteen or twenty minutes the ground was bitterly contested. Seeing his advance checked, Tarleton ordered his reserves into action; the infantry to take a position on his left, while the cavalry was to charge the American right. His object was to turn Howard's flank with the reserves, while those already engaged should entertain the main line. This was very dangerous for the Americans, but Morgan was equal to the occasion. He ordered Pickens, who had now reformed his men, to attack the enemy's left flank, and Washington to charge their right. Hence, Pickens struck the left flank of the reserves and Washington charged and broke through their cavalry just as they were about to swoop down on Howard's right. Not understanding Morgan's order, Howard seeing the danger to which his right was exposed, ordered the flank company to change their front. Here a singular thing happened. Howard's order to change front was understood that they should retire some distance to the rear, consequently they began to fall back in good order to that point. Howard, seeing this, supposed that Morgan had given the order, and Morgan supposed that Howard had given it. The enemy mistook this movement for a retreat, and in confusion, dashed forward, yelling at the top of their voices, until they were within thirty yards of Howard's men.

Seeing the confusion, especially of the enemy, Washington sent Morgan word that "they were coming on like a mob, and if he would give them one fire the cavalry would charge them." Morgan instantly ordered the men to face about and fire, which was done with such deadly effect that the enemy gave way. Howard then ordered a bayonet charge, and Washington wheeled into the rear and was about to charge, when they laid down their arms. Some others of the enemy were still trying to maintain their ground, but were soon put to flight. The conflict was now over, and a glorious victory won.

At one time on that day Colonel Howard held the swords of seven British officers who had surrendered to him. For his gallantry and faithful service Congress voted him a silver medal. The following are the devices and inscriptions: "An officer mounted, with uplifted sword, pursuing an officer on foot bearing a stand of colors. Victory (in the form of an angel) is seen descending in front over the former, holding a wreath in her right hand over his head. In her left hand is a palm branch. Legend: "John Eager Howard, Legionis, Peditum Praefects Comita Americana—the American Congress to John Eager Howard, commander of a regiment of infantry." Reverse: A laurel wreath inclosing the inscription: "Quod In Nutantem, Hostium Aciem Subito Irrueris, Praecharum Bellicae Virtutis Specimen Dedit In Pugna Ad Cowpens 17th of January, 1781—Because, rushing suddenly on the wavering line of the foe, he gave brilliant specimen of martial courage at the battle of The Cowpens, January 17, 1781."

At the battle of Guilford Court House, North Carolina, which was far from a victory for Greene, the First Maryland regiment was commanded by a Colonel Gunby until he was unhorsed, when the command devolved on Colonel Howard, who, by heroic service, did all he could to alleviate the misfortunes of the day. He was wounded, but not seriously.

He materially aided Greene in effecting his retreat from Guilford, and we next find him at the battle of Hobkirk's Hill, near Camden, South Carolina, which took place April 25, 1781, and in which Greene won one of his near victories—which means defeat. The Maryland regiment was commanded by Colonel Gunby. Against this regiment, Rawdon pitted his best troops, and a terrific struggle might have been expected, but, strange to say, the Marylanders, who fought so gloriously at Cowpens and fought half the battle at Guilford, shrank away in a panic.

The first symptom of confusion was shown by firing contrary to orders. Then Captain Beatty, who was the pride and stay of his company, fell mortally wounded. The company then halted, and Colonel Gunby dispatched Colonel Howard, with orders to the other companies of the regiment, then advancing with confidence, to halt and fall back in order that he might re-form their faltering comrades; but instead of remedying the matter, the retrograde movement only extended the panic to those who had been before without fear. While Williams, Gunby and Howard were actively and earnestly engaged in a combined effort to rally their regiment, Colonel Ford fell from his horse with a mortal wound. This so dispirited the troops that they faltered and retired.

"Nothing," says Johnson, "could exceed the surprise and disappointment of the commander at this instant. His favorite regiment, whose courage and conduct he reposed with such confidence, now blasting all his fair hopes by a retreat without making the smallest trial for victory."

At Eutaw Springs, the Marylanders were under the command of Colonel Otho H. Williams, and were divided into two battalions, one under Colonel Howard, and the other Major Hardiman. Howard's command was reduced to thirty men, and himself the only surviving officer. In his final charge he was severely wounded. This ended his Revolutinary career.

Lieutenant-Colonel Lee, in his memoirs, pays Howard the following tribute: "We have seen him at the Battle of Cowpens seize the critical moment and turn the fortune of the day; alike conspicuous, though not alike successful, at Guilford and the Eutaws, and at all times and on all occasions eminently useful. He was justly ranked among the chosen sons of the South. Trained to infantry service, he was invariably employed in that line, and was always to be found where the battle raged, pressing into close action to wrestle with fixed bayonet."

At the conclusion of the war, Colonel Howard was married to Maragaret Chew, daughter of Chief Justice Chew, around whose house at Germantown he had valiantly battled years before. In November, 1788, he was chosen governor of Maryland, which office he held for three years. In 1794, he was commissioned major-general of militia, but declined the honor. President Washington invited him to a seat in his cabinet, as Secretary of War, in 1795. That honor was also declined. These things show, notwithstanding his lofty patriotism and great services to his country, that John Eager Howard was not an aspirant to great honors. He served, however, in the State senate of Maryland, and in 1796 was elected to the United States senate, where he served until 1803, when he retired to private life.

Life and Service After Revolution

During the second war with England, when, in 1814, the city of Baltimore was threatened, Howard prepared to take the field. The battle at North Point rendered such a step unnecessary. After the disasters in Washington, when Baltimore was again threatened, it was suggested that it would be best for the city to capitulate. He indignantly opposed the mention of such, declaring that though the bulk of his property was at stake, and that he had four sons in the field, he would rather behold his property reduced to ashes and his sons weltering in their blood, than sanction the adoption of a measure disgraceful to the honor and character of his country. Was there ever a greater outburst of heroism, patriotism and love of country than this? Surely they are few.

In 1816 he was a candidate for vice-president of the United States, but was unsuccessful. At his famous residence, "Belvidere," in Baltimore, he entertained Lafayette in 1824.

There is a monument to George Washington in Baltimore, erected in 1815. It is about two hundred feet high and cost nine thousand dollars. The ground on which it stands was given by John Eager Howard.

In the former part of 1827 he lost his wife, and on the 12th of October following, he, too, left the scenes of earth at the age of seventy-five years. A eulogist has said: "Honor, wealth and the ardent love of friends were his lot in life, and few men ever went down to the grave more truly lamented than John Eager Howard."

Colonel Howard was so highly esteemed in South Carolina that at the session of the General Assembly of the State in January, 1828, Representative Davis, of Abbeville County, introduced the following eloquent preamble and resolution, which were unanimously adopted:

"Amongst the master-spirits who battled for independence, we are to remember with veneration the late patriotic and venerable Colonel John Eager Howard. His illustrious name is to be found in the history of his country's suffering and the annals of his country's triumphs. In the day of peril and of doubt, when the result was hid in clouds, when danger was everywhere, and when death mingled in the conflict of the warrior, Howard still clung to the fortunes of the struggling Republic.

"He was his country's common friend and his country owes him one common unextinguishable debt of gratitude. South Carolina, with whose history his name is identified, is proud to acknowledge her obligation.

"*Resolved, therefore,* That it was with feeling of profound sorrow and regret that South Carolina received the melancholy intelligence of the death of Colonel John Eager Howard, of Maryland.

"*Resolved,* That the State of South Carolina can never forget the distinguished services of the deceased.

"*Resolved,* That the governor be requested to transmit a copy of these proceedings to the governor of Maryland and to the family of the late Colonel Howard."

He was buried in the family vault in the cemetery of St. Paul's Church, Baltimore. There is no epitaph—just the family name—*Howard*—is inscribed over the entrance.

The Life of Lieutenant-Colonel William Washington

WILLIAM WASHINGTON, who has been styled "The Modern Marcellus—the Sword of His Country," was the eldest son of Bailey Washington, and was born in Stafford County, Virginia, on February 28th, 1752. As to his genealogy, little seems to be known beyond his father, although there is a family chart preserved in Charleston, prepared by Captain Henry DeSaussure, showing that all the Washington family came from John Washington, the first immigrant of that name to come to this country. In his correspondence with General George Washington, William gives no evidence of their relation, but it is true that General Washington, in his own diary, refers to him as his kinsman.

He was given a classical education preparatory for the church, to which he was inclined in his youth, but a peculiar situation in public affairs led him into the political field.

Trouble arising with the mother country, he early espoused the Patriot cause, and entered the American army under Colonel (afterwards General) Hugh Mercer, and received a commission as captain of infantry. His post was in the Third Virginia Regiment, and he acquitted himself with great credit in the operations about New York, being wounded in the battle of Long Island. At the battle of Trenton, December 26, 1776, he led a charge upon one of the enemy's batteries, capturing the guns, and was again wounded. He was at Trenton, and was with his beloved General Mercer when he fell at that place. Later he was transferred to Colonel George Baylor's

WILLIAM WASHINGTON

Begins His Military Career

44

Cavalry Corps, and served as major. He was with that officer at the slaughter of his corps at Gappan in 1778.

The next year he joined the army under General Benjamin Lincoln, in South Carolina, and became very active in the command of a light corps in the neighborhood of Charleston.

On the 23rd of March, 1779, Tarleton, with his dragoons, fell on a party of militia at Lieutenant-Governor Bee's plantation, killed ten of them, took four prisoners, and a number of horses. Three days later, Tarleton was met by Colonel Washington at Governor Rutledge's plantation, between Rantowles' Bridge and Ashley Ferry. Washington drove Tarleton's cavalry back and took several prisoners, including Colonel Hamilton, a North Carolina Royalist, and a British surgeon. Hamilton was a valuable prize, but Washington was hunting bigger game, and came near getting Sir Henry Clinton himself, on his visit to some newly-arrived reinforcements from Georgia.

His First Encounter With Tarleton

In early April, Colonel Washington, with his cavalry, was encamped at the head of Ashley River. For the purpose of surprise, fifty horse and five hundred infantry were detached by the enemy and marched to his encampment But Washington being apprised of the fact, fell back for some distance, and when the enemy came they found fires burning but no troops. The British, disappointed, retired; and Colonel Washington sent a party of horse after them and picked up three of their rear guards. From this point, Washington fell back to Monck's Corner at the head of Cooper River, where all General Greene's cavalry were posted. Clinton, determined to break up this force, sent Tarleton, who had been reinforced by Ferguson's Corps, to surprise Huger by night. Everything was favorable for Tarleton. Huger's forces were routed or captured. He, with Major Jameson and other officers and men, fled on foot to the swamps and escaped.

From this time until December, 1780, Colonel Washington and his cavalry remnant were out of action. On that date, he, with one hundred men (Johnson says seventy), was attached to the command of Daniel Morgan, at that time under General Gates. On December 4th, Gates was superceded by General Greene. Greene's first hours were brightened by a most brilliant, but bloodless victory, scored by Colonel Washington.

Rowland Rugeley, a Loyalist, lived on the Camden Road, thirteen miles north of that town. He had been commissioned a colonel in the British militia, and was desirous of being appointed a brigadier-general. Rugeley, with his followers, took post at his own house, which he had stockaded, together with his log barn. Washington, with his cavalry, pursued, and about ten o'clock on the 4th of December, 1780, appeared at Rugeley's Mill, on the south side of the creek. The Loyalists were strongly posted in the log barn, in front of which was a ditch and abatis. Having no artillery, Washington could make but little impression on the garrison, so he resorted to strategem. Fashioning a pine log as to resemble a cannon, he placed it in such a position near the bridge as to apparently command both the house and barn. He then made a demand for surrender, intimating the instant demolition of the fortress unless the summons was obeyed. Alarmed at the presence of a cannon, Rugeley sent out a flag, and with his whole force of one hundred and twelve men immediately surrendered. Rugeley never appeared in arms any more. Cornwallis, in a letter to Tarleton, said, "Rugeley will not be made a brigadier-general."

The Pine-Log Strategem

Soon after General Greene assumed command of the Southern army, a part of it was detached and ordered to march into South Carolina. Leaving Charlotte on December 16, 1780, Morgan crossed the Catawba and Broad Rivers and pitched his camp at the Grindal Shoals, on the east bank of the Pacolet on Christmas Day. A part of this force was eighty cavalrymen, led by Lieutenant-Colonel William Washington.

The country about Grindal Shoals had been scoured by Tory plunderers until provisions were hard to get, but Morgan's army must have supplies or go elsewhere; hence, his commissaries were sent abroad to glean whatever they could find. A party of Tories marched as far as Fairforest Creek to embarrass these operations. They were within twenty miles of Morgan's camp, and commanded by a Colonel Pearson and Major Ben Wofford. Morgan immediately sent Colonels Washington and McCall, with seventy-five cavalrymen and two hundred mounted militia, to drive these Loyalists from the country. Hearing of Washington's approach, they fell back to a place called Hammond's Store, where they halted, sup-

The Affair at Hammond's Store

posing that they were secure, as on their right Cornwallis was at Winnsboro, and on their left the post at Ninety-Six. Washington pressed the pursuit with such diligence that after a march of forty miles, he came upon them and immediately ordered a charge, and almost a massacre followed. Out of two hundred Tories, one hundred were killed, fifteen wounded, and only forty prisoners taken. This seems to have been rather severe, but the Whigs having so long and bitterly suffered at their hands, no doubt felt that it was what they deserved. A detachment of Americans then proceeded to the fort, on Mud Lick Creek, commanded by Colonel Cunningham, but the prey had flown to Ninety-Six, which was not far distant. Washington then returned to Grindal Shoals. These bold movements on the part of the Americans made Cornwallis fear the safety of the garrison at Ninety-Six. So on the 1st of January, 1781, Cornwallis ordered Tarleton, who had already advanced as far as Brierly's Ferry, on Broad River, now Strother, to move towards Ninety-Six, with special instructions that he "push Morgan to the utmost." After proceeding twenty miles, he found that Morgan was quite a distance from Ninety-Six, and proposed a joint movement against Morgan, which was agreed to. Hence, on January 1st, Tarleton resumed his march, and on the evening of the 15th he reached Pacolet River at the Easterwood Ford, about two miles below the present Pacolet Mills.

When Colonel Washington was returning to Grindal Shoals he passed near where General Pickens was encamped, between Tyger River and Faiforest Creek. Pickens, hearing of Tarleton's advance, immediately sent a verbal message to Morgan, apprising him of the fact.

In 1773, Colonel William Wofford erected his afterwards famous iron works on Lawson's Fork, in what is now Spartanburg County. The site of the works was on the south bank of that stream, at the head of the present Glendale pond, probably about seventy-five feet below where the electric railway crosses. When the intelligence of Tarleton's approach was received by Morgan, Colonel Washington was at Wofford's Iron Works having his horses shod. Upon receipt of the message, delivered by Major McJunkin, General Morgan called out to a little Frenchman, who had just come in from the iron works, but was then asleep: "Baron, get up and go back to the iron works and tell Billy, *i. e.,* Washington, that Benny is approaching, and tell him to meet me tomorrow evening at Gentleman Thompson's, on the east side of Thickety Creek." Accordingly, the next morning, which was the 15th, Morgan broke up camp at Grindal Shoals and marched to the place of juncture, which was where Thickety Station, on the Southern Railway, now is.

Being joined by Washington, the march was resumed early on the morning of the 16th, and the little army reached The Cowpens about sundown that evening and a halt was again called, and the information given out that it was here that they should meet the enemy.

Though night was soon upon them, much remained to be done. Morgan well knew the power of Tarleton's legion, and deemed it all important to strengthen his cavalry. Volunteers were called for, and they were ordered to press any horses into services not belonging to an officer or dragoon. Two companies were formed by Majors Jolly and McCall, consisting of about forty-five men. This made Washington's force about one hundred and twenty-five strong.

Col. Washington's Heroic Conduct at Cowpens

The plans of battle were arranged during the night, and early next morning when the lines were formed and placed, Colonel Washington was posted behind an eminence in front of the old Ezell place, some three or four hundred yards in the rear of the main line under Colonel Howard, and was to hold in reserve. Tarleton arrived a little after sunrise and immediately formed his lines and advanced to the attack. He was met by a volley from the front line of picked riflemen. Their fire was unerring, and a number of saddles were emptied, as they had been ordered to mark the "epaulet men." The British continued to advance, and the front line fell back to the second under Pickens. After delivering some murderous fires, this line was forced back and retreated toward Howard's flank, as they had been ordered to do. But before they could gain the cover of this line, the British cavalry charged and drove them back towards the position held by Washington. That brave officer immediately met this bold dash by a counter charge, which scattered the British horses in the wildest confusion. This enabled Pickens to promptly rally and re-form his men, and passing around the ridge behind which Washington had been posted, he reached Howard's right flank just as the enemy were about to turn it.

Howard held Tarleton's main force in check for fifteen or twenty minutes. Not making the headway that he expected, he ordered his reserves into action. Seeing this, Morgan ordered Pickens to attack the enemy's left flank, and Washington to charge their right. Both orders were promptly executed. Before these movements were understood by Howard, seeing the danger to which his right was exposed, he ordered his flank company to change front. This was understood that they should retire to the eminence some distance to the rear, and began to fall back in good order to that point. The enemy mistook this movement for a retreat, and somewhat confusedly dashed forward, yelling at the top of their voices. Seeing this break in the enemy's line, Washington sent Morgan word "that they were coming on like a mob, and if he would give them one fire the cavalry would charge them." Morgan instantly ordered the men to face about and fire, which was done with such deadly effect that the enemy gave way Howard then ordered a bayonet charge, and Washington wheeled into the rear and was about to charge them when they laid down their arms, many of them falling on their faces. The victory was now won and in a few minutes it was complete.

In one of his charges, Colonel Washington and Tarleton had a personal encounter. In the eagerness of his pursuit of that officer, **Washington-Tarleton Incident** Washington had got far in advance of his men, when Tarleton and two of his aides, at the head of his Seventeenth Regiment of dragoons, turned upon him. An officer on Tarleton's right was about to strike the impetuous Washington with his saber, when Sergeant-Major Perry came up and disabled the assailant's sword arm. An officer on Tarleton's left was about to strike at the same moment, when Washington's little bugler, about fourteen years old, disabled him with a pistol ball. Tarleton, who was in the center, then made a thrust at him, which Washington parried, and gave his enemy a wound in the hand. Tarleton wheeled, and as he retreated discharged his pistol, and the ball was received by Washington's faithful horse.

It is related that this wound was twice the subject for the sallies of wit by two American ladies, who were sisters—daughters of Colonel Monfort, of Halifax County, North Carolina. When Cornwallis and his army were at Halifax on their way to Virginia, Tarleton was at the home of an American. In the presence of

Mrs. Willie Jones, Tarleton spoke of Colonel Washington as an illiterate fellow, hardly able to write his name. "Ah, Colonel," said Mrs. Jones, "you ought to knew better, for you bear on your person proof that he knows very well how to make his mark." At another time, Tarleton was speaking sarcastically of Washington in the presence of Mrs. Ashe, a sister of Mrs. Jones. "I would be happy to see Colonel Washington," he said with a sneer. Mrs. Ashe instantly replied, "If you had looked behind you, Colonel Tarleton, at the battle of The Cowpens, you would have enjoyed that pleasure." Stung with this keen wit, Tarleton placed his hand on his sword. General Leslie, who was present, remarked, "Say what you please, Mrs. Ashe; Colonel Tarleton knows better than to insult a lady in my presence."*

For some unkown reason Cornwallis did not carry out his part in the joint movement against Morgan, but remained in his camp on Turkey Creek in York District. Tarleton being defeated, and his army practically annihilated, with a few horsemen, fled to Cornwallis' camp.

About two miles northeast from Grindal Shoals lived an aged couple, Adam and Hannah Goudelock. He was a non-combatant, but sided with the Whig cause. Not being acquainted with the country, Tarleton, in his flight, stopped at Goudelock's and forced the old man to go with him as a pilot to Hamilton's Ford on Broad River. A few minutes after Tarleton left, Colonel Washington and a squad of his cavalry came dashing up in hot pursuit. He asked Hannah how long Tarleton had been gone. Fear for the safety of her husband, in case the pursuit was continued, getting the better of her patriotism, she replied: "Almost three hours." This answer caused Washington to give up the chase and return to Cowpens, driving before him near one hundred straggling prisoners collected on the route. Had it not been for this falsehood, Tarleton would have been bagged, and his career of murder and pillage ended; and the chief crowning star of glory would have been put on that immortal day of January 17, 1781.

Congress voted Colonel Washington a silver medal for his great valor at The Cowpens. The following are device and inscription: An officer mounted at the head of a body of cavalry, charging flying troops; victory in the form of an angel is flying near the

---

*See Lossing, Field Book of the Revolution, Vol II, page 436

heads of the Americans, holding a laurel crown in her right hand and a palm branch in her left. Legend: "Guliems Washington Legionis Equitum Praefects Comitia Americans—the American Congress to William Washington, commander of a regiment of cavalry." Reverse: "Quod Parva Militum Manu Strenue Prosecutus Hastes Virtutis Ingenitae Praeclarum Specimen Dedit In Pugna Ad Cowpens, 17th January, 1781—Because having vigorously pursued the foe with a small band of soldiers, he gave a brilliant specimen of innate valor in the battle of Cowpens, 17th of January, 1781." This inscription is within a laurel wreath.

Morgan began his masterly retreat into North Carolina the same day the fight took place. Leaving the battlefield about noon, he crossed Broad River that evening. By exercising great skill, aided by Providence, with his prisoners and booty, he reached Sherald's Ford on the Catawba, where he was joined by General Greene in person, about January 30th. It is said that no officer aided more materially in this perilous retreat than did Colonel William Washington

The battle of Guilford Court House, North Carolina, took place March 15th, 1781. Four small companies of cavalry, consisting of Kirkwood's Delawares, were commanded by Colonel Washington, and were placed on the right line as a covering party. Johnson, in his "Life of Greene," says: "No language can do justice to the gallantry with which Washington conducted himself; he was everywhere where duty called, and indefatigable in searching for opportunities for service." At one time Washington saw Lord Cornwallis near him and completely within his reach, and while he waved his sword for

Colonel Washington at Guilford

some of his officers to follow him, the string that held his cap on by passing under his chin broke and the cap fell from his head. The fall of his cap obliged him to dismount, which gave the British general time to provide for his safety.

After Greene's defeat at Guilford, he withdrew into South Carolina and gave Lord Rawdon battle at Hobkirk's Hill, near Camden, April 25th. Greene went into this contest with great confidence of victory, but because of the cowardice of some troops and poor generalship, his hopes were not realized. When all seemed lost, Washington appeared and saved the artillery and put an end to the fray. But his mistake was in delaying too long. In his official communication, Greene asserts that Washington penetrated into the enemy's rear, found them flying in confusion, and made two hundred prisoners. While Greene may have received such a report, it was undoubtedly an error. Colonel Davy, an American officer, whose truthfulness and fidelity cannot be questioned, submits the following: "In turning the enemy's left, Washington made a circuit so large as to bring him into the open commons between Log Town and Camden; this space was filled with doctors, surgeons, quartermasters, commissaries, wagon masters, waiters, and all the loose trumpery of an army who had pushed out to see the battle. The cavalry immediately charged this mixed multitude, and employed in taking, securing and paroling a great number of these people, those precious moments which would have brought them in actual contact with the second line of the enemy, either before it moved up to extend the front or while this maneuver was performing, and in either case the charge would have been decisive, and the battle would not have lasted fifteen minutes. But the charge was never made on the line of the enemy, the critical moment was lost, and in battle minutes are hours. The British officers acknowledged the unfortunate effect of the clemency of our cavalry in waiting to capture and parole prisoners, when they should have cut them out of their way without stopping, and charged the rear of the British line. They were, in fact, so encumbered with prisoners they could do nothing." Another writer has said: "Not only did Washington waste his time in paroling wounded officers and non-combatants, but he encumbered his cavalry by mounting these useless prisoners behind his troopers, thus

(Col. Washington's Mistake at Hobkirk's Hill)

exhausting his horses and rendering them, while thus doubly burdened, useless for further action."

The British accounts make still less of Colonel Washington's movements in their rear. They restrict its results to the capture of a few stragglers and the paroling of some British officers, who lay on the ground. As we have already seen, Washington partly retrieved his mistakes by appearing just in time to save Greene's artillery from capture. When Greene retired, Rawdon also withdrew towards Camden, leaving Captain Coffin and some mounted men on the field of battle. Washington succeeded in drawing this party into an ambush and cut it to pieces, and as a consequence he occupied the position where Greene had drawn up his army in the morning, and thus, in a way, the Americans remained in possession of the field.

During the interim between Hobkirk Hill and Eutaw Springs, Washington was not inactive, but for the want of efficient horses he could only do ordinary service in watching the enemy and cutting off small parties, mostly by surprise At Eutaw Springs, which battle took place September 9, 1781, Colonel Washington met his Waterloo. As usual, he, with his cavalry, was held in reserve. When Greene saw that the enemy must be dislodged from the brick house which they occupied, Washington was ordered to turn Major Majoribanks' (pronounced Marshbanks) right. He attempted a charge on his front, but his cavalry was unable to penetrate the dense woods. Failing in this, Washington turned to the left, but in so doing he exposed his flank, into which the enemy poured a deadly fire, which brought Washington to the ground, and with him many men and horses, and every officer except two. Just what happened to Washington here, writers differ. All agree that his horse was shot down. Some mention his being wounded, others do not. One says that while trying to dislodge himself from his fallen horse, he received a bayonet wound and was taken prisoner. Another says: "In attempting to execute, with his usual impetuosity, an almost impossible order, his horse was killed under him, and he fell in the midst of the British infantry, very severely wounded, and would there have lost his life but for the generosity of Major Majoribanks, of the British army, who interfered and saved his life." He was made a prisoner, paroled, and allowed to proceed to Charleston, where he re-

Col. Washington Meets His Waterloo

mained until the close of the war. This ended his military career, for every effort to secure an exchange was refused.

On a bluff, or hill, near a stream running into the Stono River, known as Hyde Park, or Elliott's Savanna, about seven miles from Rantowle's Ferry, stood during the Revolutionary period the stately mansion of Charles Elliott. The plantation embraced a large body of land, consisting of several thousand acres. This plantation was known as "Sandy Hill." Here lived Miss Jane Elliott, who, as we shall see later, improvised and presented to Colonel Washington his battle flag. About the close of the war he married Miss Elliott and settled near Charleston.

His Post-War Career

He represented his district in the State legislature for some years, and was tendered the nomination for governor, but declined the honor on the grounds that he had been a citizen of the State only for a short while and that "he could not make a speech."

In 1798, when the United States was threatened with war by France, President Adams called George Washington to the position of Commander-in-Chief of the American army. General Washington recommended the appointment of his "kinsman" as brigadier-general, which was done July 19th, 1798, and in a letter to the Secretary of War, suggested that he be given the direction of affairs in South Carolina and Georgia.

Colonel Washington died on the 6th of March, 1810. A writer describes him as follows: "He was tall and majestic in person, exhibiting a manly figure, with every indication of supreme strength and corresponding activity. His countenance was composed and rather of a serious cast, but evinced the benevolence that characterized all his actions. In social life he was retiring and taciturn."

His Death

The Elliott plantation, previously mentioned, was joined by another called "Live Oak" On this plantation was the Elliott family's cemetery, and within its borders lie the mortal remains of Colonel William Washington and his wife, the spot being marked only by a slab of marble with this inscription: "My Parents, Dear, Lie Here, J. A." J A. stands for Jane Ancrum, the only daughter of the Washingtons, and she survived until 1866.

On the occasion of his death, the American Revolution Society adopted resolutions in which he was spoken of as . "Modest without timidity, generous without extravagance, brave without rashness, and disinterested without austerity, which imparted firmness to his conduct and mildness to his manners, solidity to his judgment and boldness to his achievements, which armed him with an equanimity unalterable by the frowns of adversity or the smiles of fortune, and steadiness of soul not to be subdued by the disasters of defeat or elated by the triumphs of victory."

As we have already seen, Colonel Washington, as opportunity offered, was a visitor at "Sandy Hill," the Elliott Estate. On a hurried visit there during the storm of war, the want of a flag for his cavalry was mentioned.

Col. Washington's Battle Flag

From a heavy crimson silk curtain, with handsome silk fringe, the nimble scissors cut a square, the ready needle bound its edge, and a hickory pole served as a staff. "Here is your flag, Colonel," said Jane Elliott. This historic flag, a picture of which adorns the frontispiece of a small volume entitled, "Proceedings at the Unveiling of the Battle Monument at Spartanburg, S. C.," was at Cowpens, Guilford, Hobkirk Hill, Eutaw Springs, and in numerous smaller combats, and is preserved to this day.

After about a half century had elapsed, Mrs. Washington determined to give the custody of this sacred relic to one of the military companies of Charleston. The Washington Light Infantry was her choice. At that time Captain Robert Budd Gilchrist was the commander. The ceremony took place in front of Mrs. Washington's house in Charleston, April 19, 1827. In presenting the crimson relic, this noble woman referred to the corps as "a band of citizen soldiers, who would on no occasion suffer its honor or luster to tarnish," and the corps made a pledge "to consider it more precious than their lives, as dear as their sacred honor."

In 1876 it was found necessary to repair the flag, which could only be done by quilting it on a piece of crimson silk. Mr. George F. Babbage, an English dry goods merchant in Charleston, asked to see the flag, and when brought to him he exhibited a piece of crimson silk closely resembling the original flag, and said, "I brought that remnant of silk from England a great many years ago, and I know of no better use to put it to than to restore this historic flag." This was done, and it was said that the flag was good for another hundred years. It is worthy of note than an *Englishman* furnished the silk to repair this *historic* American flag.

In 1856, when the Washington Light Infantry erected the now

battered monument on The Cowpens battle ground, this flag once more waved over the same field, where it had been followed to such a glorious victory seventy-five years before. At the Centennial in 1881, as the troops moved in procession, it was again unfurled on the streets of Spartanburg.

This precious relic is kept in a case and deposited in a bank vault for safekeeping. It is displayed annually on the 22nd of February, Washington's birthday. It is the only flag of the Revolution that is in active use by any military company in the United States.

In 1858, the Washington Light Infantry erected a beautiful monument to the honor and memory of William and Jane Washington. It stands in the Magnolia cemetery at Charleston. It is of white marble, and about seventeen feet high. The base is four-square, and surmounted by a circular column around which a spiral wreath is entwined. The four faces of the base are marked by appropriate inscriptions. The monument is enclosed by a handsome wrought-iron railing. The gate posts are made of two bronze cannon, used in the Revolution. So were the two crossed sabres that adorns the top of the gate.

Col. Washington's Monument in Charleston

The Life of Colonel John Thomas, Sr.

JOHN THOMAS was born in Wales; but being removed to America when quite young, he was brought up in Chester County, Pennsylvania. About the year 1740, he married Jane Black, a native of his adopted county, and a sister of Rev. John Black, the first President of Dickerson College. She was a woman of rare intellectual attainments, splendid education, of great force of character, and, as we shall see later, played her part as one of the noted heroines of Independence. Some ten or fifteen years after his marriage, Mr. Thomas emigrated to South Carolina and resided for some time on Fishing Creek, in what is now Chester County. About twelve or fourteen years before the breaking out of the Revolution, he removed to Fairforest, where he settled on that stream, just above the mouth of Kelso's Creek, within the present limits of Spartanburg He was one of the founders of the historic Fairforest Presbyterian Church, and Mrs. Thomas was one of its most active and zealous members. He was described as "industrious, intelligent, patriotic and highly distinguished for his devotion to the public welfare." For quite a number of years before the commencement of the Revolution, Mr. Thomas held commissions from the Royal Government as magistrate and captain of militia, but when the mutterings of hostilities began to rumble, he resigned these positions.

That which has rendered the name of John Thomas immortal was his connection with the Spartan Regiment. How that regiment got its name should be a matter of concern, for there is no doubt but that the name Spartanburg was derived from it. The most common view is this: That William Henry Drayton, who was sent out by the Council of Safety to explain the differences between the Colonies and the Mother Country, did on the 21st of August, 1775, assemble a goodly number of citizens at Wofford's Iron Works, on Lawson's Fork. Writing to the Council of Safety on the same day, Mr. Drayton says: "I had this day a meeting with the people in this frontier. Many present were of the other party, but I have the pleasure to acquaint you that those became voluntary converts Every person received satis-

The Spartan Regiment

faction and departed with pleasure. I have also ordered matters here, that this whole frontier will be formed into voluntary companies, but as they are at present under Fletchball's (Fletchall or Fletcher) command, they insist upon being formed into a regiment independent of him, and I flatter myself you will think this method of weakening Fletchball to be considered sound policy. These people are active and spirited, they are staunch in our favor; are capable of forming a good barrier against the Indians, and of being a severe check upon Fletchball's people, on whom they border. For these reasons, and to enable them to act with vigor, I shall take the liberty of supplying them with a small quantity of ammunition, for they have not an ounce, when they shall be formed into regular companies. Several companies will be formed by this day week."

The following letter is taken from Gibb's Documentary History:

"Spartan Regiment, Sept. 11th, 1775.
"*To the Honorable Wm. H Drayton, Esq.*

"MAY IT PLEASE YOUR HONOR:—I this moment received your Honor's favor of the 10th inst., and very fortunately, the command for this district was just assembled at my house in order to address the Council of Safety almost on the very purport of your Honor's letter, as we had all the reason in the world (and still have) to believe from good information that the malignants are forming the most hellish schemes to frustrate the measures of the Continental Congress, and to use all those who are willing to stand by those measures in the most cruel manner. Your Honor will be fully convinced of the truth of this by perusing the papers transmitted, to which I refer your Honor.

"I shall comply with your Honor's orders as far as is in my power. Your Honor must suppose it impossible to raise the whole regiment, as several have families and no man be left about the house, if they should be called away. I shall take as large a draft as possible from every company, and in short, do everything to the utmost of my power, and when encamped shall transmit to your Honor, as quick as possible, an account of my proceedings.

"JOHN THOMAS"

Dr. Landrum says that the organization was effected on the above named date, and it was called the *Spartan Regiment*. He furthermore says that the name "was doubtless suggested by the Hon. Wm. Henry Drayton, who was at that time President of the

Provincial Congress, then convened, who desired to express his appreciation of the patriotic sentiments which he knew to prevail in said section visited by him during the previous year." This appears plausible, but it is not certain. Under the Royal Government, the territory between the Broad and Saluda rivers formed a regimental district over which Colonel Fletcher, or Fletchall, presided; and there are reasons for believing that the upper part of the district was called *Spartan* before the regiment under Thomas was rearranged. A careful reading of his letter above will show that the regiment called for by Drayton had not been raised, although he says, "The command for this district (undoubtedly Fletcher's, or at least a part of it) was just assembled at my house," etc. He believed it impossible "to raise the whole regiment," but promised Mr. Drayton to "do everything to the utmost of my power." Evidently, then, the troops called for by Drayton were not at that time collected and organized for the patriot service; yet Thomas writes his letter from *"Spartan Regiment"* Saye, in his "Memoir of McJunkin," says: "Upon the refusal of Colonel Fletcher to accept a commission under the authority of the Province, an election was held and John Thomas was chosen colonel of the *Spartan Regiment,* having previously resigned the commissions that he had held under the Royal Government." Then the regiment under Fletcher appears to have been called the Spartan previous to Drayton's visit; and most of them, at least, being convinced of the righteousness of the patriot cause, resolved to resist the British yoke, and when Fletcher refused to go with them they reorganized and elected John Thomas colonel. Whether they originally gave themselves the name; or some one else, because of their ancient Spartan spirit, we cannot tell; hence the truth in the matter is enveloped in uncertainty.

Mr. Saye, being informed by Major Joseph McJunkin, a son-in-law of Colonel Thomas, says: "In the month of November, the Provincial Congress raised an army for the purpose of subduing the Tories and reducing the Indians to peace, as they were now committing depredations along the frontiers. General Richardson was appointed commander-in-chief of this expedition Colonel John Thomas, who resided on Fairforest Creek, just above the mouth of Kelso's Creek, was ordered by Richardson to raise a regiment and meet him at Granby The regiment was raised without drafting a man." This may have been the first real completion of the regiment; for if it had been perfected a few weeks before, we can see no reason for raising another so soon. This regiment consisted of two hundred men, and with them Colonel Thomas proceeded to join Richardson, whom he found encamped at McLaurin's store, in the Dutch Fork, in early December. From the heavy snow that fell during its latter part, it was called "The Snow Campaign."

The nearness of this regiment to the frontiers imposed a large amount of active service on the men belonging to it, and great responsibilities upon the commander. In the spring of 1776, British emissaries incited the Indians to an uprising for general destruction. Soon the work of pillaging, burning and massacreing began. In May, a number of soldiers assembled under General Williamson at a camp on Fairforest near the residence of Colonel Thomas. Williamson pursued the Indians and overtook a number of them at Richard Pearis' (Parris), on the present site of Greenville. Here considerable property belonging to Pearis was taken and destroyed by Colonel Thomas. The Indians and their Tory associates, that escaped capture, fled. In September, Pearis memorialized the General Assembly, seeking redress for his losses. Colonel Thomas and his followers shared in the perils and hardships suffered by Williamson's army, while in the heart of the enemy's country, which brought the Indians to sue for peace.

On March the 26th, 1776, the Provincial Congress resolved itself into a General Assembly. Those who thus became members of the first Assembly were John Thomas, Michael Leitner, Jonas Beard, William Wofford, William Henderson and John Prince, from the Spartan District.

In April, 1776, election precincts were arranged for the Ninety-Six District. For the Upper, or Spartan District, the precinct was to be near the Fairforest meeting house, and the commissioners were Colonel John Thomas, Captain Andrew Berry, Captain Thomas Brandon, Captain Ralph Smith, and John Thomas, Jr.

Colonel Thomas retained the command of his regiment until after the fall of Charlestown in May, 1780. Soon after that event, Major Patrick Ferguson was sent to the up-country to complete its subjugation. His policy was to use persuasion first, and where that failed he would use coercive measures. About the last of June, Ferguson reached the Fairforest region, where the family of Colonel

Thomas resided. The Whig families were mercilessly plundered—what property was not taken off was wantonly destroyed. The country between the Broad and Saluda rivers was overawed, and about all that the patriots could do was to take British protection, or abandon the country. By the former course they hoped to remain unmolested with their families. Colonel Thomas, then quite advanced in life, with such choice spirits as Andrew Williamson, Isaac Huger, Andrew Pickens, Isaac Hayne and others, took protection; but poor protection it was, for Cornwallis used the severest measures, hoping thereby, says a writer, "to crush and extinguish the spirit still struggling and flashing forth like hidden fire among the people whom the arm of power had for a season brought under subjection." But the continual witnessing of the sufferings inflicted on the helpless Whigs was too much for a gallant spirit like that of John Thomas. Therefore, he cast aside the pretended protection and was taking steps to organize a regiment in his community when he was arrested by the notorious Tory leader, Sam Brown, and sent to prison at Ninety-Six. After remaining there for awhile, he was carried to Charlestown, where he remained until the end of the war. Brown carried off Colonel Thomas' negroes and horses.

After his father's capture, it appears that John Thomas, Jr., raised a regiment, which Draper calls the *Fair Forest,* while Mrs. Ellett, in her "Women of the Revolution," calls it the *Spartan.* While there may have been some in it that belonged to the original Spartan, it was really a new regiment. John Thomas, Jr., was colonel, and the place of rendezvous was at the Cedar Spring This noted spring derived its name from a large cedar tree that, in early times, stood on its banks. It was then about fifty feet in circumference and three feet deep. This spring is only a few miles southeast of Spartanburg, and is now rendered famous by the State's magnificent institution for the education of the deaf, dumb and blind being located there. In early July, Mrs. Thomas paid a visit to Ninety-Six, where her aged husband and two sons were incarcerated in the loathsome prison there, hoping thereby to render them such assistance as she could. While there, Mrs. Thomas overheard a conversation between some Tory women, and her quick ear caught these words: "The Loyalists intend, tomorrow night, to surprise the Rebels at Cedar Spring." This intelligence was indeed ominous,

The First Battle of Cedar Spring

and, naturally, enough to fill a mother's heart with great anxiety; for Cedar Spring was not far from her home, and the little regiment there was commanded by her own son, and numbers of the men were her neighbors, friends and kinsmen. No time was to be lost—she determined, if possible, to apprise them of their danger before the cowardly blow could be struck. Early the next morning she mounted her horse and reached Cedar Spring in the evening, delivered her message, and then quietly retired to her Fairforest home, having ridden about sixty miles, but conscious that she had performed her duty to her kindred and to her country.

Colonel Thomas' force numbered only about sixty men, and as soon as he received the intelligence brought by his mother, a brief consultation was held as to the best means of defense. Their decision was to rekindle their camp-fires so that they would burn brightly, and then to retire a short distance from them in the woods.

They had just completed their preparations and gotten to their positions when they heard, in the distance, the cautious advance of their assailants. What followed is thus described by a writer: "Slowly and warily, and with tread as noiseless as possible, the enemy advanced, till they were already within the glare of the blazing fires, and safely, as it seemed, on the verge of their anticipated work of destruction. No sound betrayed alarm; they supposed the intended victims wrapped in heavy slumber; they heard but the crackling of the flames and the hoarse murmurs of the wind as it swept through the pine trees. The assailants gave the signal for the onset, and rushed towards the fires, eager for indiscriminate slaughter. Suddenly the flashes and shrill reports of rifles revealed the champions of liberty. The enemy, to their consternation, found themselves assailed in the rear by the party they had expected to strike unawares. Thrown into confusion by the unexpected reception, defeat, overwhelming defeat, was the consequence to these Loyalists."* Although the enemy numbered about one hundred and fifty strong, the affair was short, quick and decisive. Several were slain, and the survivors scampered off badly demoralized. Among the slain was a Tory by the name of John White, who was well known to some of Thomas' party, and had in the early part of the war declined to bear arms against the Indians, on the trumped-up plea that he was a non-combatant. After all, it was fortunate for

---

*Mrs Ellet's "Women of the Revolution"

the patriots, that it was a night attack, as it rendered the enemy unable to discover the inferiority of Thomas' numbers. Doubtless, they retired believing that there were several hundred. The victory was achieved without loss to the Americans, but who can tell what the consequences would have been had it not been for the heroine, Jane Thomas. This affair took place on July 12th, 1780.

Some time early in the war, Governor Rutledge sent a quantity of arms and ammunition to the house of Colonel Thomas, to be in **Another** readiness for any emergency that might arise on **Heroic Deed** the frontier. The house was prepared to resist assault, and put under the guard of twenty-five men. Intelligence was received by Colonel Thomas that a large party of Tories led by Colonel Moore, of North Carolina, was advancing to attack him. Thomas and his guard considered it unwise to risk an engagement with a force so much larger than their own; consequently, they withdrew to a place of safety, carrying as much of the ammunition with them as possible. Josiah Culbertson, a son-in-law of Thomas belonged to the guard, but refused to leave the house with the others He and little William Thomas were the only occupants of the house, except the women. At length, Moore and his band appeared before the house and prepared for the capture of the booty, which did not turn out to be such an easy task. Their demand for admittance was answered by an order to leave the place The old-fashioned "batten door," strongly barricaded, resisted their efforts to demolish it, and their fire did little or no execution because of the heavy logs of which the house was built. Their fire was returned by the faithful defenders from the upper story and proved to be much more effective than that of the assailants. Mrs Thomas and her daughters, aided by the youthful William, loaded the guns as fast as Culbertson could fire them. Culbertson, being an expert marksman, was doing so much execution, and the rapidity with which the guns were fired, led the enemy to believe that a considerable force was concealed in the house, and that further effort was useless. Getting things together, Moore and his crowd retreated as rapidly as their wounds and wounded would permit.

After waiting a reasonable length of time, and reconnoitering the best she could from her position, Mrs. Thomas descended the stairs and opened the doors. As a writer has expressed it: "When her husband made his appearance, and knew how gallantly the plunderers had been repulsed, his joy was only equalled by his admiration of his wife's heroism." This same powder was again marvelously preserved when Colonel Brandon's camp was surprised and broken up by a force under "Bloody Bill" Cunningham. It eventually served as the principal supply for Sumter's army in the battles of Rocky Mount and Hanging Rock.

Mrs. Thomas was not only distinguished for her bravery and heroism, but for indomitable energy, perseverance, eminent piety, **The Family of Colonel Thomas** discretion and industry. She is described as being "below the ordinary stature, with black eyes and hair, rounded and pleasant features, fair complexion and countenance sprightly and expressive."

Mrs. Thomas was the mother of eight children—four sons and four daughters. John was the eldest son and took an active part in the war. He was colonel of his regiment, and several of his brilliant acts and achievements have been mentioned in different parts of this work. He was with General Sumter in some of his most important engagements. His speech at Bullock's Creek, in June, 1780, revealed his unflinching patriotism and undaunted bravery *

Independence having been won, only a few years elapsed until the wheels of civil government were put in motion. The records show that the first court that was ever held in Spartanburg County convened at Nickoll's Mill, which, according to Dr Landrum, stood at, or near, Anderson's Mill on North Tyger, where Captain David Anderson afterwards lived.

The following entry is made:

"June Court, 1785.

"At a court began to be holden at Nickoll's Mill, on the third Monday in June, one thousand and seven hundred and eighty-five, for the County of Spartanburg, in the State of South Carolina.

"Present—Baylis Earle, John Thomas, Jun'r, Henry White, John Ford and Henry Machan Wood, Gentlemen Justices.

"Court being opened, *John Thomas, Jun'r, being previously appointed clerk*, the court proceeded to the choice of a sheriff for said county. Thereupon casting up the votes, Mr. William Young was duly appointed to that office, and Josiah Buffington duly appointed coroner for said county.

---
*For a synopsis of this speech and the circumstances under which it was delivered, see "Life of Major Joseph McJunkin." page 230

"Court adjourned until court in course."

It will be seen from the above that John Thomas, Jun'r, was the first clerk of the court in Spartanburg. His bond was given September 19th, 1785, and his bondsmen were Richard Harrison, William Prince and William Smith. The amount was one thousand pounds.

There are good reasons for believing that if Colonel Thomas, Jun'r, ever married at all, it was not until he passed middle life; for in none of the family narratives that we have seen is there any mention of his marriage; and when he sold his Fairforest plantation to Joseph Wofford in 1795, no one signed the deed except himself. Undoubtedly, if he had been married, his wife would have signed it, and thereby renounced her dower. At the time of this transaction, he was a resident of Greenville County, his father having moved there shortly after the war was over.

Captain Robert Thomas, another son, was mortally wounded at the battle of Mud Lick, or Roebuck's defeat Abram was wounded, taken prisoner and died in confinement at Ninety-Six.

William, the youth, who aided in defending the house on the occasion already mentioned, took part in other activities, but we find no further mention of him.

The four daughters married staunch Whigs, and all held commissions in the war and rendered their country substantial service in the cause of freedom. Martha married Josiah Culbertson, who was the most effective scout in the country, and figured in many daring and single-handed adventures. Mrs. Culbertson was said to be a woman of exceedingly rare beauty, and her sister, Ann, was a close second Ann married Major Joseph McJunkin, whose career is given in another part of this work.

Jane, the third daughter, married Captain Joseph McCool, and Letitia married Major James Lusk. Both of these were brave and patriotic officers, but little or nothing is now known of their achievements.

On the north side of Fairforest, near the mouth of Kelso's Creek, a beautiful elevated ridge rises and extends in the direction of the present White Stone Station on the Southern Railway. From the time of the earliest settlements, it has been known as Rich Hill. This tract of land has also been long pointed out as the reputed homestead of Colonel John Thomas, Sr., during and after the Revolution. A short distance to the westward from the public highway leading from White Stone to Foster's Mill and bridge on Fairforest, the site of the house and family burying ground are said to be. This site is about one mile from the Forest. In 1904 the D. A. R's. of Spartanburg placed a marker over the supposed graves of Colonel John and Mrs. Jane Thomas, which is a granite block with a bronzet tablet embedded in it, bearing the following inscription:

"Erected, 1904, to the memory of Colonel John Thomas and his wife, Jane Thomas, by the Spartanburg D A. R's."

Later this marker was enclosed by an iron fence.

These acts of patriotism are greatly to be admired; but there is one unfortunate thing about it—the marker is at the wrong place. The records in the office of the Register of Deeds at Spartanburg show, most conclusively, that the beautiful tract of land described above never belonged to Colonel John Thomas, Sen., at all It was originally granted to Peter Johnson by William Tryon, Governor of North Carolina, December 11th, 1770.

The following are extracts from Deed Book "F," pages 101 and 102:

"JOHN THOMAS TO MOSES FOSTER
Deed—14th April, 1798.

"Know all men by these presents, that I, John Thomas, of Spartanburg and State aforesaid, for and in consideration of the sum of two hundred dollars, to him in hand paid by Moses Foster, of the said county and State, have granted, bargained, sold and released, and by these presents do grant, bargain, sell and release unto the said Moses Foster a certain parcel or tract of land lying in Spartanburg County on the north side of Fairforest, on a certain ridge or hill generally known as Rich Hill, bounded as follows· Beginning at a black oak on the west side of Rich Hill and branch called Long Branch—running thence N. 70, E 52 chains and fifty links—containing four hundred acres, more or less," etc., etc

This deed was signed by John Thomas, Shands Golightly and Martha Golightly. It was witnessed by James Smith, John Foster and M Louvina Smith The date was March the 21st, 1798.

The following is quite interesting:
"State of South Carolina—Spartanburg County.

"I, Isham Harrison, one of Judges of the county aforesaid,

Colonel John Thomas, Sr.

do hereby certify unto all whom it may concern that Martha Golightly, *mother to the within named John Thomas,* did this day appear before me, and being privately and separately examined by me, did declare that she does freely, voluntarily and without any compulsion, dread or fear of any person or persons whosoever, renounce, release and forever bequeath unto the within named Moses Foster, his heirs and assigns, all her interest and estate—also all her right and claim of dower of, in, or to all and singular the premises above mentioned and released. Given under my hand and seal this 9th day of April, 1798.   "Martha Golightly (Seal)
"(Seal) I Harrison, Judge of County."

The John Thomas who sold the Rich Hill lands to Moses Foster could not have been Colonel John, Sen., who was born in Wales between the years of 1715 and 1720. The natural inference is that a man by the name of Thomas obtained the Peter Johnson grant. He probably died at an early age and left the plantation to his son John; his wife, Martha, retaining her dower. Later Mrs Thomas married Shands Golightly, who became a share-holder, and when they sold out to Foster, all three signed the deed.

The following entry is also made in Book of Deeds "D," pages 436 and 437:

December 1st, 1796, John Thomas, Jun., of Greenville County, conveyed to Joseph Wofford, "all that plantation, tract, or parcel of land situated in Spartanburg County, *on both sides of Fairforest Creek,* containing two hundred and fifty acres, including the plantation whereon the said John Thomas formerly lived, joining lands laid off for John Thomas, Sen., Josiah Culbertson and James Tillette—except a few acres sold to said Culbertson—when said land was granted to the John Thomas, Jun., in the year of our Lord 1771, under the hand of William Tryon, then Governor of North Carolina."

This deed was signed by John Thomas, Jun., only, November 28th, 1795, in the presence of George Roebuck and Andrew Thompson. The next year Joseph Wofford conveyed the property to James Barnette In 1799, James Barnette conveyed that portion lying on the south side of Fairforest to Richard Barnette, and in this deed it is spoken of as a part of the plantation belonging to John Thomas. In 1800, Richard Barnette sold to William Lancaster; and in 1802 he conveyed this tract of one hundred and sixty-seven acres to Zachariah McDaniel. In 1829, McDaniel conveyed to William M. Kennedy four hundred acres on Fairforest Creek called McDanielsville. This deed states that it was composed of sundry tracts described in the records.

The name of McDanielsville implies that a rural postoffice had been established at McDaniel's; for in those early times the post-offices frequently took the name of the person at whose place they were, with *ville* attached. Examples of this are Meansville, in Union; Gowdysville, in Cherokee, and Cashville, in Spartanburg.

The records show that James Barnette, the second owner of the Thomas lands, conveyed to William Lancaster a tract of three acres on Fairforest which contained a shoal, and that Lancaster and McDaniel built a grist mill there. This is described as "Buffington old tract." Subsequently Lancaster and McDaniel conveyed this property to Daniel White. Undoubtedly, this site is the one on which Foster's Mill now stands.

In 1830, William Kennedy conveyed the McDanielsville plantation to George Kellock, "but not including the three acre tract on which Antioch Methodist Church now stands."

As Antioch Methodist Church yet stands—1924—the immediate vicinity of the Thomas homestead is easily located, and shows that Mr Saye was right when he said that Colonel John Thomas, Sen, "lived on Fairforest just above the mouth of Kelso's Creek"

Nothing is found among the records in either North or South Carolina which shows that any lands on Fairforest were ever granted to, or sold by, John Thomas, Sen.; therefore, we conclude that he settled on his son's grant, a part of which was laid off for him. In the deed of conveyance given by the younger Thomas to Joseph Wofford, mention is made of the property "joining lands laid off for John Thomas, Sen."; not granted to, nor owned by, but *"laid off for"*

The proof is, therefore, conclusive that the Rich Hill lands, the reputed Thomas homestead on which the family marker stands, was never at any time before, during, or after the Revolution owned by the Colonels Thomas who figured so prominently in the struggle for independence.

Mr Saye says: "Soon after the war closed, Colonel Thomas removed to Greenville District, where he resided till the time of his death."

Colonel John Thomas, Sr.

There is on record at the courthouse in Spartanburg a conveyance dated March 21st, 1786, by Thomas Tod and his wife, Ann, to John Thomas, Sen., conveying four hundred and forty acres of land on the northeast side of the "South Fork of Tyger River above the ancient boundary in the State aforesaid granted to Major Parsons."

This deed describes John Thomas, Sen., as "Commissioner of Locations for the north side of Saluda River." By this we presume that he was a surveyor and had to do the arranging and laying off homesteads for prospective settlers. The fact that he held that position at the time of the above mentioned purchases leads us to believe that he had removed to Greenville District for some time previous. An examination of the records at Greenville would, doubtless, reveal the exact location of the last earthly home of the old hero and his wife, a heroine who played her part so well in the Revolutionary drama. There their ashes quietly sleep, awaiting the time when "the Lord, Himself, shall descend from heaven with a shout, with the voice of the archangel, and with the trump of God; and the dead in Christ shall rise first." I Thess. 4:16.

We have not been able to find the exact date of their deaths.*

We have in hand a copy of a grant made to John Thomas, Sen., of a tract of land containing eight hundred acres, situated in St. Mark's Parish, Craven County, on the north side of the Santee River. The date of this grant is August 13th, 1766. This may be the date of Colonel Thomas' advent into South Carolina. He could have removed from there to Fishing Creek in Chester District—his residence there is only a supposition of his descendants—and from thence to Fairforest, and finally, as we know, to Greenville.

---

*Mr Saye says "A number of years before the war Mr Thomas removed to South Carolina, and his descendants suppose, resided for some time upon Fishing Creek Before hostilities commenced with the mother country he was residing upon Fairforest Creek, in the lower part of what is now Spartanburg District"

The Life of Colonel James Williams

JAMES WILLIAMS, a son of Daniel and Usurla Williams, was born near the Old Fork Church, Hanover County, Virginia, in November, 1740. His father was a native of Wales, therefore he descended directly from Welsh stock. Losing his parents at an early age, young Williams' opportunities for an education were quite limited, but he seems to have possessed a good stock of common sense. While quite a youth, he left his native heath in Virginia and migrated to Granville County, North Carolina, where his brother, Colonel John Williams, an able and distinguished jurist, resided. General William Henderson and Major John Henderson, once residents of the Grindal Shoals vicinity in Union District, were his cousins. In 1762 he was married to a Miss Clark. Eight children were born unto them—five sons and three daughters Ten years later (1772), he left Granville, came to South Carolina and settled on Little River, in what is now Laurens County. He engaged in the combined avocations of farmer, miller, and merchant.

JAMES WILLIAMS

Williams' Entrance Into Public Life

Williams had been in his South Carolina home only a short time when war clouds began to gather. The intolerant spirit manifested by England towards her American colonies caused public meetings to be held all over the country, and a result was the assembling of the Continental Congress in Philadelphia in October, 1774. In order to strengthen the actions of this Congress, the people of South Carolina planned to convene a Provincial Congress. Delegates were elected from every parish and district in the Province to attend this Congress. James Williams was one of the representatives chosen by the Broad River and Saluda District. This body held its first meeting in January, 1775. The acts of the Continental Congress were approved, and a General Committee and Council of Safety appointed. James Williams was made a member of the local committee.

The emissaries of the Royal government having incited the Indians to insurrection, it became necessary for the liberty men to **The Snow** take up arms for the defensive and the offensive. **Campaign** Consequently, in obedience to an order from the Provincial authorities, Colonel Richard Richardson assembled quite an army and succeeded in quelling the insurgents for a time. Richardson's army suffered terribly for want of clothes, shoes, tents, and all other necessary supplies, which suffering was greatly increased by the falling of an unprecedented snow while they were in the field. This snow gave it the name of Snow Campaign. James Williams went through this campaign, and was made a captain.

Not long after the disbanding of Richardson's army, there was a far greater Indian outbreak than before. It was along the whole **Williamson's Ex-** frontier, including parts of North Carolina and **pedition Against** Georgia. Such shocking massacres as that of the **the Cherokees** Hamptons, Hannons and Bishops, in the Spartanburg District, were numerous. This savage butchery was another call for the Patriots to arm. The first expedition was led by a Captain Howard, who, with his small command and guided by a friendly Indian, Schuyuka by name, entered a gap in the mountains, since known as Howard's Gap. By the aid of his friendly guide, Howard was enabled to surprise the Indians under Big Warrior and totally defeat them. This was known as the battle of Round Mountain. But Captain Howard's victory was not sufficient. Two other expeditions were formed, one in North Carolina, under the command of Colonel Griffith Rutherford; the other in South Carolina, under Colonel Andrew Williamson. The details of Williamson's campaign have been chronicled in the "Life of Major Joseph McJunkin," so we will not repeat them here.

Captain James Williams was one of the heroes in that expedition, and served as lieutenant-colonel of militia.

It appears that after Williamson's expedition, Williams returned home, where for a year or two he was actively engaged in the Patriot cause, raising troops and defending **About Home** the territory about Ninety-Six, which was a hot- **for a Season** bed of Toryism. In 1778 he ran for the office of State senator, but was defeated by the strong Tory influence of his section. The same year he led his command on the Florida expedition, a detailed account of which is given in the life of Colonel Joseph Hughes

Early in the year 1779, the British retreated from Augusta towards Savannah. General Lincoln, hoping to be able to confine the enemy to the seacoast, separated his army into two divisions and crossed into Georgia. A detachment, consisting of fifteen hundred men under General Ashe, marched as far as Brier Creek. Here they were surprised by the British under General Prevost, and routed with great slaughter. Captain Williams shared in this disastrous affair.

Brier Creek, Stone Ferry and Savannah

After Ashe's defeat, Prevost marched into South Carolina and threatened Charleston, but finding it too strong for him, he again retired toward Savannah. About a week after this, the battle of Stono took place. The Americans were defeated, but the losses on both sides were about equal. Williams took part in this battle, serving according to his rank as lieutenant-colonel, and commanded a detachment of militia.

Early in September, 1779, Count DeEstaing, with a large French fleet, arrived off the coast of South Carolina. It was determined that the united French and American forces should storm Savannah, but the assault was unsuccessful. Colonel Williams was struck by a spent ball on his forehead. Shortly after this affair, he went on another expedition against the Cherokees. Later still, he was engaged for a while in guarding prisoners at Ninety-Six.

Soon after the fall of Charleston, in May, 1780, Major Patrick Ferguson, with some two hundred of the King's Rangers, was dispatched from the lower part of the State in the direction of Ninety-Six. This was the signal for the uprising of Tories and Loyalists in that section, and their name was "legion, for they were many." Williams realizing the danger to which his property was exposed, he, together with some of his friends on Little River, with such movable goods as they could carry, transferred them to North Carolina, probably to Granville, his old settlement, for safekeeping.

A Dark Page in Colonel Williams' History

At this time Colonel Sumter was on Clem's Branch of Sugar Creek, east of the Catawba, organizing his forces. Williams repaired to Sumter's camp. He frankly informed the Colonel that he brought no men and could claim no command, yet he was anxious to serve his country in some position of usefulness. Colonel

Hill being acquainted with him, suggested to Sumter that as he was in need of an efficient commissary, he might give him that position. He accordingly commissioned Williams to serve in that capacity. Major Charles Miles, with twenty-five others, with four wagons and teams, were put under his charge. Everything went on satisfactorily until after the battle of Hanging Rock, which occurred on the 6th of August. While Sumter was camped on Cane Creek, in Lancaster District, one morning, about the middle of the month, it was discovered that Williams had suddenly left the camp. Colonel Brandon, with a small party, had gone with him. They had taken with them a number of public horses, considerable provisions, and camp equipage. Sumter and his subordinates were greatly vexed at this ungenerous treatment. As they regarded it, Williams had not only shown ingratitude for the position conferred upon him, but he had betrayed a public trust.

Colonel Edward Lacey, a man of great personal prowess, and one of the best officers in Sumter's command, was sent out with a small party in pursuit of Williams and his followers. Their chief object was to recover the public property. Lacey came up with them on the west side of the Catawba, but finding that the Williams' party was too strong to attempt coercive measures, Lacey resorted to other means to accomplish his purpose, so invited Williams to take a walk with him. When some distance from the camp, he suddenly presented a pistol at Williams' breast and threatened him with instant death if he made the least noise or called for assistance. With pistol still drawn, Lacey remonstrated with Williams for his baseness of conduct, whereupon he pledged his word and honor that he would take back all the public property and as many of the men as he could prevail upon to return with him. Not willing to take his word for it, Lacey required him to make oath to the same purpose, and Williams readily consented. But when he was free from restraint he disregarded both his word and oath, and instead of returning as he had sworn to do, he proceeded to Smith's Ford on Broad River, where he joined Colonel McDowell, who had just come to that place from the Cherokee Ford, a few miles above.

Just here the writer wishes to say that the details of this trouble is taken from Draper's "Kings Mountain and Its Heroes," and that Draper got them from Colonel Hill's own narrative, so doubtless in part, they are true; but we should remember that this is only one side of the question, and that it is presented by one who was involved in the difficulty. We are bound to believe that Williams thought that he had some grounds to at least partially justify his conduct, and others thought so too, for such men as Colonel Thomas Brandon, Colonel James Steen, and Major Joseph McJunkin, men of irreproachable character, followed him, stood by him, and with him joined Colonel McDowell at Smith's Ford. It is hardly probable that such men would have remained faithful to him if he had been so base as represented by Colonel Hill.

Saye, in his "Memoir of McJunkin," says: "On this march (i. e., from Hanging Rock toward Charlotte), Sumter was joined by Colonel James Williams, and also received instructions from General Gates to co-operate with him in the contemplated attack on the British forces at Camden."

"Williams, preferring to return towards Ninety-Six to a march down the Wateree, took that direction. Such of Sumter's force as desired it joined Williams. Among these were Steen and McJunkin. Colonel Williams, having separated from Sumter, turned his face towards the British post at Ninety-Six. He was probably induced to take this course from several considerations. He resided but a short distance from that place, and his friends were suffering from the domination of the British and Tories. General McDowell had advanced with a considerable force into the northern portion of the State. The Northern army, under Gates, was advancing towards Camden. The recent spirited conflicts in which the command of Sumter had been engaged had rekindled the spirit of liberty and taught the militia that it was possible for them to conquer a foe superior to them in numbers and equipment. Williams, therefore, crossed the Catawba, and took post near Smith's Ford, on Broad River."

Mr. Saye got his information direct from Major McJunkin, and McJunkin being one of the Williams party, we get the other side of the matter first-hand.

In other articles we have given the generalities of this contest and detailed the parts acted by the officers of whom we were writing; but now it is our purpose to give full details of the whole, because, as we believe, Colonel James Williams was the commander-in-chief and deserves

Battle of Musgrove's Mill

full credit for such a complete victory, which meant so much to the Patriot cause in this, the darkest, period of the Revolution.

In this account, while availing ourselves of all data we could find, we are much indebted to Saye's "Memoir of McJunkin," but more especially to Lyman C. Draper, who, though a resident of Wisconsin, did more to preserve the Revolutionary history of upper South Carolina than any other one man that ever lived.

It will be remembered that when Williams and his party left Sumter their purpose was to go toward Ninety-Six. When they arrived at Smith's Ford, on Broad River, Colonel McDowell, with a considerable force, lay at the Cherokee Ford, ten miles above, and with him was the noted leaders, Colonels Elijah Clarke and Isaac Shelby. At that time, Major Patrick Ferguson, with his forces of Rangers and Loyalists, were in the upcountry, but accounts differ as to where he was posted. Draper says that he was at the Fairforest Shoal in Brandon's settlement. McCrady says this is a mistake, that according to Allaire's diary (Allaire was one of Ferguson's lieutenants), he was at Winn's plantation, eight miles from Winnsboro. Major McJunkin says that on their way to Musgrove's they passed Ferguson to their right. This would put him somewhere, so it seems, in the Fairforest region, and would preclude his being near Winnsboro. At any rate, McDowell's faithful scouts kept him well informed of the movements of Ferguson and his outposts. Hearing that a large Tory force was posted at Musgrove's Mill on the Enoree, the next day after Williams' arrival at Smith's Ford, McDowell detached a force, under Clarke and Shelby, to join Williams in the Musgrove expedition

It was rumored that a military chest was either at Musgrove's or was being conveyed from Ninety-Six to Ferguson's camp, and the Whigs may have hoped to intercept it on the way. Whether this story was true, or just a camp yarn gotten up for the occasion, we do not know, but nothing more was heard of it.

The success of such a daring adventure into the enemy's country would necessarily require rapid movements, with as much secrecy as possible A night march was, therefore, chosen, for they would be less likely to be observed, and cooler for their horses to travel.

Their plans being completed, a short while before sundown on August 17th, the combined forces under Williams, Clarke and Shelby, consisting of about two or three hundred horsemen, crossed

Smith's Ford and proceeded toward Musgrove's. Colonel Thomas Brandon, Major Joseph McJunkin, and their men knew the country well and acted as guides. They traveled through the woods until dark, and then fell into a road and pushed on all night, much of the way in a gallop, crossing Gilky and Thickety creeks, Pacolet, Fairforest, Tyger, and several lesser streams. Draper says that they passed within three or four miles of Ferguson's camp on their left, which was at that time at the Fairforest Shoals in Brandon's settlement. Saye, in his "Memoir of McJunkin," says that they turned off the route to avoid the army of Colonel Ferguson, which lay in their way. McJunkin himself says: "Continuing our march and leaving Ferguson a little to our right, we reached the Tory camp, three hundred strong, forty miles from Smith's Ford, at the dawn of day." It will be readily seen that a forty-mile ride on a short, hot August night would be hard and tiresome, and that the Patriots would not be in the best physical condition for the difficult task before them. Nevertheless, as we shall soon see, it was marvelously executed.

When within a mile north of Musgrove's Ford, the Whig party halted in an old Indian field and sent out some five or six scouts to reconnoiter. This party crossed the mouth of Cedar Shoals Creek, close to the Spartanburg line, a short distance below Musgrove's Mill, and then passed up a by-road to Head's Ford, a mile above Musgrove's, where they forded the Enoree, and stealthily approached near enough to the Tory camp to make observation. Having obtained intelligence, the scouts returned by the same route, and when on top of the ridge west of Cedar Shoal Creek, they met a small Tory patrol, which had crossed over at Musgrove's Ford during their absence above. Sharp firing ensued, which resulted in one of the enemy being killed, two wounded, and the other two fleeing to their camp. Two of the Americans were slightly wounded, but all promptly returned to their commands with the intelligence gained, and the particulars of their skirmish.

This firing, and the precipitate arrival of the two patrolmen, put the Tory camp in the wildest confusion. Colonel Innes, Major Fraser, and other officers who had their headquarters at Musgrove's residence (Draper says his name was Edward; Horseshoe Robinson, that it was Allen) held a hurried council. Innes' plan was to cross the river at once and catch the "Rebels" before they had time to retreat, while others contended for delay, at least till after breakfast, hoping that by that time a party of one hundred mounted men, who were some eight miles below, might return and add very materially to their strength. Innes' counsels prevailed, for he did not want to miss such a fine opportunity to "bag a scurvy lot of ragmuffins," as he regarded the adventurous Americans. So, leaving one hundred men in camp as a reserve, Innes and his associates made preparations for an immediate advance to meet the unexpected invaders. In the meantime, Williams, Shelby, and Clarke had taken their position on a timbered ridge, some little distance east of Cedar Shoal Creek, and about half a mile from Musgrove's ford and mill. At this juncture, a countryman, who lived nearby, came up and informed the Americans that on the evening before the British had been reinforced by the arrival of Colonel Alexander Innes, from Ninety-Six, with two hundred Provincials and one hundred Tories, destined to join Colonel Ferguson. Captain Abraham DePeyster, of the King's American regiment and the noted Loyalist partisan captain, David Fanning, were there; also Colonel Daniel Clary, the leader of all the Tories of that region.

So minute were the details of the information brought by the countryman that no doubt was entertained of its truth. What could be done? To give battle to so formitable an enemy appeared rash, and to attempt a retreat, with wearied and broken-down horses, seemed almost impossible. Williams and his associates instantly concluded that there was but one alternative, and that was to fight; for as a writer has expressed it, "Death was before them and destruction behind them." Securing their horses in the rear, they formed their lines across the road, extending along the ridge about three hundred yards. The form was that of a semi-circle, both wings being concealed and protected by woods. Old logs, fallen trees and brush were hurriedly dragged together and piled upon each other, so that within thirty minutes they had a very respectable protection breast high. Shelby occupied the right, Clarke the left, and Williams the center; the whole force forming one extended line. A party of almost twenty horsemen were placed on each flank, shielded as much as possible from the enemy's observation. Josiah Culbertson had command of those on Shelby's right, and Clarke had a reserve of forty men in easy reach.

At his own suggestion, Captain Shadrack Inman, who had figured prominently in fighting the British and Tories in Georgia, was sent forward with about twenty-five mounted men, with orders to fire upon and otherwise provoke the enemy to cross the ford; then skirmish with them and retire, so as to draw them into the net so adroitly prepared for them by the wily Americans. This strategem worked admirably, for the British infantry seemed much elated over their success in driving Inman at the point of the bayonet, but he kept up a show of fighting and retreating While yet two hundred yards from the American breastworks, the enemy hastily formed their line of battle, and then advancing fifty yards nearer, opened a heavy fire, in which they generally shot over their antagonists. When trees were convenient, the Patriots used them, while others were shielded by their rude breastworks; and some, to some extent, were partially protected by a fence on the roadside. The Americans had had their usual caution to reserve their fire until they could see the whites of the enemy's eyes, and then not to discharge their rifles until orders were given, when each man was to make his object sure. These orders were strictly obeyed.

The British center, upon whom Inman had made his feigned attacks, seeing him retire in apparent confusion, pressed forward, under beat of drum and blast of bugle, but in considerable disorder, shouting, "Huzza for King George." When within seventy yards of the American lines they were unexpectedly met by a deadly fire, from which they at first recoiled. But their superior numbers enabled them to continue their assault, notwithstanding the advantage which the breastworks gave the Americans. A strong force, composed of the Provincials, led by Innes and Fraser, forming the enemy's left wing, drove from their breastworks the right wing under Shelby at the point of the bayonet. It was a desperate struggle. Shelby's men were contending against large odds, and the flank of his right wing gradually giving way, but fortunately his left maintained its connection with the center at the breastwork. Clarke, maintaining his ground and seeing Shelby's need of succor, sent his small reserve to his aid, which proved a most timely relief. Fortunately for the Americans, at the critical moment when Innes was forcing Shelby's right flank back, the British leader was badly disabled, fell from his horse, and was carried back. He was shot, it was reported, by one of the Watauga volunteers, William Smith, who exultingly exclaimed, "I've killed their commander." Shelby then rallied his men, who raised a regular frontier Indian yell, and rushed furiously upon the enemy, who were gradually forced back before the enraged riflemen. Culbertson's flanking party acted a conspicuous part on this occasion.

In this desperate contest, the enemy lost one captain killed, and five out of seven of the surviving officers of their Provincial corps were wounded. Innes was shot down by Smith, and another Watauga rifleman, Robert Beene, wounded Major Fraser, who was seen to reel from his horse. Captain Campbell and Lieutenants Camp and Chew were also wounded.

These heavy losses of officers had a very disheartening effect upon the British troops. The Tories also failing to make any impression on Clarke's line, and having already lost several of their officers and many of their men, began to show signs of wavering, when Captain Hawsey, a noted leader among them, who was striving to re-animate the Loyalists, and thus retrieve the fortunes of the day, was shot down. In the midst of the confusion that followed, Clarke and his brave men followed Shelby's example, leaped over their breastworks, yelling, shooting, and slashing like mad men. Just at this time, the Tory Colonel Clary, had the bits of his horse's bridle seized at the same moment by two stalwart Whigs. Having the ingenuity and presence of mind, he extricated himself from his perilous situation by exclaiming, "D—n you, don't you know your own officers!" They released him instantly, and he fled at full speed By this time the British and Tories were in full retreat, closely followed by their victorious assailants. It was in this exciting chase that the brave Captain Inman was killed, while pressing the enemy and fighting them hand-to-hand. He was shot by the Tories seven times, one a musket ball, which pierced his forehead.

He fell near the base of a Spanish oak that stood where a recent road left the old mill road. We are glad to say that his grave is now marked. He was the only American officer that fell in this battle, and his name deserves to be enshrined in our memories as one who paid with his life's blood the price of our civil redemption. Draper says: "Great credit is justly due to Captain Inman for the successful manner in which he brought on the action, and the aid he rendered in conducting it to a triumphant issue "

Continuing, Draper says: "The yells and screeches of the retreating British and Tories, as they ran through the woods and over the hills to the river, loudly intermingled with the shouts of their pursuers, together with the groans of the dying and wounded, were terrific and heartrending in the extreme. The smoke, as well as the din and confusion, rose high above the exciting scene. The Tories ceased to make any show of defense, when halfway from the breastworks to the ford. The retreat there became a perfect rout, and now, with reckless speed, they hastened to the river, through which they rushed with the wildest fury, hotly pursued by the victorious Americans, with sword and rifle, killing, wounding or capturing all who came in their way."

Many of the British and Tories were shot as they rushed pellmell across the Enoree at the rocky ford. When they were over, there was one who was not too weary to display his arrogance, and seeking to attract attention, turned up his rump in derision at the Americans. One of the Whig officers, probably Colonel Brandon or Steen, said to Golding Tinsley, "Can't you turn that insolent braggart over?" "I can try," replied Tinsley, who was known to possess a good rifle, and suiting his action to his word, he took good aim and fired, and sure enough, turned him over, when some of his comrades picked the fellow up and carried him off.

The name of Golding Tinsley deserves more than a passing mention. This faithful old hero, who rendered so much service in the **Golding Tinsley** up-country of South Carolina during the Revolution, was born in Culpepper County, Virginia, about 1754 Emigrating to South Carolina about 1771, he settled in Newberry District. At the commencement of the Revolution, he, with three brothers, enlisted, probably in Captain John Caldwell's rangers. Two of these brothers were killed by Tories on Fairforest, near the present Murphy's Shoal, in Union County. He and his brother James served throughout the war. Golding was at Kings Mountain, after which he joined Sumter and was at Blackstock. Later he joined Morgan and was at Cowpens. After this he proceeded to Virginia and was at Yorktown.

After the war, Golding Tinsley lived quite a number of years in Spartanburg District, where he lived the balance of his days. O'Neal, in his annals of Newberry, pays him the following tribute· "Was for the last thirty years of his life a member of the Methodist Church; his life was adorned by every Christian grace, which showed itself in his conversation, in his precepts and his examples. He died near Cross Anchor, Spartanburg District, on May 11, 1851, having attained the great age of ninety-six or ninety-seven years. He left two children, Isaac and Amelia. The estimation in which he was held was evidenced by the immense concourse who followed the body to the grave. He was buried with the honors of war, not less than two thousand persons present. In closing this account of that gallant soldier, we may well say: 'Blessed are the dead which die in the Lord,' etc."

He was probably the last Revolutionary survivor to die in Spartanburg County. There are numbers yet living that are old enough to have seen Golding Tinsley.

The action at Musgrove's resulted in a complete rout of the British and Tories. As to the number of troops engaged in that action, accounts widely differ. Saye, in his "Memoir of McJunkin," says that the number of horsemen that left Smith's Ford on the evening before the engagement was seven hundred. In a statement made by Colonel Shelby, he says the number was about seven hundred. McCall, the historian, says about three hundred and fifty. Major James Sevier says, according to the reports of his neighbors who were in the engagement, that the number was two hundred and fifty. Colonel James Williams says two hundred, and Major McJunkin corroborates this, when he says that after the battle "we were only about one hundred and fifty strong." The British and Tory forces are estimated from three hundred and fifty to seven hundred, and then reinforced by four hundred more. Such great disparity among those actually engaged is hard to account for, but, however, when it comes to losses, all are agreed. The British loss was sixty-three killed, about ninety wounded and seventy prisoners. The American loss was only four killed and eight or nine wounded. In numbers the Whig loss was trivial, but the fall of Captain Shadrach Inman rendered it heavy.

Eager to follow up the great advantages which they had gained, the daring officers resolved at once to pursue the demoralized Tories and make a dash for Ninety-Six, which they understood to be in a weak condition, and only twenty-five miles away. Draper says· "Returning to their horses and mounting them, while Shelby was counseling Colonel Clarke, Francis Jones, an express from Colonel McDowell, rode up in great haste with a letter in his hand from

General Caswell, who had on the sixteenth shared in General Gates' total defeat near Camden, apprising McDowell of the great disaster and advising him and all officers commanding detachments to get out of the way or they would be cut off. McDowell sent word that he would at once move toward Gilbert Town. General Caswell's hand-writing was, fortunately, familiar to Colonel Shelby, so he knew it was no Tory trick attempted to be played off upon them. He and his associates instantly saw the situation; they could not retire to McDowell's camp, for his force was no longer there. Gates' army was defeated and incapacitated, and Sumter's were soon destined to meet the same fate, in the rear was Cruger with whatever of Irvines' and Fraser's detachments remained, with Ferguson's strong force on their flanks. There was no choice; further conquests were out of the question." . . . "It was, therefore, determined in a hasty council on horseback that they would take a backwoods route to avoid and escape Ferguson, and join Colonel McDowell on his retreat toward Gilbert Town."

Major McJunkin says: "The reason of our rapid march to North Tyger was this: The Tory prisoners told us that there were four hundred British soldiers, under the command of Colonel Innes, encamped just over the river, and knowing that Colonel Ferguson, whom we had just passed a little on our right, must also have heard the firing, and not knowing but that they would break in upon us, who were only about one hundred and fifty strong, and serve us worse than we did the Tories." Anyway, the situation brought about hurried movements. The prisoners were first grouped and then distributed for as safe transportation as circumstances would allow. Just at this time an amusing thing happened. Colonel Williams, riding along the ranks viewing the prisoners, he recognized an old acquaintance, Saul Hinson by name, a very small man, and one who had served in his command at the battle of Stono, when the Colonel pleasantly exclaimed, "Ah! my little Sauly, have we caught you?" "Yes, Colonel," replied the little fellow, "and no d——d great catch, either."

This produced a laugh—nothing more. Encumbered with their prisoners, the gallant troopers set out in a northwesterly direction, stopping neither day nor night, only long enough to snatch a drink from a passing brook and to pull peaches and green corn from the roadside, which they ate raw. After a forty-eight hour march, with faces and eyes bloated and swollen from hunger and fatigue, they rejoined Colonel McDowell near Gilbert Town, in North Carolina. Here the prisoners were turned over to Colonel Clarke for the purpose of conveying them to a place of safe-keeping. Starting in the direction of Charlotte, Clarke soon concluded to return to Georgia. The prisoners were then placed in the care of Colonel Williams, who safely conducted them to Hillsboro, where he met Governor Rutledge, of South Carolina, who was at that time a refugee, and giving an account of the battle of Musgrove's, the Governor at once commissioned Williams a brigadier-general in the South Carolina militia as a reward for his gallantry and success in that battle. Now, as to the part taken by Williams in the battle of Musgrove's and the amount of credit due him, historians differ. That most eminent historian, Lyman C. Draper, who is usually so fair, regards him as a very small factor. He merely makes mention of his joining McDowell at Smith's Ford with a few run-aways the day before the expedition, and when McDowell detached Clarke and Shelby, Williams and his men were no more than guides; and when the battle was fought he was placed in the center without any special command; yet when he met Governor Rutledge at Hillsboro he gave himself credit for the victory, and thereby obtained the commission of brigadier-general. This does Colonel Williams an injustice.

It is probable that in his great elation over such a brilliant victory, and it won in his own section, too, that he might have given himself a little more credit than he deserved, but we believe he had some rights to his claim. Governor Nash, of North Carolina, writing September the 10th, 1789, says: "Colonel Williams, of South Carolina, two days after Gates' defeat, with two hundred men engaged four hundred of the British cavalry in a fair, open field fight and completely defeated and routed them, killing sixty-three on the spot and taking seventy-odd prisoners, mostly British." Orandates Davis, a prominent public character, writing from Halifax, N. C., seventeen days later, states the following: "Colonel Williams, of South Carolina, three days after Gates' defeat, fell in with a party of the enemy near Ninety-Six and gave them a complete drubbing, killing seventy on the spot and taking between sixty and seventy prisoners, mostly British, with the loss of four men only." These two statements appeared in the North Carolina University Magazine for March, 1855. Draper charges that they doubtless were based on Williams' statements.

We have already seen that Saye, in his "Memoir of McJunkin," says that Williams separated from Sumter because he preferred to go in the direction of Ninety-Six, and that such of Sumter's force as desired to, joined him. Saye furthermore says: "It has been previously stated that Colonel Williams met Colonel Sumter a few days after the battle of Hanging Rock, that part of Sumter's force united with Williams, and were led by him to Musgrove's Mill, and thence fell back toward North Carolina." In his personal reminiscenses, Major McJunkin says: "About this time, *i. e.*, the time of the battle of Hanging Rock, Colonel James Williams joined Sumter, the latter having a disposition to go southward and the former towards the west. Disagreeing in their notions, the troops joined with Sumter or Williams, just as their inclinations led them. Colonel Williams and Colonel Steen and myself, one of his captains, with those who had a disposition to annoy the British and Tories at Ninety-Six, by various marches, went up to Smith's Ford, on the Broad River, and lay one day, and on the evening of the 17th of August took up our line of march to Musgrove's Mill, on the Enoree River." So we have it direct from the pen of one who was with Williams, and whose veracity cannot be questioned, that when he left Sumter his intention was to go to Ninety-Six, and that he had such of Sumter's force as desired to go with him. It is furthermore stated (Saye's Memoir of McJunkin) that when Williams arrived at McDowell's camp that he (McDowell) detached a part of his force under Colonels Clarke and Shelby to unite with Williams for the purpose of the Musgrove's expedition.

Mills, in his statistics of South Carolina, published in 1825, gives Williams credit for the whole. He says: "On the 18th of August, 1780, Colonel Williams attacked a considerable party of British and Tories at Musgrove's Mills, on the Enoree River." He does not mention either Clarke or Shelby. Chapman, in his school history of South Carolina, says: "On August 18th, 1780, Williams gained a decided victory over the British at Musgrove's."

Moultrie, in his Memoirs of The American Revolution, says: "On the 18th of August, 1780, Colonel Williams attacked a large party of British and Tories at Musgrove's Mills, on Enoree River, under the command of Colonel Innis, of the South Carolina Loyalists, whom he defeated, and wounded Colonel Innis." But the clearest and most satisfactory evidence is given by Dr. Howe in his history of the Presbyterian Church in South Carolina. He says: "A large body of Tories were encamped near Musgrove's Mill, in the southeast corner of Laurens District, on the south bank of the Enoree River, where they commanded a bad rocky ford. They were joined on the 17th of August, 1780, by the British officers, Innis and Fraser, and all amounted to about three hundred men. Colonels Williams, Shelby and Clarke, with a force much inferior, posted themselves on the north side, on a small creek emptying into the Enoree just below the Spartanburg line about two miles above Musgrove's Mill. *It was agreed that Williams should have the chief command.* He drew up his little army in ambush in a semicircle within a wood, and advancing to the ford with a few picked men, fired on the enemy. Innis immediately crossed the ford to dislodge the rebels. Williams retreated, with Innis in hot pursuit."

This doubtless refers to the little party sent forward under Captain Inman to provoke the enemy and draw them in the trap set for them. When they reached the area of the ambuscade, a shot from Colonel Shelby gave the signal, when the Patriots arose with a shout and immediately surrounded the Tories. Innis was slightly wounded, but escaped with a larger part of the regular troops. Major Fraser and eighty-five others were killed. Most of the Tories were made prisoners; the Americans lost four killed and eighteen wounded.

It will be noticed that Dr. Howe says that it *was agreed* that Williams should have the chief command, and we have no reason to doubt that statement, for Hunter in his sketches of Western North Carolina says the same thing. Of course, the agreement was on the part of Clarke and Shelby. This would be natural, as they were detached by McDowell for the purpose of uniting with Williams in the Musgrove's expedition. The summary of evidence in Williams' favor is that when he, with his followers, parted company with Sumter, he designed to go to the Ninety-Six region, that McDowell sufficiently reinforced him to make the expedition successful, that Clarke and Shelby agreed that he should have the chief command, and when the battle was on he occupied the center; not as Draper says without a command, but as commander-in-chief. Hence, we think it is quite clear that Colonel Williams had justifiable grounds on which to base his claims as they were presented to Governor Rutledge

It will be remembered that Governor Rutledge honored Colonel Williams with a brigadier-general's commission in the South Carolina militia for the glorious achievement at Musgrove's Mill. With this commission in his pocket, he set out for Sumter's camp on the east side of the Catawba. He had it publicly read and then ordered both officers and men to recognize his right to command them, at the same time declaring that Sumter had no authority to do so. A serious difficulty now arose. At this time Sumter bore the title of, and performed the office of general, but he had no commission. The men under his command were such as had been forced from their homes and banded together for mutual protection; at the same time designing to strike such blows in the behalf of liberty as opportunity might afford. Being thus gathered, they felt independent and at liberty to do pretty much as they pleased. So they had chosen Sumter as their leader and recognized his rights as such. The trouble that arose between Sumter and Williams while he was commissary, a few weeks before, was still fresh in their minds The result was that Sumter, his officers and men unanimously agreed to have nothing to do with Williams. Meeting with such a reception, he soon left Sumter's camp.

Trouble Between Williams and Sumter Party

Shortly after Williams' departure, a council of the field officers of Sumter's command were called together and it was decided to lay conditions before Governor Rutledge, giving their reasons for rejecting Williams as their commander. Five prominent officers were appointed to wait on the governor at Hillsboro, viz.: Colonels Richard Winn, Henry Hampton, John Thomas, Jr., and Charles Myddleton; Colonel Thomas Taylor, supposed to be the fifth. In the meantime, it was decided that Sumter should retire until the matter was decided, and the command was given to Colonels Lacey and Hill. For some reasons, perhaps having some scruples as to his conduct in the matter, Williams did not seek redress before Governor Rutledge, but repaired to the field.

Governor Nash, of North Carolina, granted Colonel Williams the privilege of raising and organizing a corps of one hundred men. By this authority he set about enlisting them. The call was dated September 23rd, and was headed, "A call to arms—beef, bread and potatoes." This was quite a tempting offer for that time, and was probably based on the fact that Governor Nash had ordered the commissaries of the State to furnish the party with the necessary supplies. Colonel Thomas Brandon and Major Samuel Hammond were quite active in this work. Colonel Hill, who never let an opportunity pass to make a fling at Williams, says that these North Carolinians who enlisted under him were men who shirked duty under their own local officers. We do not know what they had done up to this time, but Major Hammond states in his pension application that this little force "constituted the largest portion of Williams' command at Kings Mountain," and as we shall see later, no part of the line stood firmer, and displayed greater bravery, than that commanded by Colonel Williams.

With his little band of North Carolina followers, the Colonel pushed in the direction of the Catawba, where he found Sumter's command under Hill and Lacey encamped in the fork of the main and south branches of that stream. Sumter and the most of his principal officers were still absent on their mission to Governor Rutledge. Thinking that this might be a favorable opportunity, Williams marched into the camp and again read his brigadier-general's commission, and commanded the officers and men to submit to his authority Hill told him frankly, but in no uncertain language, that there was not an officer nor a man in the whole company that would for a moment submit to him, exhibiting signs of harsh treatment if he persisted. Thinking it the part of prudence, Williams retired, forming his camp some distance from that of Sumter.

It will now be necessary for us to leave Williams in his camp for a while, in order that we may take note of some events that **The Gathering** were transpiring elsewhere, so that the reader of **of the Clans** this narrative may be better able to understand it. It will be remembered that when the battle of Musgrove's Mill was fought that Major Ferguson, with his British and Tory forces, were encamped in the Fairforest settlement not far from that point.

Two days before this battle, the Southern army under General Gates was totally defeated at Camden. On the same day Sumter's force was cut up on Fishing Creek. Ferguson was now the undisputed master of upper South Carolina, for McDowell was rapidly retreating from Smith's Ford northward, and there was no "game" for Ferguson to pursue except the heroic victors of Musgrove's. This he did, passing through Union and Spartanburg Districts, going as far as Gilbert Town, N. C., near the present site of Rutherfordton. As already seen, Colonel McDowell camped near this place after leaving Smith's Ford, where he was rejoined by Williams, Clarke and Shelby on their retreat from Musgrove's. Before they separated here, Colonel Shelby proposed that an army be raised on both sides of the mountain sufficiently strong to cope with Ferguson. Ferguson remained at Gilbert Town for quite a time, hoping to intercept Colonel Clarke as he passed back from North Carolina to Georgia. The first to resist Ferguson in that quarter was Colonel Charles McDowell, who surprised and defeated a detachment of his army near Cowan's Ford, a crossing on Cane Creek. McDowell, says Judge Schenk, "being unable to resist the large British force now in North Carolina, retreated across the Blue Ridge to the Watauga settlement, then the homes of Sevier and Shelby." Here he urged them to join the mountain men on the other side to resist further British invasion and devastation.

Ferguson, hearing the mutterings of the gathering storm over the mountains, paroled Samuel Phillips, a relative of Colonel Shelby, whom he had taken prisoner, with the following message: "That, if they did not desist from their opposition to the British arms, he would march his army over the mountain, hang their leaders and lay their country to waste with fire and sword." Phillips went direct to Shelby with the message, but instead of causing them to desist, it fired the Patriots to greater determination.

A few days later, Colonel Shelby rode forty miles to a horse race, near the present site of Jonesboro, Tenn., to confer with Colonel Sevier. The result was that these brave troopers resolved to call their own forces together and if possible secure the assistance of Colonel William Campbell, of Virginia. The place of rendezvous was at the Sycamore flats on the Watauga. The forces of Shelby and Sevier met there on September 25th, and an express was at once sent to Colonel Campbell soliciting his assistance. At first, Campbell was not favorably impressed with the undertaking, but later decided to take one-half of his force, and at the same time he apprised Colonel Benjamin Cleveland, of Wilkes County, N. C., of the matter, and requested him to meet them on the eastern side of the mountains. The place appointed for the meeting of the combined forces of Shelby, Sevier, Campbell and Cleveland was the "Quaker Meadows," in Burke County. Consequently, in due time Colonels Shelby, Sevier and Campbell appeared with two hundred men each. They were soon joined by McDowell and a little later by Colonel Cleveland. The whole force now numbered about fifteen hundred men, and says a writer, "They made the welkin ring with their glad acclaim."

Two deserters from the American ranks informed Ferguson of the coming of the determined mountaineers, at which he took fright and hurriedly pressed in the direction of Earl's Ford, on North Pacolet. From thence he marched down on Broad River, and for two days he lay encamped at Tate's place, near the mouth of Buffalo Creek. On the morning of the 6th of October he left Tate's place, and passing to the right of the present town of Blacksburg late in the afternoon, took his chosen position on Kings Mountain, where he "defied God Almighty and all the rebels out of hell to overcome him."

We will now return to the camps of Hill, Lacey and Williams. Hill and Lacey had planned to join General Davidson, but aban-
Final Juncture at Cowpens doned the idea on hearing of the approach of the mountaineers and determined to join them in the pursuit of Ferguson. Hill then suggested to Lacey that he thought it best to come to terms with Williams, if they could get him to desist from his ambitious purpose of being recognized as brigadier-general. At first he "spurned" their offer, but later accepted and a commander was chosen for the whole. They then proceeded until they reached the Cherry Mountain, in the eastern part of Rutherford District, where they took up temporary quarters. While here, Colonels Williams and Brandon visited the camp of the mountaineers and told them the place of their meeting was at the old iron works on Lawson's Fork. This was considered by Hill and Lacey as a design on the part of Williams and Brandon to allure the troops into the Ninety-Six region, instead of assailing Ferguson After some effort, matters were set right and "The Cowpens" was agreed upon as the place where the juncture of forces should be effected the following evening.

The first to arrive at "The Cowpens" were the South Carolinians, the Lincoln County men under Hambright getting in near sunset. About a half hour later they were joined by the mountaineers under Colonels Campbell, Cleveland, Sevier and McDowell.

We are fully aware of the fact that in detailing the troubles between the Sumter party and Williams, that some things are brought out greatly to the detriment of his character, but it is the duty of the honest chronicler to tell the bad as well as the good. But, notwithstanding the fact that he attempted to deceive and mislead the mountain men, Williams was a good man and possessed a deeply religious nature; but like David, Peter and others under the strong impulses of the hour, he failed. We do not for a moment believe that he wished to avoid a combat with Ferguson, for there was not a cowardly drop of blood in his veins; but he had a burning and insatiable desire to lead an adequate force into his own neighborhood to punish the marauding Tories at whose hands he and his community had suffered so bitterly. Mills says: "Colonel Williams, of the district of Ninety-Six, in particular, was indefatigable in collecting and animating the friends of Congress in that district. With these he frequently harrassed the conquerors." It was undoubtedly this unconquerable ambition to rid his own locality of British and Tory pests that led to his unscrupulous conduct.

For an hour or two after the assembling of the gallant Whig troopers, there was a lively time at "The Cowpens." A wealthy **The Battle of** English Tory by the name of Saunders lived there, **Kings Mountain** and the country being well adapted to the business, he reared many cattle, and had numerous pens built in which to herd his stock—hence the name Cow-Pens. Saunders was in bed at the time, either not well or feigning sickness, from which he was pulled out and treated quite roughly. When asked to tell when Ferguson had passed that way, he positively declared that neither the Major nor his army had passed at all, and that he had plenty of torch pine in his house which they could light and make search; and if they found any sign of a passing army they might hang him, or do what else they pleased, but if they found no such sign he hoped that they would treat him with greater consideration. Search was made, but no evidence of a passing army was found. A number of the old Tory's cattle were shot down and butchered for the suppers of the hungry soldiers, and a large field of corn was harvested in a few minutes. Everywhere bright camp fires lighted up the surroundings; strips of beef were broiling on the coals, while the corn was thrown to the weary horses. Both men and beasts were thus refreshed.

Either while encamped at the Cherry Mountain, or shortly before, Joseph Kerr, the crippled spy, who belonged to Williams' command, was sent out to obtain intelligence as to Ferguson's strength and whereabouts. Being a cripple and in a strong Tory neighborhood, his real character was not suspected and he found no difficulty in entering the British camp. After inquiring about the welfare of the friends of King George and making such observations as he could, he quietly withdrew, mounted his fleet charger, and set out to rejoin his countrymen. Knowing that they were on the wing, probably, after a circuitous route, he came upon them at "The Cowpens" soon after their arrival at that place. Shortly after Kerr came in, a council of war was held, in which all the officers participated, except Williams, who was absent on account of the friction existing between him and them. Colonel Campbell, of Virginia, was given the chief command in courtesy to him and his regiment for having marched the greatest distance. Kerr was present and reported that he found Ferguson encamped at Peter Quinn's old place, just six miles from Kings Mountain, and that he intended to move to that place the same afternoon. But it was deemed advisable to gain the very latest intelligence concerning Ferguson's positions, so Enoch Gilmer, one of Graham's men, was sent forward to reconnoiter, but soon returned. No time was to be lost. Selecting the best-equipped men and horses, amounting to about nine hundred and ten, between eight and nine o'clock in the evening they set out towards Kings Mountain in quest of Ferguson. About two hundred, including footmen and those with jaded horses, were left behind to make their way the best they could.

The night was very dark, and to add to the difficulty of march, a drizzling rain set in, which Colonel Shelby said was at times excessively hard. Their first intention was to cross Broad River at Tate's Ferry, a short distance above where the Southern Railway now crosses that stream; but fearing some obstructions there, they decided to cross at the Cherokee Ford, lower down. It was near daylight when the Patriots reached the hills adjacent to the ford. A halt was made, and Gilmer sent forward to see if the way was clear. While awaiting his return, orders were given to keep the guns dry, for it was still raining. Soon Gilmer's voice was heard in a hollow nearby, singing, "Barney Linn," a favorite song of the times, which was sufficient notice that the way was open. It was about sunrise when they reached the river. Orders were given for those who had the largest horses to ride on the upper side, but very little attention was paid to the order. The river was deep, but it was said that not a single soldier got a ducking. After crossing the river, Gilmer was again sent forward to make observations, and dashed off at full gallop. The officers rode slowly in front of their men, and when they reached a point about three miles from the ford they came across Ferguson's former encampment. Here a short halt was made, and those that had it took such a snack as their saddle-bags and wallets afforded, but many had nothing at all, and on coming to a corn field by the roadside, they pulled the corn and ate it raw from the cob. The rain continued to fall so heavily during the entire forenoon that Colonels Campbell, Sevier, and Cleveland concluded that owing to the weary and jaded condition of both men and beasts it would be best to halt for refreshments, for a number of the horses had given out.

Riding up to Shelby and apprising him of their ideas, he replied roughly with an oath: "I will not stop until night if I follow Ferguson into Cornwallis' lines." Without reply, they returned to their respective commands and continued the march. The men could only keep their guns dry by wrapping their blankets and hunting shirts around the locks, thus leaving their bodies exposed to the drenching rain that had fallen without intermission since leaving The Cowpens. As they proceeded onward, they came to the house of Solomon Beason, who was half Whig or half Loyalist, as the occasion required. Here they learned that Ferguson was only six miles away, and also they captured two Tories, who were made to pilot them the balance of the way.

About noon the rain ceased, the clouds broke away and a fine breeze sprang up. A little later they reached the house of Jacob Randall, five miles from Kings Mountain. Here a brief halt was made, for the purpose of drying their guns and priming them afresh. For fear that Randall might in some way apprise Ferguson of their approach, they put him under arrest. The weather now being favorable, and their guns in good trim, they left Randall's house in a gallop, some whipping their horses with switches and others with their hats.

Just here we wish to say that the site of Randall's house is well known to some of us Signs of the old road over which the Patriots traveled are yet plainly visible, and a pear tree which stood on the side of it, in front of Randall's door, still lives, although it was old enough to bear fruit when the army passed. It must be near one hundred and sixty years old.

Crossing Whisonant's Mill Creek, they passed up and along the ridge right by the present Antioch Baptist Church. Reaching a point three miles from Ferguson's post, which was probably the east end of the Antioch ridge, they saw Gilmer's horse fastened at a gate, some little distance ahead. Dismounting, and going into the house, they found Gilmer at the table eating, for he pretended to be a great King's man, and was received with a royal welcome. "You d—d rascal," exclaimed Colonel Campbell, "we have got you." Having provided himself with a rope, he put it around Gilmer's neck, and declared that he would hang him to the bars of the gate. Major Chronicle begged that he should not be hung there, as his ghost would haunt the women, who were present and looking on with tearful eyes. To this Colonel Campbell acquiesced, and decided to move on, reserving him for the first convenient limb. Once out of sight, the rope was taken off, and he gave the information which he had received. One of the women, who talked quite freely, stated that she had been in Ferguson's camp that morning to carry him some chickens, and that he was posted on a ridge between two branches, where some deer hunters had a camp the previous autumn. Major Chronicle and Captain Mattocks stated that the camp was theirs, and hence were familiar with the ground. When at or near the same place, some of Sevier's men called at the house of a Loyalist and sought information, but about all they would say was that Ferguson was not far away. As they left the building a girl followed them and inquired, "How many are there of you?" "Enough to whip Ferguson if we can find him," was the reply. "He is on that mountain," she said, pointing to the eminence, three miles away.

Being now acquainted with Ferguson's position, the officers rode a short distance ahead and planned the attack, even going so far as to agree upon the location that some of the corps should occupy. They crossed Ponder's Branch, and coming to King's Creek, forded it a short distance above the present crossing, and passed up the ravine, which leads out just back of the old Colonel Hambright homestead, which is still in the possession of one of his descendants. In the meantime, some of Sevier's advance captured two or three Tories, from whom they secured evidence similar to that given by Gilmer. Presently, a youth, named John Ponder, was seen riding rapidly across an open field. Being acquainted with him, Colonel Hambright ordered his prompt arrest. Upon examination, a fresh dispatch was found on his person from Ferguson to Cornwallis. It was the information given by Ponder that prompted Colonel Hambright's famous saying. He stated that Ferguson was the best uniformed man on the mountain, but wore a checked shirt or duster over it. Hearing this, Hambright turned to his men, and in his Pennsylvania German exclaimed: "Vell, poys, vhen you see dot man mit a pig shirt on over his clothes, you may know whom he is, and mark him mit your rifles!" Proceeding a little further, they met George Watkins, a good Whig, who had been a prisoner with Ferguson, but having been released on parole, was now on his way home. He was able to assure them that the British major still maintained his chosen position on the mountain. A brief halt was made for better arrangements

Up to this time, the men had been marching singly or in squads, as might best suit their convenience, but they were formed into two lines—two men deep—Colonel Campbell leading the right line, and Colonel Cleveland the left. The officers were still agreed on the plan of attack, before suggested, to surround the enemy; but Hill, still after Williams, says: "Williams dared not appear at the council in consequence of his recent effort to mislead the Whig colonels." Orders were now given that no talking should be indulged in, which was faithfully obeyed, every man appearing to be as dumb as the beast he rode. Near three o'clock in the afternoon the mountaineers reached a point about half a mile from Ferguson's camp, and here the word "Halt!" was given. The order then came to "dismount, and tie horses," then to "take off and tie up great coats, blankets, etc., to your saddles," as they were wet because of the amount of rain that had fallen since leaving The Cowpens. A few men were detailed to take charge of the horses, and then came the final and general order: "Fresh prime your guns, and every man go in to battle firmly resolving to fight until he dies"

Before taking up the line of march, Colonel Campbell and all the leading officers appealed earnestly to their men—to the higher and nobler instincts of their natures, to all of their patriotic impulses— to fight like heroes, and never give up an inch of ground unless forced to do so, and then, if in their power, retake it at the earliest possible moment. Campbell visited in person all the little corps and said unto them "that if any of them, men or officers, were afraid, to quit the ranks and go home, that he wished no man to engage in the action who could not fight, that as for himself he was determined to fight the enemy a week if need be to gain the victory." None acceded to this proposition, but like faithful fox hounds, these brave mountaineers had for days and nights followed Ferguson's trail, and as the opportune moment was at hand they were eager to catch the object of their pursuit   Many of the men threw their hats aside and tied handkerchiefs around their heads, so as not to be hindered by bushes and overhanging limbs during the engagement. Forming a line two men deep, each little corps, led its own officers, marched towards the battle hill.

The ridge on which the battle was fought belongs to the Kings Mountain range, and is situated about a mile and a half south of the North Carolina line, in the extreme western part of York County. It is in the shape of a horseshoe, only somewhat more elongated, the toe pointing to the northeast and the heel to the southwest. It is some four or five hundred yards in length, and one hundred and fifty or sixty yards from base to base in the widest place. The height is sixty or seventy feet, and the top is narrow and tapering, so much so that Mills is correct when he says "that a man standing on it may be shot from either side." It was upon the crest of this ridge that the defiant Ferguson, with his Provincials and Tory followers, were posted. Because of the thickness of the intervening forest, it appears that the approach of the daring Whigs was not discovered until they were within a quarter of a mile. Drums were then ordered to beat to arms, and the shrill blast of Ferguson's silver whistle was heard throughout the camp, calling his followers to repair to their places in the ranks, for, as he dubbed them, "The Back Water Men" were upon him.

Approaching from the west, it is natural that the Whigs should reach the northwest side of the mountain first, which they did, and here Shelby took his position on the extreme right. The plan being to surround the mountain, Colonel Campbell passed up a small ravine, crossed the neck of the ridge, just a little to the right of the Centennial Monument, and gained his position on the opposite side facing Shelby, while Lacey occupied the center at Williams' left. Colonel Cleveland, who was delayed a few minutes because of the marshy condition about the branch, stationed himself on the north side, next to Lacey Colonel Hambright took his position at the end of the ridge, where the old monument stands. McDowell, Winston and Sevier passed around the northeast end, proceeded up the ravine, and took their places on the opposite side. McDowell occupied the center, where the traditional grave of Ferguson now is. Sevier took his place between McDowell and Campbell, while Winston occupied the ground between McDowell and Hambright, which made the circle around the mountain complete.

There is a tradition which states that inasmuch as Colonel Lacey rode from the Cherry Mountain to the camp on Greene River and apprised the Patriots as to Ferguson's true position, that Colonel Campbell gave him the honor of commencing the battle, but this is hardly credible.

Draper says: "The first firing was heard on the north side of the mountain—evidently made by the enemy upon Shelby's column before they were in a position to engage in the action. It was galling in its effect, and not a little annoying to the mountaineers, some of whom, in their impatience, complained that it would never do to be shot down without returning the fire. Shelby cooly replied, 'Press on to your places, and then your fire will not be lost.' But before Shelby's men could reach their places, Colonel Campbell had gained his position on the opposite side of the mountain, facing Shelby, had thrown off his coat, and while leading his men to the attack he yelled at the top of his voice, 'Here they are, my brave boys, shoot like h— and fight like devils.' Immediately the woods resounded with the shouts of his little corps, in which they were heartily joined, first by Shelby's, and then by the others. When Captain DePeyster, Ferguson's second in command, heard these frightful and almost deafening yells—he had not yet forgotten these same kind which he heard at Musgrove's Mill—he said to Ferguson: 'These things are ominous—they are the d— yelling boys.'"

Colonel Williams, who felt so greatly offended at the harsh and cruel treatment which he had received at the hands of his fellow colonels, at first hesitated to take part in the battle, but when the pinch came, he could not resist such a glorious opportunity to do his country a service, so he wheeled chivalrously into line, and advancing to the head of his column, he exclaimed, "Come on, my boys, the old wagoner never yet backed out!" It was probably ten minutes from the time the attack was made on Shelby's and Campbell's columns until all the colonels had reached their respective places, but immediately upon gaining their positions they poured a deadly and unerring fire into the ranks of the over-confident Britons. As a writer has expressed it, "The mountain was covered with flame and smoke, and it seemed to thunder." In a speech delivered in Congress, January 16, 1834, the Honorable Bailie Peyton, of Tennessee, said: "When the conflict began the mountain appeared volcanic. There flashed along its summit, and around its base, and up its sides, one long sulphurous blaze." The Indian war whoop and shouts of the determined mountaineers, the peals and cracks of hundreds of rifles and muskets, the loud commands and encouraging words given by the various commanders, and high above the din and confusion of battle the shrill scream of Ferguson's silver whistle, the groans of the wounded and dying on every part of the mountain, all combined, will convey some idea of the dreadfu' carnage of that memorable day.

For one hour the battle thus raged, the Whig troopers from every side were pouring into Ferguson's ranks the most deadly and destructive fire, while their own was receiving but little damage. When the British charged their antagonists with bayonets, they would scamper down the hill out of reach while those on the opposite side would rush up and inflict terrible execution upon their rear. Mills says: "Three times did the British charge with bayonet down the hill; as often did the Americans retreat, and the moment the British turned their backs the Americans shot from behind every tree and every rock and laid them prostrate." Though the numbers that fought under Colonel Williams at Kings Mountain were few, probably not exceeding one hundred, he was ably assisted by several brave and experienced subordinates. Among them were Brandon, Hammond, Hayes, Steen, Roebuck and Dillard. Taking all things into consideration, we doubt if more real courage and dauntless bravery was ever shown, and more thrilling incidents occurred, than in this short but decisive conflict In these things, Williams and his intrepid followers were not a whit behind their colleagues. Major Thomas Young, a youthful hero from Union District and a member of Williams' command, makes the following statement: "Major Ferguson had taken a very strong position upon the summit of the mountain, and it appeared like an impossibility to dislode him, but we had come there to do it, and we were determined, one and all, to do it or die trying. The attack was begun on the north side of the mountain."

"The orders were, at the firing of the first gun, for every man to raise a whoop, rush forward and fight his way as best he could. When our division came up to the northern base of the mountain, we dismounted, and Colonel Roebuck drew us a little to the right and commenced the attack. I well remember how I behaved. Ben Hollingsworth and myself took right up the side of the mountain, and fought from tree to tree, our way to the summit. I recollect I stood behind one tree and fired until the bark was nearly all knocked off, and my eyes pretty well filled with it. One fellow shaved me pretty close, for his bullet took a piece out of my gun stock. Before I was aware of it, I found myself apparently between my own regiment and the enemy, as I judged from seeing the paper which the Whigs wore in their hats and the pine tops the Tories wore in theirs, these being badges of distinction."

After the battle had raged some forty or fifty minutes, the mountaineers were pressing Ferguson so hard on all sides that his men were so busily engaged that they could not go to each other's assistance, however much they were in need of it. At length, the Provincial Rangers, led by the brave DePeyster, began to show signs of discouragement, because they were rapidly decreasing in number and were making little or no headway against their assailants. The circle occupied by the British and Tories was made to grow less and less as they were forced back to the center on the crest of the eminence. Dr. Ramsay, in his History of Tennessee, says: "The Tories had begun to show flags in token of surrender even before Ferguson was disabled, seeing which, he rode up in two instances and cut them down with his own sword." Captain DePeyster and some other officers advised a surrender, as further resistance was useless; that they were being hemmed "like ducks in a coop," to be slaughtered without any loss on the enemy commensurate with their own. But the boastful and defiant Ferguson would not listen to such proposals. He would not entertain the idea of surrendering, for he despised his enemies and hated them with such venomous hatred that he swore "he would never yield to such d—d banditti."

The Fall of Ferguson

Finally, he was forced to realize that all was lost; but he determined not to fall into the hands of the despised "Backwater Men."

With a few chosen comrades, he made a desperate attempt to break through the Whig lines on the east side of the mountain, opposite where Winslow's column was originally posted, and if possible make his escape Such an effort was as bold and daring as it was foolhardy, but it showed the spirit of the proud, haughty and defiant, but doomed Briton. When the dash was made, Ferguson wielded his sword mightily in his left hand, cutting and slashing until he broke it.

At this moment, one of Sevier's men, named Gilliland, who had been wounded several times and well-nigh exhausted, seeing Ferguson and his party approaching, made an effort to bring the career of the brilliant leader to an end, but his gun snapped—when he called out to Robert Young, one of the same corps: "There's Ferguson; shoot him!" "I'll try and see what 'Sweet Lips' can do," muttered Young, as he drew a sharp sight and fired, when Ferguson fell from his horse. It appears that several others espied him and fired at the same time, as he received six or eight balls, one of them passing through his head.

Draper says: "He was unconscious when he fell, and did not long survive." He furthermore says: "He is said to have received six or eight bullet holes in his body, one penetrating his thigh, another reshattering his right arm just above the elbow, and yet he continued to raise his sword in his left hand, till a rifle ball piercing his head put an end to his further fighting or consciousness." Dr. A. L. Hammond, son of Major Samuel Hammond, in an article on Kings Mountain, says: "As he (his father, Major Hammond) passed where Ferguson fell, he saw that he was not dead, and stooping down, took him gently under the arms and raised him to a sitting posture, placing his back against a tree by the side of which he had fallen, receiving the dying man's thanks for his attention, and hastened forward after the flying enemy." He again says: "Colonel Hammond passed where Ferguson had been left and found him fallen over on his face, and dead." Doctor Ferguson, in his memoir

COLONEL FERGUSON

of Colonel Ferguson, says: "He received a number of wounds, of which, it is said, any one was mortal, and dropping from his horse, expired while his foot yet hung in the stirrup."

On the authority of John Spelts, who fought in the battle, Draper says that one "Powell and three others were seen at the close of the surrender, bearing off in a blanket their fallen chief to a spring near the mountain's brow on the southern side of the elevation, and there gently bolstered him up with rocks and blankets. A little later, Colonel Shelby rode up, and thinking, perhaps, that Ferguson might yet be sensible of what was said to him—though he evidently was not—exclaimed: 'Colonel, the fatal blow is struck—we've "burgayned you."' The life of this restless British leader soon ebbed away."

It will be readily seen that these statements differ. Some say that Ferguson was unconscious when he fell, others say that he retained his consciousness for a short while afterward. Some say that he expired where he fell, others that he lived until after he was borne to the foot of the mountain. Whether conscious or unconscious, it is most probable that he survived until after he was carried to the spring below, although there was a tradition in the Kings Mountain neighborhood that his body lay where it fell until the next day, when it was carried down to the branch and buried.

Although his choice of ground was much against him, it must be said that Ferguson's conduct in his last contest was that of a hero. He did everything that mortal man could have done under the circumstances to save himself and his army from destruction. He seemed to be almost omnipresent—his person, his voice and his whistle were everywhere seen and heard, encouraging his men to renew their bayonet charges or to maintain a firm stand against the terrible assaults of the determined mountaineers.

Ferguson having fallen, the contest was soon brought to a close. Immediately white flags and handkerchiefs were displayed, both with and without DePeyster's orders, but it seems that at first little attention was paid to them. Mills, in his Statistics of South Carolina, says: "When the British found themselves pressed on all sides, they hung out white handkerchiefs upon guns and halberds. Few of the Americans understood the signal, and the few that did chose not to know what it meant; so that even after submission the slaughter continued until the Americans were weary of killing."

While Mills' statement is probably somewhat exaggerated, there is no doubt that the firing was kept up after the signs of surrender were raised.

Some of the Whigs, especially the younger ones, pretended that they did not know what the white flag meant, while others were so exasperated that they were crying, "Buford's play," "Tarleton's quarters," etc., and it was with difficulty that the officers restrained them. They have been severely censured in some quarters because of this unfortunate affair, but we have reason to believe that some of them, at least, tried to do their duty. Andrew Evins, a Virginian, with some other soldiers, were firing on some demoralized Tories, when Colonel Campbell ran up and knocked up the soldiers' guns and exclaimed: "Evins, for God's sake, don't shoot. It is murder to kill them so, for they have raised the flag." Campbell ran along the lines repeating the order, "Cease firing; for God's sake, cease firing!" Then Colonel Campbell called out, "Officers, rank by yourselves; prisoners, take off your hats and sit down." By this time, the enemy had been driven in a group sixty yards in length and less than forty in width. The victors were now ordered to close up and surround the prisoners, "first in one continuous circle, then double guards, and finally four deep." Colonel Campbell then proposed to the troops that they give three "huzzas for liberty," which they did. Thus, the mountain which had for one hour trembled beneath the rushing tread of soldiery, the sharp crack of rifles, and the roar of musketry, now gave way to the shouts of victory.

> "This being indeed, we shouted amain,
> Our voice was heard seven miles on the plain;
> Liberty shall stand, the Tories shall fall;
> Here's an end to my song, so God bless you all."

Fall of Colonel James Williams

"But," says Draper, "an occurrence now transpired that for a few moments changed the whole scene in that quarter, and threatened for a brief period the most tragic consequences. It is known, as a British account relates it, that a small party of the Loyal militia, returning from foraging, unacquainted with the surrender, happened to fire on the rebels. The prisoners were immediately threatened with death if the firing should be repeated. Whether it was the volley from this party, who probably scampered off, or whether from some Tories in the general huddle, exasperated, perhaps, that proper respect was not instantly paid to their flag, now fired upon and mortally wounded Colonel Williams, who was riding toward the British encampment. Colonel Williams, wheeling back, said to William Moore, one of Campbell's regiment: 'I'm a gone man'."

According to Draper, Colonel Williams was not wounded until after the enemy had surrendered and the firing ceased, but during an unexpected outbreak, while the surrounding hills and valleys were yet filled with reverberations of the shouts of victory. The whole scene changed in a moment and twinkling of an eye. The expressions of joy and gladness instantly gave way to the sounds of rifle volleys as they were again brought to bear on the Tories by the maddened followers of Colonel Williams.

Joseph Hughes, one of Williams' command, in his pension application says: "Was at Kings Mountain, where General Williams was mortally wounded after the British had raised their flag to surrender, by a fire from some Tories." This account substantially agrees with that of Draper. Dr. John Whelchel, another of Williams' command, a man of much intelligence, and likely an eyewitness, says: "Colonel Williams received his fatal shot immediately after the enemy had hoisted a flag to surrender."

Major Thomas Young, one of Williams' faithful subordinates, gives this graphic account: "On the top of the mountain, in the thickest of the fight, I saw Colonel Williams fall, and a braver or better man never died upon the field of battle. I had seen him but once before that day; it was in the beginning of the action. as he charged by me at full speed around the mountain. Toward the summit, a ball struck his horse's under jaw, when he commenced stamping as if he were in a nest of yellowjackets. Colonel Williams threw the reins over the animal's neck, sprang to the ground and dashed onward. The moment I heard the cry that Colonel Williams was shot, I ran to his assistance—for I loved him as a brother—he had ever been so kind to me, almost always carrying a cake in his pocket for me and his little son, Joseph. They carried him into a tent and sprinkled some water in his face. As he revived his first words were: 'For God's sake, boys, don't give up the hill!' I remember it as well as if it had occurred yesterday. I left him in the arms of his son, Daniel, and returned to the field to avenge his fall."

There are several accounts which say that Williams sought a personal encounter with Ferguson and determined to kill him or die in the attempt. Mills, in his Statistics of South Carolina, says: "Colonel Williams behaved here with the greatest bravery, and proved his patriotism. He had the good fortune to encounter personally in battle Colonel Ferguson, who attempted to force his way at this point. They both fell on the spot, being shot, it was supposed, by a ball from the British side—it was the last gun fired."

Ramsey, the Tennessee historian, asserts that Colonel Williams "fell a victim to the true Palmetto spirit, an intemperate eagerness for battle. Toward the close of the engagement, he espied Ferguson riding near the line, and dashed toward him with the gallant determination of a personal encounter. 'I will kill Ferguson, or die in the attempt,' exclaimed Williams; and spurring his horse in the direction of the enemy, received a bullet as he crossed their line. He survived till he heard that his antagonist was killed and his camp surrendered, and amidst the shouts of victory by his triumphant countrymen, said, 'I die contented,' and with a smile on his countenance, expired."

Dr. A. L. Hammond, in an article published in the *Charleston Courier* in 1859, says: "Just then Williams' horse, wounded and snorting with foam and blood at every bound, dashed forward. Ferguson turned to receive him, their swords crossed, nothing more, for at that moment a deadly volley came from both sides and the two combatants fell mortally wounded." Ensign Robert Campbell states: "Colonel Williams was shot through the body, near the close of the action, in making an attempt to charge on Ferguson; he lived long enough to hear of the surrender of the British army, when he said: 'I die contented, since we have gained the victory'."

John H. Logan, the historian, among his manuscript traditions, gathered the following: "Williams and Ferguson fell nearly at the same time on the eastern side of the mountain. Williams, from a more favorable position than those occupied by Campbell and Hambright, saw the magic influence of Ferguson's whistle. Dashing to the front, his horse throwing bloody foam from his mouth that had been struck by a ball, he was heard to exclaim, 'I'll silence that whistle or die in the attempt.' Quickly Ferguson was no more; and soon after, a ball from the enemy laid Williams mortally wounded on the hillside."

But the most romantic of all is that of Sims in his History of South Carolina: "Tradition reports that Williams and Ferguson perished by each other's hands; that after Ferguson had fallen by the pistol of Williams, and lay wounded on the ground, the latter approached and offered him mercy, and that his answer was a fatal bullet from the pistol of the dying man." A similar statement is made by Colonel Samuel Hammond in a private letter written to a friend in 1823. "Sir: I feel much mortified at the manner in which Colonel James Williams and his family have been neglected by all the writers, as well as those who ought to have written on the subject of the celebrated and fortunate battle of Kings Mountain. That patriotic officer died in personal combat with the British commanding officer; both fell at the moment, and their bones are bleaching together on the brow of that hill."

We do not believe that there is any truth in these latter statements that either Williams or Ferguson perished by the hand of the other; and Draper thinks that all of them relative to a personal encounter are "more romantic than probable." He says: "It could hardly have been so, since Ferguson was shot some distance from where Williams must have received his wounds, and on the opposite side of the hill." It could be true that no such thing as a personal encounter was even sought for, but we can hardly see how such a report could have gained credence among participants in the battle, and the older historians, if it had been utterly without foundation. Neither can we determine at this late day just where Williams fell. True, when the battle began, he was on the opposite side of the mountain from where Ferguson was shot; but before its close the British and Tories were driven together and huddled in such a small space that Williams might have come in quite close proximity to Ferguson, and seeing and hearing the magical effect of his whistle, determined if possible upon a hand-to-hand conflict. That he fell at or near the close of the action there is little or no doubt. In this the various accounts are pretty well agreed. It is quite sure also that Ferguson fell first, but not very long. Of one thing, however, we are certain, and that is when victory was already perched upon his brow, the gallant Williams received a death missile which laid him prostrate on the field of glory.

Two accounts are before us as to where the fatal ball struck him.

One says it passed through the groin; the other that the ball fired from the mountain struck him between the shoulders and ranged downward through the body.

The battle lasted about one hour, and probably ceased shortly after 4:00 o'clock. As soon thereafter as possible, such attention was given to the wounded as circumstances would permit. The Patriots, having neither baggage nor camp equipment, Colonel Williams was taken into one of the British tents, and it appears that he received some attention from Doctor Johnson, of Ferguson's corps, as there was not a single surgeon in the Whig ranks. Johnson seems to have been the good Samaritan of the occasion, rendering such professional services as he could, both to the Whigs and his fellow Britons alike.

A Night on the Battle Hill

As soon as circumstances would permit, a number were appointed to count the losses, and after considerable difficulty it was found that the Whigs had lost about 28 killed outright, and about 60 wounded. Ferguson's losses amounted to 150 killed, about the same number wounded, and six or seven hundred prisoners taken. In Colonel Williams' command there was only one killed besides himself, and William Giles was slightly wounded. It necessarily took considerable time to properly secure the prisoners, for their number was only a hundred or two less than that of their captors. One of Campbell's men said: "It was dark when we got the prisoners under guard." Night having fallen upon them, the only thing that could be done was to remain on the battle hill and wait for the light of another day.

It should be remembered that the Patriots had not slept any since leaving their camp on Green River thirty-six hours before, and but few had tasted food since they had left "The Cowpens" twenty-four hours previous.

Situated as they were, on Kings Mountain, they had to pass another night with little or nothing to eat, and we may judge with but little sleep, since they had such a large number of prisoners to guard, and were in the midst of such terrible surroundings. Says Major Thomas Young: "Awful indeed was the scene of the wounded, the dying and the dead on the field, after the carnage of that dreadful day." Benjamin Sharp states: "We had to encamp on the ground with the dead and the wounded, and pass the night amid groans and lamentations." Colonel J. H Witherspoon remarks: "My father, David Witherspoon, used to describe the scenes of the battleground the night after the contest as heart-rending in the extreme, the groans of the dying, and the constant cry of 'Water! Water!'" John Spelts says: "The groans of the wounded and dying on the mountain were truly affecting, begging piteously for a little water; but in the hurry, confusion and exhaustion of the Whigs, these cries, when emanating from the Tories, were little heeded." Such was the awful night on Kings Mountain immediately following the battle.

The next morning, which was Sunday, October 8, the sun shone out bright and clear for the first time in several days, and the Patriots were astir quite early. They were prompted to this because of two very pressing motives—one was to get away as quickly as possible, in order to secure a much-needed supply of food; the other to get beyond the reach of the dreaded Tarleton, for it was rumored in the camp that he was not far away and would make an effort to release the prisoners. A goodly number were busily engaged in preparing horse litters for the conveyance of the wounded. These litters consisted of blankets or pieces of tent cloth, to which poles were attached on each side, and the poles fastened to a couple of horses that stood side by side and the disabled soldiers were placed on the cloth suspended between them. With these litters they could travel with more ease and make greater speed over a rough and broken country than they could with wagons. Of these they had none of their own, and not caring to be encumbered with any of the seventeen that belonged to Ferguson, they were pulled over the camp fires and burned.

There are statements, both traditional and historical, which say that in their haste the dead were left unburied. Mills, in his Statistics of South Carolina, says: "The victors, dreading the arrival of Tarleton, who was only about two days march distant, hastened from the scene of action; nor durst they attend to bury the dead, or take care of the wounded, many of whom were seen upon the ground two days after the battle, imploring a little water to cool their burning tongue; but they were left to perish here, and this long hill was whitened with their bones. The vulture and the wolf divided their carasses between them, and so audacious had the latter grown that in some cases showed a disposition to attack living men." This is not altogether true; for upon the authority of Joseph Phillips, one of Cleveland's men, and Wm. Snodgrass and John Craig, of Campbell's regiment, Draper says: "When the army marched, some ten o'clock in the forenoon, Colonel Campbell remained behind with a party of men to bury their unfortunate countrymen. A place of sepulture was selected upon a small elevation some eighty or a hundred yards southeast of Ferguson's headquarters; large pits were dug and a number of the slain were placed together, with blankets thrown over them, and thus hurriedly buried."

It is very likely that in their haste Colonel Campbell and his party buried but few, if any of the Britons, and no Tories; but it should not be forgotten that there remained on the ground a hundred or more wounded Tories who were still alive. These, of course, were left behind in their anguish until relieved by death. It was upon the carcasses of these, and their comrades already dead, that the wolves and vultures fed, and whose "bones whitened the long hill."

We will add in this connection that these bones lay exposed until 1815, when, through the instrumentality of Dr. William McLean, of Lincoln County, N. C., a day was set apart for their gathering up and burial. At the same time, and at his own expense, Dr. McLean erected the old monument at the branch which marks the graves of Major William Chronicle, Captain John Mattocks, William Rabb and John Boyd. These belonged to Hambright's Lincoln County men and were from the south fork of the Catawba. They were killed when the British made their first charge down on that end of the mountain. The monument bears this inscription on the north side: "Sacred to the memory of Major William Chronicle, Captain John Mattocks, William Rabb and John Boyd, who were killed at this place on the 7th of October, 1780, fighting in defense of America." On the south side: "Colonel Ferguson, an officer of his Britannic majesty, was defeated and killed at this place on the 7th of October, 1780."

'Tis sad, but nevertheless true, that vandal hands have chipped away and disfigured this monument until the inscriptions are no longer legible. But thanks to the D. A. R.'s they have set up beside it a substantial granite rock with the inscriptions engraved upon it, and have enclosed the whole by an iron fence.

About ten o'clock the next morning, the army took up its line of march, and though encumbered by so large a number of prisoners, they were strongly guarded, and at the same time the tenderest possible care was bestowed upon the wounded, who were placed on the horse-litters. None received more attention that the heroic Colonel Williams, for, notwithstanding several reports to the contrary, he did not die on the battle hill. They set out in the direction of what was then called Deer's Ferry, on Broad River, and for several miles traveled the same road over which they had journeyed the day before. Early in the afternoon, they again reached Jacob Randall's place, where they had made a brief halt the evening before. At this place, on the roadside, stood a large chestnut tree with wide-spreading branches, producing a most inviting shade. Reaching that spot, the little party having Colonel Williams in charge, seeing that he was rapidly sinking, halted under this tree, where he quietly breathed his last. As a writer has expressed it, "The spirit of the gallant Williams quit forever the fields of carnage and blood below for realms of peace and life above." Such was the earthly end of this brave, uncompromising, unflinching and "martyr hero" of the Revolution.

More than twenty-five years ago the late Ira Hardin, of Blacksburg, S. C., informed the writer that this tree stood near the edge of his father's yard, and when a boy he had often shot birds off of it. The tree has long since disappeared, but Mr. Hardin kindly located the spot for us, and at our request, Mr. F. H. Dover, who at that time owned the place, set up a long, rough stone with these words chiseled upon it: "Where Colonel Williams Died." During the short halt made at Randall's, John Rainey, a young private from Georgia, who had been mortally wounded, expired; and his remains were carried about one hundred yards to the southwest of the Randall residence and buried on the slope overlooking the little stream that passes below. Colonel Williams' death was a matter of sincere grief to the whole army. His friends resolved at first to convey his body to his old home at Mt. Pleasant, in Laurens County; so carrying the remains with them, the army proceeded on their march towards Deer's Ferry. Passing over, or near the site of the present town of Blacksburg, they proceeded until they came to the deserted plantation of a Tory by the name of Matthew Fondren, just twelve miles from the battle ground. Here they found a good camping ground, with plenty of dry rails and poles for making fires, and luckily a sweet potato patch, sufficiently large to supply the whole army.

This, says Benjamin Sharp, "was most fortunate, for not one in fifty of us had tasted food for the last two days and nights—since we left 'The Cowpens.' " Later in the evening, they were joined by Colonel Campbell and the party who had been left behind to bury the dead. The location of this camp, which will be more fully described later, has long been known as the Mintz place. The next morning, for want of suitable conveyance and not thinking it wise to go in the direction of Colonel Williams' home, it was decided to bury his remains where they were. They were, says Draper, "accordingly interred with the honors of war between the camp and the river, a little above the mouth of Buffalo Creek, on what was long known as the Fondren place, now belonging to Captain John B. Mintz. Having performed this touching service, and firing a parting volley over the newly-made grave of one of the noted heroes of the war of Independence, the army, late in the day, renewed its line of march, apparently up Broad River." In a footnote, Draper further says: "Colonel Logan (John R.) adds that he learned from Captain Mintz that a tradition had been handed down that Colonel Williams was buried in that neighborhood, and no little pains had been taken to identify the grave by various people, and even by some of Colonel Williams' descendants, but without success. At length Captain Mintz employed some men to shrub off a field, long overgrown, and requested them to watch for the long-forgotten grave, and sure enough they found a grave, with a headstone and footstone composed of a different kind of rock from those abounding there, and well overgrown with grape vines. Though there was no inscription on the headstone, there is no doubt but that it is the grave of 'Old Kings Mountain Jim.' "

The following letter, published many years ago in the *Yorkville Enquirer*, throws additional light on, and corroborates the foregoing statements:

Thursday, November 19, 1857.

Grave of Colonel Williams

It is well known that Colonel Williams—the hero of Kings Mountain—fell mortally wounded in the moment of victory. With a vow that he would silence the whistle of Ferguson, whose shrill, clarion notes rang out above the din of battle, and brought again the wavering Red Coats to the charge, he rushed upon the foe and fell just as the enemy was giving away—just as the whistle ceased to ring—just as the shouts of the victors were going up from the "Grand Old Mountain." It was a fit requiem for the gallant soldier, the music which sounded so sweetly in the ear of Wolfe on the plains of Abraham. But it is not generally known that the spot of earth where sleeps the hero can be distinctly identified. The tread of pilgrim feet have echoed through the ravines of the mountain, baptized in the blood of heroes; but patriotism has never sought out, nor love and veneration consecrated that little mound—the "narrow house" of the big-hearted Williams. Two rude stones mark that sacred spot, and oral and traditionary evidence have alone given it a "local habitation and a name."

But the chain of testimony by which it is identified has recently been traced out, link by link, by William G. Black, Esq. From him we gather the following evidence, which he has taken the trouble to collect: "William Camp, Esq., a highly respectable citizen of this district, now upwards of 70 years of age, who has resided in the immediate neighborhood for the last fifty-eight years, says that tradition and the oldest citizens, contemporaries of the battle of Kings Mountain, have uniformly designated a grave on the plantation of Mr. John B. Mintz as the final resting place of Colonel Williams. The plantation of Mr. Mintz lies between Buffalo and Broad River, and was pointed out to him forty-odd years ago by Mrs. David Quinn, the daughter of Anthony Morgan, who resided within forty rods of the grave when Colonel Williams was buried. She was a full-grown lady at the time. The American army, on the night after the battle, camped near her father's spring, and early next morning their dead commander was interred." This evidence accords with the well-known facts that the army retreated immediately after the battle for fear of Cornwallis; that Colonel Williams died under a chestnut tree, which we have often seen, which until recently stood near the residence of A. Hardin, Esq., and that the army, then in full retreat, did not stop to bury him, but carried him along with them.

The statement of Mrs. Quinn was confirmed by Peter Morgan, her brother. Mr. Collins, who lived in a mile of the encampment at the time, likewise attested the same. A quixotic adventure brought him to the American camp. He was a quiet, harmless person, whose sole ambition was to live and let live; and a few days previous to the battle, a neighbor, a violent Tory, told him that the

British had possession of the entire country, and that he would be "hung, drawn and quartered" if he did not carry immediately to their camp a supply of provisions. He was credulous enough—like the witless Cornwallis—to believe that the country was conquered, and so he posted off with a bag of meal for the British. This was the very day of the battle. In the meantime, the mountaineers, like eagles from their aeries, had swooped down upon the confident Ferguson. Before the meal intended for the Tories could reach them, many of them had lost their appetites forever. The pliable Collins was met by a neighbor, who, discovering his intention, told him the result of the battle in the following unique language: "Ferguson has been in hell three hours, and the Whigs will send you after him if you don't change your course immediately." He took the hint from the gentle Mercury and returned home. That night he carried his meal to the American camp.

Silas Randall, who recently died at the age of 90, gave Mr. Camp the following information: He was with Colonel Williams at A. Hardin's; raised his head and gave him a drink, when he immediately went to sleep—his soul passed quietly away, so that it scarcely seemed like death. Mr. Randall also asserted that he (Colonel Williams) was carried on to the camp and buried as above stated. No man ever possessed a fairer character than the last witness, and therefore his evidence is conclusive.

The grave itself appears to be a fitting abode for the hero of Kings Mountain. It is situated on the side of a hill, in full view of the blue mountain top, so that at the resurrection morn his eye will rest first on the scene of his glory and earthly immortality. Was it the native taste of the rude mountaineers, or the directing hand of that Providence "which shapes our ends"—which we call chance— that selected this site and this position, ere in the haste of retreat, they left the hero "alone in his glory?"

Feeling that the grave of such a noted hero should be identified if possible, this writer set about more than a quarter of a century ago to make some investigations. Accordingly, on the morning of April 25, 1898, in company with some friends, we visited the supposed place of Colonel Williams' burial. It answered Draper's description exactly. He says that on leaving the battle ground, the army marched "on the route towards Deer's Ferry, on Broad River, and marching some twelve miles from the battle ground, they encamped that night near the eastern bank of Broad River and a little to the north of Buffalo Creek." At this point a large hill rises, and about midway between its top and bottom, on the eastern slope, is where the grave was found. A little higher up, running almost exactly east and west, the old road to Deer's Ferry passed. The signs of that road were then visible, and at the nearest point, just ninety yards north of the grave. Standing there, facing the southeast, the river is about a quarter of a mile to the right, and Buffalo Creek about a half mile in front—both river and creek being in plain view. We have seen that tradition also pointed to that locality as the burial place of Colonel Williams, though the exact spot was long lost sight of; that where Captain Mintz cleared a particular field, command was given that search be made, the result of which was the finding of a lone grave, etc

Mr. D. D. Gaston, a son-in-law of Captain Mintz, informed the writer that he had often heard his father-in-law say that when he first came to the place an old negro woman told him (Mr Mintz) that Colonel Williams was buried on that hill—the one where the grave was found—for she, when a girl, went with her mistress to the newly made grave. Hence, search was made in that particular place with the results already mentioned So history and tradition agree exactly, and both point to the single grave on the hill as that of Colonel Williams.

As we went up the hill from the river toward the grave, one of the party picked up a large, round-leaden ball, just such as have been found on the Kings Mountain and Cowpens battle grounds. Balls of that kind were picked there occasionally for thirty years previous. No doubt but that they were discharged when the parting volley was fired by the Patriots over the newly-made grave of their beloved, but fallen leader.

Arriving at the spot, we found a black oak growing on or near the grave. Captain Mintz had this tree left when the field was cleared for the purpose of marking it. Armed with ax, pick and shovel, we began the work of excavation on the south side of the tree, but without success. We then began on the north side, and soon had reason to believe that we had struck the grave, and sure enough we had Going about three feet, we first found a rib bone, and then almost the entire skeleton, and in a fair state of preservation. The skull was perfect from the base to the eyesockets. All the bones removed were put back at once, except the skull, which was kept out long enough to be photographed, when it, too, was replaced. No military relic was found, but when we reached the skeleton the dirt contained considerable amounts of short hair, which looked liked cow hair, and we believe that it was indicative of the shroud in which he was buried—a cowhide. With this vast array of fact, we have no doubt about finding the grave of Colonel James Williams, "a martyr hero of the Revolution."

Having located the grave of Williams beyond dispute, we set about to enlist his descendants, and any others who would, in the erection of a suitable monument to his memory, **His Bones Removed** but did not succeed. A few years ago the D. A. R. had the bones disinterred, placed in an iron chest, removed to Gaffney and deposited in the yard of the public library. A granite marker was placed over the deposit, which is surmounted by two small cannon and some cannon balls.

Colonel Williams was about five feet nine inches high and quite corpulent. His complexion was very dark; his hair and eyes were black; his nose uncommonly large, turned up, and **His Personal Appearance** round at the end. His nostrils, when distended by passion or excitement, were so large as to give rise to the coarse jest gotten off by one of his militiamen as an excuse for his tardiness at muster: "The boys," he said, "had been hunting and had treed a 'possum in the colonel's nose, and hence he was not in attendance."

Notwithstanding the fact that Colonel Hill, in his manuscript narrative, makes some damaging charges against him, Colonel Williams was a man of much personal piety, and pro- **His Religious Character** foundly religious in his character. He was a member and elder in the Little River Presbyterian Church, in Laurens District, and the last time he was ever at home he worshiped with this church and performed the duties of his office. He came near being captured by Tories, just barely making his escape by mounting a horse and dashing off through a field.

The sentiments expressed in his private letters to his wife reveal the religious status of the man In one of these he begins by saying, "I trust in God that His guardian care has been over you for your protection; I have earnestly requested the favor of heaven on you."

and concludes with this request, "But let our joint prayers meet in heaven for each other and our bleeding country."

Amos Lee, who resided on the west side of Fairforest, in Union District, and a soldier of the Revolution, says: "I knew Colonel James Williams before the war commenced, and spent a night at his house soon after it began. I remember that Williams prayed in his family and that he was a Presbyterian."

Johnson, in his traditions of the American Revolution, says, "Colonel Williams was a Presbyterian, and, like all of that faith, his religion placed him on the side of freedom. He and they thought with John Knox, that if they suffered the twins—liberty and religion— either to be infringed on or taken from them, that nothing was left them whereby they might be called men. In the bloodiest trials and the darkest hour of the Revolution, his faith upheld him and enabled him to say with the Psalmist, 'The Lord is my light and my salvation, whom shall I fear. The Lord is the strength of my life, of whom shall I be afraid.' "

Many writers and historians unite in paying the highest tributes to Colonel Williams as a man, as a soldier, and a hero. Bancroft, **Opinions of Colonel Williams as a Soldier and a Man** the historian, speaks of him as "a man of exalted character, of a career brief but glorious." Moultrie, in his "Memoirs of the Revolution," says: "He was a brave and active officer, and warm in the American cause." Lee, in his "Memoirs," states that, "Among the killed was Colonel Williams, with his adherents from the district of Ninety-Six, and was among the most active and resolute of this daring assemblage." Ramsay, in his "History of South Carolina," says: "The Americans lost comparatively few, but in that number was that distinguished militia officer, Colonel Williams." Johnson, in his "Life of Greene," says: "The loss of the Whigs was inconsiderable as to numbers, but rendered distressing to the Carolinians by the fall of Colonel Williams. When this State shall perpetuate her own gratitude and the memory of the worthies of the Revolution by dedicating a column to the preservation of their name, let not that of Williams be forgotten." Dr. Johnson, in his "Traditions," affirms that "All who knew him concurred in ascribing to him great personal bravery, and from a review of his conduct at Musgrove's Mill and in the events preceding the defeat of Ferguson, he is entitled to have it said that he exhibited great partisan skill."

Says Lyman C. Draper: "Fighting and dying, as he did, for his country, Colonel Williams well deserves to be judged in charity. He was every inch a Patriot, and a man of strong religious feelings. He was rough, rash and fearless. As a soldier, he was much after the style of Cromwell and Thomas J. Jackson in more recent times; and it may be added, his ambition for glory, mingled doubtless with a true love of country, led him, perhaps unconsciously, to the use of means not over scrupulous in the accomplishment of his ends. While he differed and chaffered with Sumter, Hill, and their associates, yet, when the tug of war came, he plunged fearlessly into the thickest of the fight and freely poured out his blood and yielded up his life for his country. Let his unquestioned patriotism, like a mantle of charity, cover all his seeming shortcomings. An ungenerous enemy revenged themselves for his virtues by nearly extirpating his family; they could not take away his right to be remembered by his country with honor and affection to the latest time."

When Colonel Williams fell at Kings Mountain, he left besides his wife, five sons, Daniel, Joseph, John, James, Jr., and Washington; three daughters, Elizabeth, Mary, and Sarah.

His Family James and Washington alone lived to be fathers of families. Daniel and Joseph were murdered at Hayes' Station by Bloody Bill Cunningham, aged, respectively, eighteen and fourteen years.

The daughters married John Griffin, James Atwood Williams, and James Tinsley.

The Life of Colonel Samuel Hammond

SAMUEL HAMMOND was born in Richmond County, Farnham's Parish, Virginia, on the 21st of September, 1757. His career of public service began in 1774, when he was but seventeen years of age. At that time he volunteered in an expedition sent out by Governor Dunmore, of Virginia, against the Western Indians, and was engaged in the desperate battle fought at the mouth of the Great Kenahaw River, on October 10, 1774.

When the strained relations between the Colonies and the mother country came to the breaking point, Samuel Hammond at once arrayed himself on the side of liberty, and joined a company of volunteers, or minute men, and was commissioned captain. At the head of this company, he fought at the battle of Long, or Great Bridge, near Norfolk, under Colonel Woodford, in December, 1775. He also served with the Virginia troops in Pennsylvania and New Jersey, under Colonel Matthews, General Maxwell, and others.

His Revolutionary Career

In 1778, he volunteered as aide to General Hand and went with him as far as Pittsburgh, Pa.

In January, 1779, he removed with his father's family from Virginia, and settled in Edgefield District in South Carolina. He immediately joined the Patriot army under General Benjamin Lincoln, according to permission received from General McIntosh, who had superseded General Hand in Western Pennsylvania. When he reported to General Lincoln, the Virginia troops, among whom he was to have served, were about to return home, their time of enlistment having expired. Hammond remained with Lincoln, and subsequently served under his brother, Colonel Leroy Hammond, in Georgia. Having been the aide of General Hand, and in com-

SAMUEL HAMMOND

116

Colonel Samuel Hammond

mand of a volunteer company in Virginia, he entered the Southern army with the rank of captain; and on the 2nd of February received orders from General Andrew Williamson to enroll a company of mounted volunteers, to be attached to Colonel Leroy Hammond's regiment. This he did, and on the 2nd or 3rd of March, 1779, was commissioned by Governor Rutledge captain of that company.

During the British invasion, under Provost, Captain Hammond was attached to the command of Colonels Henderson and Mahmudy, and with them was engaged in the battle of Stono, and several previous skirmishes. At the siege of Savannah, Hammond fought under General Huger, and was in the gallant attack made on the left of the British lines. He then continued to serve under General Williamson until the fall of Charleston, in May, 1780.

The fall of Charleston came perilously near wrecking the cause of Independence in South Coralina. The skies of hope were blackened by the dense clouds of British soldiery, from which rumbled the thunder of their guns. The terrible mutterings of the storm, accompanied by such merciless, savage butchery as that perpetrated by Tarleton on Colonel Buford at the Waxhaws, caused many strong knees to tremble and stout hearts to fear and quake. The British offer of protection, with life and property safeguarded, was the only rift to be seen in the clouds by many; hence, quite a number took advantage of it, even such officers as Generals Andrew Pickens and Williamson.

Hammond's Dauntless Courage in a Critical Hour

On the other hand, it aroused many to greater determination than ever before. A council of officers was called to meet near Augusta, Georgia, to determine what should be done. Captain Samuel Hammond was present at this council, and has left an account of what took place, which is important in indicating the condition of public opinion at the time in that part of the State.

There were present at this council General Williamson, with a number of field officers from South Carolina, and Governor Howley, of Georgia, his Secretary of State and council, with Colonels Clarke, Clary, Dooley, and several other Continental officers. Williamson presented a copy of the Articles of Capitulation at Charleston, which was read. Various plans were proposed and discussed, but none decided upon. Governor Howley and his council decided, however, to fly to the North with such State papers as they could conveniently carry with them. General Williamson decided to discharge the few militia then on duty, to retire to his own place, called White Hall, where he would call together the field officers of the brigade and the most influential citizens to consult what course to pursue. The Georgia Colonels, Clarke and Dooley, promised to co-operate with Williamson in any plan that should be adopted by the council at White Hall.

Williamson went at once to his place and assembled a large number of officers, and before going into the council high hopes were entertained by Captain Hammond that the determination would be to move into North Carolina, without loss of time, with all who chose to go and meet the expected army coming to the South. Williamson had under his command three independent companies of regular infantry, raised by Carolina, well-disciplined troops with good officers Besides these, there were also present between one hundred and fifty and two hundred unorganized men from different parts of the State. Andrew Pickens, then on his march toward the lower country, was halted about three miles below Ninety-Six; and with this additional force, Captain Hammond thought a movement into North Carolina could be made safely, as the enemy had no force near, who were equal to them, either in numbers or discipline.

The council met, and the terms of capitulation in Charleston were read, General Williamson commented on them, briefly reviewing the situation of the country, and concluded by advising an immediate movement; but said he would be governed by whatever action the majority of the council should adopt. The decision being rendered, Captain Hammond says he was struck dumb when he found that there was only one officer of the staff—one field officer and four or five captains—but what were ready to accept the British terms of capitulation. It was then proposed that a flag be sent to the British Captain Pearis, informing him of their action, and to settle the place and manner of surrender.

Williamson did not, however, yet give in. Hammond says he still persevered, and tried to induce the people to continue the struggle. He again addressed the council, urging them to change their verdict, and induced a number of officers to accompany him to Pickens' camp, which was only a few miles off, that he might confer with him and address the troops under his command. Arriving there, Williamson had a short consultation with Pickens and then addressed his command, all of which were mounted and drawn up in a square. The address was said to have been quite spirited and patriotic. He told them that with his (Williamson's) command alone, he could drive all the British forces in their district before him.

The Articles of Capitulation at Charleston were then again read and another address delivered to the troops. Williamson declared that there was nothing in the way of a safe retreat to North Carolina, and that he had no doubt but that they would soon be able to return with sufficient forces to keep the enemy, at least, confined to Charleston. He reminded them of what they had already done and urged them to persevere, but left it to them to say what they would do, and that he would go or stay as they should decide. Pausing for a short while, as if to give them time to consider, Williamson called to them, saying: "My fellow citizens, all of you who are for going with me on a retreat, with arms in your hands, will hold up your hands, and all who are for staying and accepting the terms made for you by General Lincoln, will stand as you are." Two officers, with three or four privates, held up their hands; all the rest stood as they were. The question was again put, with the same result. Not even General Andrew Pickens held up his hand. Certainly this was a dark day for the lovers of "liberty" in upper South Carolina. General McCrady, in his "History of South Carolina," gives the explanation of the above proceeding as follows: "The truth was that the people of Ninety-Six, who had never taken an active or an enthusiastic part in the Revolution, refused to go on in the face of disaster with a movement they had not generally or cordially espoused, and were ready to accept the terms offered at Charleston."

If Williamson is, at this time, to be condemned for acquiescing in the decision of his people against his urgent advice, still more so must Pickens, who refused to join in his earnest appeals to them not to submit. Pickens remained for six months, and those of the most stirring times and events, as quietly at home as did Williamson. Ultimately, Williamson went to Charleston, was taken under the special protection of the British, and in some way was employed by them. Pickens, later, joined the Americans, and as Johnson, in his "Life of Greene," observes, "fought literally with a halter around his neck." The story of these two men is not a mere episode in history. It illustrates the struggle which was going on in the minds and hearts of the people generally throughout the State.

There was one young captain present that day, Samuel Hammond by name, who refused to obey the decision of Williamson's council He immediately withdrew from the majority and raised an independent company, numbering seventy-six men, and determined to seek assistance from the North, or die with arms in hand. In a little while more than half of the number first collected withdrew from Hammond's party and hid out in secret places, but were afterwards made prisoners of war, sent to prison, where many of them died Thirty-three remained faithful, and made good their retreat into North Carolina. By concealing themselves all day in swamps and canebrakes and traveling all night, they passed the Saluda and Bush rivers, and were kindly supplied by friends, but could hear of no body of Whigs that they could join.

Passing on to the foot of the mountains, they came to the house of a good Whig, by the name of Calvin Jones. Jones was not at home, and Mrs. Jones was found in a great deal of trouble. That very day she had been ill-treated and her house plundered by a party of Tories. They had taken the children's clothes and her sidesaddle, for which they had no use, and had wantonly destroyed everything of value which they could not carry off. Mrs. Jones said that there were seventy or eighty of them. Although Hammond's little band only numbered thirty-five, they determined to follow and chastise them, if possible. Mrs. Jones being informed of their purpose, she sent for her son, a boy of twelve or fourteen years old, to guide and aid them in the pursuit. He cordially joined in the expedition, and, following the Tory trail, they were overtaken the next morning while at their breakfast. A charge was made upon them, and Hammond's men were in the midst of their camp before they knew of their approach. All their arms were taken, and most of them destroyed. Four of the enemy were killed and eleven prisoners taken, which were released on parole. All of Mrs. Jones' valuables were returned to her She supplied the brave Whigs with everything needed that was in her power, and they went on much encouraged, having a number of captured horses and a fine supply of ammunition.

After a day or two, while broiling their bacon and eating parched corn as a substitute for bread, they were alarmed by the sound of horses' feet, and soon saw a party approaching on the other side of the creek from where they were encamped. They had come within the reach of Hammond's guns before they were discovered, and, being hailed, answered: "Friends of America." "So are we," was the reply, "but let us know you. Men, stand to your guns." The other side gave the same order, and they paused with guns pointed at each other's breasts. Captain Edward Hampton advanced with a flag, and, being well known, was cordially welcomed by all of Hammond's men. Hampton and his party being actuated by the same motives, adopting the same resolutions, were pursuing the same course, and thus were happily united with the Hammond party.

The united party continued their march and soon came on the trail of a party, supposed to be enemies, and perhaps as numerous as their own. They determined to attack them, so quickened their march. After an hour's pursuit, they discovered a horse in front and a man lying down, with a bridle in his hand, fast asleep. They surrounded and hailed him. He leaped up and boldly replied: "Friend to America, if I die for it!" His name was Harrison, and he informed them that he belonged to Colonel Elijah Clarke's command, which was not far ahead; that he had been overcome with fatigue and want of sleep and had dropped from the ranks to take a nap, expecting to rejoin his command soon. Clarke was overtaken that same evening, and the Patriots found that they now numbered more than two hundred, but being out of provisions they resolved to push on to the frontier, and return when fed and rested.

Upon their arrival in North Carolina, they were informed that there were several parties of Whigs who, like themselves, had crossed over into that State. One of them was commanded by General Sumter, one by Colonel James Williams, and one by Colonel Thomas Brandon; that General McDowell had assembled a considerable number of militia not far distant from their resting place. Messengers were sent to each of these officers, informing them of the number and intentions of Hammond's party. They were joined by Captains McCall and Liddle, of Pickens' regiment, with a detachment of about twenty men. Being refreshed by their sojourn on the frontier, and having gained intelligence of the enemy's operations, it was agreed that all should return to South Carolina, under command of Colonel Clarke, to annoy the enemy as much as possible, to give opportunity to their friends to join them, and thereby encourage the cause of Independence where it was so much needed.

Although Colonel McDowell was near, for want of confidence in his activity, or from some other cause, Clarke pushed on and joined Sumter, who was then on or near the Catawba. Sumter, hearing of Ferguson's inroads beyond Broad River, in what is now Union and Spartanburg counties, he directed Colonel Clarke and his Georgians, together with such persons in his camp as resided in that region and desired to aid in its protection, to repair to that quarter. The order was quickly obeyed, and when Clarke arrived at the Cherokee Ford, on Broad River, he met Colonel McDowell, who had assembled his forces at that place.

The first blow struck by these joint forces was the capture of Thickety Fort, in what is now Cherokee County, on July the 30th. **Thickety Fort, Second Cedar Springs and Musgrove's Mill** Ninety-three Loyalists and one British sergeant-major, with their leader, the notorious Patrick Moore, and one hundred and fifty stands of arms, all loaded with ball and buck shot, were taken without firing a gun. They immediately returned to McDowell's camp at the Cherokee Ford.

A few days later, McDowell again detached six hundred men, under Colonels Clarke, Shelby, and Graham, to watch Ferguson's movements, and on August the 8th the second battle of Cedar Springs or Wofford's Iron Works was fought.

It is unknown to us as to whether Captain Samuel Hammond was in these daring expeditions or not; but, with his little force, having joined Clarke in North Carolina, it is reasonable to suppose that he was.

The Americans again returned to their headquarters at McDowell's camp. A few days later, moving down to Smith's Ford and being joined by Colonel James Williams and his followers, McDowell detached a small force, under Colonels Clarke and Shelby, to accompany Williams in an expedition against the Loyalists at Musgrove's Mill, whom they defeated on the 18th of August. Captains Samuel Hammond and James McCall were with Colonel Clarke at that place. The perilous retreat of the victorious Patriots is described on pages 81-83.

The time of enlistment having expired for Shelby's men, he turned the prisoners over to Colonel Clarke for safekeeping. After continuing some distance, Clarke decided to return to Georgia, and transferred the prisoners to Colonel Williams, who, with Captain Samuel Hammond, conducted them safely to Hillsboro. There they met Govenor Rutledge, of South Carolina, who was there as a refugee. Acquainting the Governor with the victory at Musgrove's, he commissioned Williams a brigadier-general, and Hammond as major.

With Rutledge's commission in hand, Williams proceeded to Sumter's camp and asserted his right to command the troops. To this Sumter and his forces would not agree A second effort on the part of Williams was made, with no better success. He then returned to North Carolina and got permission from Governor Nash, of that State, to raise a company of troops. Under this call he enlisted about seventy men. Colonel Thomas Brandon and Major Samuel Hammond joined the Williams party. Much bickering and strife arose between Williams on one side and Sumter and Hill on the other, and many aspersions of the most malicious character were heaped on Williams and his followers. Colonel Hill tells us "that these North Carolinians, who enrolled under Williams, were men who shirked duty under their own local officers; and besides the tempting offer of 'beef, bread and potatoes,' Colonel Williams had furthermore promised what was regarded as still better in the estimation of men of easy virtue—the privilege of plundering the Tories of South Carolina of as many negroes and horses as they might choose to take." Such accusations were unfair, unjust, and unbecoming in a fellow-officer. The fact that officers of such character as Colonel Thomas Brandon and Major Samuel Hammond were active in enlisting men for Williams' command would offset Hill's charges. Says Major Hammond in his pension application: "This little force constituted the largest portion of Williams' command at Kings Mountain," and all know that none played their part better in that immortal struggle.

While the "over-mountain-men," who were bent on the destruction of Ferguson, were yet in North Carolina, Colonel Williams was joined by that noted officer from Spartanburg, Benjamin Roebuck, and his company of twenty or thirty men.

Though feeling the mistreatment by Hill, Lacey and others very keenly, when the partisan leaders made their final juncture at The Cowpens on the evening of October 6th, Colonel Williams and his men, including such faithful officers at Thomas Brandon, Samuel Hammond, Benjamin Roebuck, James Steen, James Dillard and others were there.

Major Samuel Hammond at Kings Mountain

Before beginning their night march toward Kings Mountain, a council of war was held. To this Colonel Williams was not invited, but when the troops began to move Williams and his followers were in line. Arriving at Kings Mountain in the early afternoon of the next day, Ferguson's position was soon surrounded and the mighty struggle begun. It is said that because of his ill-treatment by the other officers, Williams at first refused to take part, but seeing such a glorious opportunity, he wheeled chivalrously into line on Shelby's left, and exclaimed: "Come on, my boys, the old wagoner never yet backed out."

While the battle raged, the Americans charged up the mountain and retreated down again as many as three times. In one of these charges, Major Hammond, full of his usual dash and intrepidity, broke through the British lines, with a small squad of brave followers, when the enemy tried to cut off their return. Seeing the perilous situation of himself and soldiers, Hammond instantly faced about and ordered his men to join him in cutting their way back, and by their most heroic efforts they succeeded.

Major Hammond used to relate a very singular incident in connection with this contest. One of the men in his command had fought in many a battle, and had always proved himself true as steel. On the night preceding the action, in some snatch of sleep, or perhaps while on the march, he had a presentiment that if he took part in the impending battle he would be killed. Before reaching Kings Mountain, he concluded that he would for once in his life be justifiable, under the circumstances, in skulking from danger, and thereby, as he believed, preserve his life for future usefulness to his country. So he stole off and hid himself. He was missed, when an orderly went in search of him and finally discovered him in an out-of-the-way place, all covered up, head and body, with his blanket. Though taken to the front, he soon found means to absent himself again, but his lurking place was again found, and he once more hurried to the front, just before the final attack.

He evidently now made up his mind to do his duty, and let consequences take care of themselves, and during the action he had posted himself behind a stump or tree, and evidently peering his head out to get a shot, received a fatal bullet in his forehead, killing him instantly. Subsequently learning the cause of his singular conduct in endeavoring to evade taking part in the contest, Major Hammond regretted that he had not known it at the time, so that he could have respected the soldier's conscientious convictions, but at the moment, suspecting that he was under the cowardly influence of fear, the Major could not and would not tolerate anything of the kind in his command.*

The battle having raged with all the fury of the gods, for about one hour, as all the world knows, Ferguson was laid low, his army captured, and "The Turning Point of The Revolution," in favor of the Colonists, had come.

Although victory was never more complete, the reported nearness of the British Colonel Tarleton, with his forces, caused the victors to return to North Carolina for safety. In a short time, Major Hammond returned to South Carolina, joined Sumter, and took part in the stirring scenes enacted in the Ninety-Six region during the latter part of 1780.

Just before Ferguson retreated from Gilbert Town towards Kings Mountain, Major Dunlap, one of his officers, noted for his barbarity, was wounded at Cowan's Ford. While in bed he was again shot through the body by Captain Gillespie, of the Fairforest region. Dunlap had seized and carried off the beautiful Mary McRae, who, refusing his amorous advances, was kept in confinement until she died of a broken heart. This lady was the affianced of Gillespie, and he shot Dunlap in revenge.

Though left for dead, it was not long until he sufficiently recovered to return to Ninety-Six, and was soon at the head of his henchmen, making a clean sweep of the country. Notwithstanding the fact that General Pickens was under British protection, with the promise of his belongings being safeguarded, Dunlap plundered his home and wantonly destroyed his property. Pickens, up to this time, had scrupulously regarded the terms of his parole, but it having been violated

---
*Draper's "Kings Mountain and Its Heroes"

by the other party, he felt himself at liberty to take up arms again in defense of his country, which he did, but not until he had fully explained to a British officer.

This state of things was made known to the commanding officer of the Georgia troops, and he again came into the Ninety-Six neighborhood to favor the assemblage of Pickens and his friends in that quarter. The officers held a council, and Colonel McCall was sent to invite the co-operation of Pickens, and Major Samuel Hammond was dispatched to White Hall, the residence of General Williamson, who, it will be remembered, upon the fall of Charleston, had in vain urged his companions and followers in Ninety-Six to retreat with him into North Carolina and carry on the war there, but accepting the decision of his comrades not to go, had given his parole and taken British protection. The British having violated its terms, he was to be appealed to once more to join his old friends in resistance. Major Hammond was ordered to bring him into camp, either with or without his consent. Although willing six months before, during the darkest days of the war, to leave home and continue the struggle, even in another State, Williamson refused to resume arms and rejoin his friends. He was taken by Hammond and brought to the Whig encampment at Long Cane, but he escaped and made his way to Charleston. It was believed that he took a British commission, but there is no evidence of his having done so, and he certainly did not engage in any active military movements in their service. It is said that he was one of those in the town from whom General Greene later obtained information of the British movements about that place.

Pickens was a great accession to the Patriot cause, and he being the senior officer in Ninety-Six, assumed the command of those who would act with him, and was soon on the way to join General Morgan, who was advancing into South Carolina, and in a few days took post at the Grindal Shoals, on Pacolet. Pickens was the first to inform Morgan of Tarleton's approach, which caused him to fall back to The Cowpens, where he achieved that brilliant victory, January 17, 1781. In that fight, Major Hammond commanded the left of the front line, and after the victory was won, Morgan detached him and a small number of men to watch the movements of the British army under Cornwallis. This duty he faithfully performed until the Britons reached Ramseur's Mill, in North Carolina. Hammond then joined General Greene, and did service for him mostly by maneuvering. At one time he escorted some prisoners to Virginia, and rejoined Greene a few days before the battle of Guilford, in which Hammond took a part.

While in North Carolina, the little party under Pickens was not idle; but affairs in their own State demanded their return. In addition to the large British force in South Carolina, there were threatenings of a serious outbreak by the Indians on the frontier. General Greene himself became anxious about the unprotected Whig families. Pickens being joined by Hammond, with about one hundred men, in early March, he was ordered to repair to the back parts of South Carolina to protect the unprotected, suppress the Loyalists, and cooperate with Sumter in his active enterprises. So, in a short time, Pickens was again engaged in arousing the people of the Ninety-Six District, urging them to join their friends in arms, and to aid in expelling their enemies. In this he was most zealously and ably seconded by the two Hammonds—Leroy and Samuel. Samuel Hammond being joined by Major James Jackson, of Georgia, he was urged to pass into that State for similar purposes. Proceeding through the Ninety-Six section, they reached a point near Pace's Ferry, on the Savannah River, in what is now Edgefield County. Here he was joined by Captain Thomas Kee, of Colonel Leroy Hammond's regiment, with a number of men. The next day, Captain Kee was detached to attack a party of Tories, assembled under a Captain Clarke, at his residence on Horner's Creek, in what is now Edgefield County. Clarke was killed, and all his company made prisoners. The party then marched to Colonel Leroy Hammond's mill, on the Savannah, attacked a British post there, broke up the mill, and took all the provisions belonging to enemies.

Being joined by two or three hundred men from Colonel Leroy Hammond's regiment, Major Samuel Hammond's force was sufficiently increased to justify the detaching of Major Jackson to cross into Georgia, and join the troops collecting on that side of the river. In a few days, the combined forces commenced the siege of Forts Cornwallis and Grierson in Augusta Major Samuel Hammond remained with Pickens, aiding in the reductions of these forts until they finally capitulated, June 5th, 1781. Here Hammond was raised to the rank of lieutenant-colonel.

Trouble having arisen on the account of the killing of the British

Colonel Grierson, after he had surrendered and was confined, caused Pickens to write the following to General Greene: "The people are so much exasperated against some individuals, I have found it necessary to give orders to cross the river with the prisoners under the care of Colonel Hammond's regiment, and Captain Smith's detachment of North Carolinians, and march them to Ninety-Six, or till I meet your order respecting them, being fully persuaded that were they marched for Savannah they would be beset on the road, but think they may go to Charleston by way of Ninety-Six, if you should so order."

It appears that the suggestion to carry the prisoners "by way of Ninety-Six" was carried out. At any rate, Hammond still remaining under Pickens, they soon joined Greene, who was before that place. When Lord Rawdon advanced, the siege was raised, and Hammond was ordered to retreat with Pickens to the westward from Ninety-Six, and ultimately to rejoin Greene, on the Congaree, below its confluence with Broad River. Lieutenant-Colonel Hammond remained active and took part in the battle of Eutaw Springs, fought September the 8th, 1781. Draper says that he was wounded in that engagement. Others mention the wounding of Lieutenant Hammond, but leave the impression that it was not Colonel Samuel. If wounded at all, it must have been slight, for only nine days later he was appointed colonel of a regiment of cavalry by Governor Rutledge, with instructions to raise and equip it immediately. The term of enlistment was for three years, or to the end of the war. A number of Hammond's State troops, who had long served under him as volunteers, now enrolled themselves in his regiment. With these, and a portion of Colonel Leroy Hammond's militia, he remained under General Greene until the preliminaries of peace were signed and announced. At this time he was encamped with Greene at Bacon's Bridge, near Charleston, and received orders to discontinue recruiting his regiment. A short time after this, the greater part of them were discharged. Previous to this, however, two companies of his regiment were detached, one under Captain Richard Johnson, the other under Captain George Hammond, to join Pickens in an expedition against the Cherokee Indians. Being successful, they returned and were also discharged.

Colonel Samuel Hammond remained in arms until peace was declared, and then settled in Savannah, Georgia. During his residence

Colonel Hammond Settles in Georgia in that State, he was honored with several positions of trust. He was appointed State commissioner to act with such men as General Lincoln, Judge Silas Griffin, etc.

In 1793, he was appointed to the command of the first regiment in Chatham County militia by Governor Telfair, and immediately ordered to the frontier, where he rendered important services.

His term having expired, he returned to Savannah, raised a volunteer troop of horse, and again repaired to the frontier. He represented Chatham County several times in the State legislature, and in October, 1802, he was elected to represent the State of Georgia in Congress.

In 1805, Colonel Hammond was honored by President Jefferson with the appointment of military commandant of what was then **Moves to Missouri** called Upper Louisiana, but now Missouri. He moved to that place and remained until 1824, occupying in the meantime such exalted positions as governor and member of Congress. He was appointed, lastly, receiver of public money in that State, and was in office in that unfortunate period when the rage prevailed for chartering banks, almost without number or restriction, in every part of the United States. The immense number of notes issued by the banks, not only deluged the country with a depreciating currency, but involved the country in hazardous speculations, by which many were financially ruined.

The banks which had loaned out their money to these speculators could not collect it, and were, therefore, unable to redeem their notes. Colonel Hammond was authorized to receive good bank notes in payment for the public lands, and the Secretary of the Treasury received them from him without hesitation, but when a large amount of bank notes had accumulated in the hands of Colonel Hammond, and the banks ceased to redeem them, the Secretary of the Treasury refused to receive them, and the loss was thrown on Colonel Hammond. In vain did he show by his entries that these notes were received before the banks stopped payment, and were generally believed to be good notes at that time.

The Government still refused them, and a great and good man was sacrificed after a lifetime of public service. He had acquired a handsome property in the city of St Louis, and he gave it all up to the Government, reserving nothing for himself and family—*"all was lost except honor."*

In 1824, he returned to South Carolina, the theater of his early military career. The Government not yet satisfied, the next year he was imprisoned in Charleston as a defaulter. He was admitted to bail, and notwithstanding the public sale of his property and the embarrassments of the day, the amount claimed by the United States was completely satisfied, and a balance of four thousand dollars left over.

Colonel Hammond Returns to South Carolina

Colonel Hammond was cordially welcomed and befriended in South Carolina by her grateful citizens as long as he lived. In 1827, the legislature elected him to the office of surveyor-general, and in 1831 he was made Secretary of State. On this occasion, General Sumter, his old friend and comrade in arms, came forward voluntarily and commended him to the legislature, and bore testimony to his gallantry and usefulness during the struggle for Independence. He distinctly attributed the victory at Blackstocks to the bravery of Colonel Hammond.

In 1835, being borne down by age and its infirmities, he withdrew from public life and retired to his farm, Varello, near Hamburg, where he resided until his death. Although so much of his early life was given to war and bloodshed, it is said that he preserved his natural gentleness and suavity of manners to the last, and would enliven every circle where he went with cheerfulness and sallies of good humor.

He passed away at his Varello farm, near Hamburg, on Sunday, September 11, 1842, in the eighty-seventh year of his age. The next day, Monday, the 12th, the military of Hamburg was joined by that of Augusta, all under the command of Major Samuel C. Wilson. These, together with the Masonic lodges of Hamburg and Augusta, and the citizens of both places, formed the funeral procession. Minute guns were fired from the site of the old fort, on Shultz's Hill, by the artillery, while the procession followed the body of the deceased veteran, with the solemn sound of muffled drums. When they arrived at the family burial ground above Campbelltown, the remains were lowered into the grave with Masonic honors, and a volley fired over it by the escorting infantry.

It is worthy of notice that from the fall of Charleston, in May, 1780, until the enrollment of his regiment in September,

1781, neither Samuel Hammond, nor any of his citizen soldiers, called for, or subscribed to a payroll. They furnished themselves as well as they could with their own clothing, often very scant, with their own arms, horses, and provisions, the last of which were frequently very scarce. Colonel Hammond, on more than one occasion, used his own property for the purchase of horses to mount the recruits in his regiment, and sold his negroes to raise the necessary money for their equipment. Such heroic sacrifices and unselfish devotion should have rendered his name immortal and inspired every American with undying loyalty to country. His body is embedded in South Carolina soil; it has only been eighty-one years since he went from the scenes of earth; a part of his deeds of valor were performed within sight of the present City of Spartanburg; and yet the name of Colonel Samuel Hammond is almost unheard of. Shame upon us!

The Life of Lieutenant-Colonel Benjamin Roebuck

COLONEL BENJAMIN ROEBUCK was born in Orange County, Virginia, about 1755. His father, Benjamin Roebuck, Sr., with his family, removed to South Carolina in 1777, and settled on Tyger River, a short distance above Blackstock's Ford, in what is now Spartanburg County. Being in moderate circumstances, the elder Roebuck came to South Carolina hoping to better his condition. Young Benjamin's education consisted of reading, writing and arithmetic, which was considered pretty good in those days. This, backed up by a noble character and manly virtues, was calculated to make the great and good man that he was. Doubtless the pious training of his mother had much to do with it, as she was a devout Baptist. His father was taken by Tarleton after the battle of Blackstocks, who sent him to jail at Camden, where the old man died with smallpox.

When the first call was made for soldiers, after the elder Roebuck's advent into South Carolina, his son Benjamin turned out and joined Captain William Smith's company and was elected first lieutenant. Governor B. F. Perry, in his eulogy of him, says: "He espoused the cause of his country with order and firmness. His patriotic associates rallied around him and looked to him as their leader in war as well as in peace." In this capacity he served under General Lincoln, in Georgia, and took part in the battle of Stono and the siege of Savannah.

Beginning of Roebuck's Military Career

Charleston having fallen in May, 1780, Roebuck, with many others, fled to North Carolina, and while there it is said took part in the brilliant affair at Ramseur's Mill. During his absence he was appointed a major in the First Spartan regiment, of which John Thomas, Jr, was about that time appointed colonel. This regiment having joined Dunbar, who was on the east side of the Catawba, upon his return from North Carolina, Major Roebuck was with the "Game Cock" long enough to take part in the battle of Hanging Rock. On the 1st of August, Sumter assaulted some British fortifications at Rocky Mount, but was unsuccessful and had to withdraw. The same day, Major Davie, with about eighty men, approached Hanging Rock, and while reconnoitering found that three companies of Loyalists infantry, who were returning from an excursion, had halted at a house in full view of Hanging Rock.

Davie at once determined to fall upon the party. Advancing cautiously, he eluded the sentinels and posted his infantry in one quarter and also gained the other point of attack with his mounted riflemen unobserved. The enemy were thus between the two divisions. The riflemen, dismounting in the lane leading to the house, gave them a well-directed fire. The surprised Loyalists fled to the other end of the lane, where they were met by a bold charge from the dragoons. Finding their front and rear occupied, the Loyalists attempted to escape in another direction which they thought to be open. Davie, having anticipated the movement, detached a party of his dragoons in time to meet them there, which rendered escape impossible. The Loyalists were all, except a few, killed or wounded, for there was no time for taking prisoners. Sixty valuable horses and one hundred muskets were the valuable booty taken. This took place in the face of the whole British camp at Hanging Rock. Their drums beat to arms, but Davie was out of reach before their forces were in motion. He reached his camp safely, without the loss of a single man.

Trouble having arisen between Sumter and Hill on one side and Colonel James Williams on the other, Williams and all who desired to do so left Sumter and moved in the direction of Ninety-Six. Such men as Colonels Thomas Brandon, James Steen, and Majors McJunkin and Roebuck chose to go with Williams, and they, with some others, joined Colonel McDowell at Smith's Ford, on Broad River, August the 16th.

Governor Perry says, "Colonel Roebuck was under Colonel Clarke in the second battle of Cedar Springs or Wofford's Iron Works, and he took an active part." This was impossible, unless he preceded his companions, Brandon, Steen, McJunkin, etc., for they did not reach McDowell's camp until August 16th, while the second Cedar Spring took place on the 8th, or eight days earlier. From no other source have we ever seen any intimation that Roebuck was in that battle; therefore we conclude that Governor Perry was mistaken.

The next day after the arrival of the Williams party at Smith's Ford, McDowell hearing that there was a large party of Loyalists at Musgrove's Mill, on the Enoree, he detached a part of his forces, under Colonels Clarke and Shelby, to unite with Williams to surprise them. An all-night ride brought them to Musgrove's in the early morning. Selecting their ground, the Americans hastily built an improvised fortress of logs, brushwood, etc. Being in readiness, a small party was sent forward to provoke the enemy to cross the river and decoy them into the trap set for them. The strategem worked admirably, and after an hour's bitter fighting the Tories fled across the river, pursued by the victorious Patriots. The British losses were sixty-three killed, seventy wounded and seventy-three prisoners. That of the Americans was four killed and nine wounded. After a most perilous and fatiguing retreat, the prisoners were safely delivered at Hillsboro, North Carolina. Colonel Roebuck was in this most wonderful battle, for that eminent historian, Lyman C. Draper, mentions the fact. For a more detailed account of the battle, see pages 74-81.

The Battle of Musgrove's Mill

On the account of Gates' disastrous defeat at Camden and the destruction of Sumter's forces on Fishing Creek, the partisan leaders in upper South Carolina had to flee to the mountains of North Carolina for safety. This left the mastery of the up-country in the hands of the British Major Patrick Ferguson. Nothing being in his way, Ferguson pursued as far as Gilbert Town, North Carolina. Although partly in hiding, the love and lovers of liberty had not been crushed, and they determined to unite their forces and crush Ferguson. Hence, the clouds began to gather and the lightning to flash. Leader after leader, party after party, and individual after individual began to unite until the final juncture came at The Cowpens, October 6th, 1780. Ferguson having fallen back and taken post on Kings Mountain, the fatal storm burst upon him on the evening of October the 7th. After one hour of the thunder of musketry and the pelting of the hail of lead, Ferguson was laid low and his army practically annihilated. Roebuck had been promoted captain, and with his company had joined the command of Colonel James Williams, in North Carolina, hence he commanded a company in Williams' division at Kings Mountain. Major Thomas Young, who took part in the battle, says:

At Kings Mountain

"When our division came up to the northern base of the mountain we dismounted, and Colonel Roebuck drew us a little to the left and commenced the attack." This makes it clear that Benjamin Roebuck took part as a commander in this momentous battle, the turning point of the Revolution.

The victory at Kings Mountain was quite complete, but the British Colonel Tarleton was not far away, and Cornwallis was at Charlotte; therefore, it was necessary for the brave heroes to retrace their steps back to the mountains in order to conserve and preserve the fruits of their victory.

Just how long Roebuck remained in North Carolina we do not know, but he was back in due time to join General Morgan at the Grindal Shoals, previous to the battle of Cowpens.

Ferguson being out of the way, and the shattered forces of the Southern army reorganized under General Greene, he detached **Roebuck Does His Bit at Cowpens** about six hundred men to march into upper South Carolina to relieve that Tory-infested and suffering region. Daniel Morgan was commander-in-chief, and was accompanied by Colonels John Eager Howard, William Washington, and Major Triplett. Morgan left Charlotte, December 16th, 1780, and took post at the Grindal Shoals, on Pacolet, the 25th of December. In a few days the Spartan regiments, under Colonels John Thomas and Thomas Brandon, took post in close proximity to Morgan, and with them came Benjamin Roebuck.

When Morgan was apprised of Tarleton's approach while at Grindal, he at once entrusted the dangerous but important mission of watching his movements to Colonel Thomas Brandon and Benjamin Roebuck. This was faithfully done, and while Tarleton was crossing the Pacolet at Easterwood Ford, on the morning of the 16th, Brandon and Roebuck, with some others, were sitting on their horses counting his men, a report of which was immediately forwarded to Morgan. All that day they hung on Tarleton's rear, and in the evening he reached the camp that Morgan had vacated the morning before. Here he remained until three o'clock a. m., when he resumed his pursuit of Morgan The eagle eyes of Brandon and Roebuck remained on Tarleton's camp until he began to move; then hurrying to The Cowpens informed Morgan and took their places with their commands in the lines of battle. Roebuck commanded a company of militia, and according to a great historian, distinguished himself and had a horse shot from under him.

The great victory being won, the Patriots, like those of Kings Mountain, feared the approach of the British; so, as soon as circumstances would admit, cumbered with prisoners and booty, Morgan began his perilous, but famous, retreat into North Carolina. It is probable that Roebuck accompanied Morgan as far as the Yadkin, where he advised the South Carolinians to return for the protection of their homes.

Roebuck ranked as a lieutenant-colonel at the battle of Cowpens, and soon after that event John Thomas, Jr., commander of the First Spartan regiment, received a colonel's commission in a different department of service, and Roebuck succeeded him as colonel and commander of the First Spartan. Samuel Smith, a fellow soldier, says: "As soon as Colonel Roebuck returned to the neighborhood after the battle of Cowpens, he engaged actively in warfare with the Tories, who came up from the direction of Ninety-Six, to harrass the Whigs in that region."

In Abbeville District, on Mud Lick Creek, there was a fort called Williams' Fort. It was occupied by British and Tories, who were

The Battle of Mud Lick

terrors to the surrounding country because of robberies and ravages. Colonel Roebuck and his lieutenant, Henry White, determined to break up this nest of plunderers. Roebuck's force did not exceed one hundred and fifty men, while that of the enemy was much larger, and had the protection of a strong fortress besides He could only hope to be successful by resorting to strategem, which he did. His main force was placed in ambush, while a number of mounted militia went up in front of the fort, then was to retreat, and thus, if possible, draw the enemy out of their fortifications and bring them within the range of the men in ambush. The ruse was successful, for when the Loyalists saw the militia retreating they came out and commenced a hot pursuit, confident of an easy victory.

This was in a measure checked by Colonel White and his riflemen. As soon as the "green cavalry" made their appearance, White leveled his rifle at one of the officers in front and brought him to the ground. This successful shot was immediately followed by those from the mounted riflemen, which brought the cavalry to a halt until the infantry came up. By this time all the hidden forces of Roebuck were engaged, and the battle raged furiously for nearly an hour. At length the British and Tories gave way and were entirely routed and their fortress taken. Their loss was considerable in proportion to their numbers. That of the Whigs was nothing like as great in numbers, but they had to lament the loss of several officers and brave soldiers. Among the officers was the gallant and beloved Captain Robert Thomas, son of Colonel John Thomas, Sr. Lieutenant-Colonel White was badly wounded, but recovered. This affair took place on the 2nd of March, 1781, and has been called "Roebuck's Defeat," meaning, of course, that Roebuck defeated the other party.

Accounts before us differ as to what happened to Colonel Roebuck. Saye, in his "Memoir of McJunkin," to which we are almost entirely indebted for our information as to this fight, mentions the death of Captain Thomas and the wounding of Colonel White, but says nothing about Roebuck being hurt. In his reminiscences, Samuel Smith, a neighbor and associate of Roebuck, tells of his capture about a week later, but says nothing of his being wounded. Governor B. F. Perry, who had interviewed a number of Roebuck's men, in his eulogy, written more than eighty years ago, says nothing of it. But that eminent historian, Lyman C. Draper, says that, "In a fight at Mud Lick with the Tories, March 2, 1781, he was badly wounded, the ball penetrating under the shoulder blade, and could not be extracted." He furthermore says,"He died in 1788 from the effect of his wounds." From what follows in Samuel Smith's narrative, we think that Draper has made some mistakes. True, Mr. Saye, in his "Memoir of McJunkin," says: "He was several times wounded, and suffered much from his wounds," but he does not tell us when nor where.

Samuel Smith says: "When Roebuck came back from North Carolina, I was with him in several excursions in search of squads of Tories. After one of our excursions, Roebuck, with Captain Mat Patton, went to stay at a neighbor's house to get some clothing which was in preparation for him, but it was not ready, so he had to stay through the day, and at night some Tories came and took him and Patton. I was taken the same night, and perhaps a dozen others in different places. This was the 10th of March. (Notice this was just eight days after the battle of Mud Lick.—Author.) "We were taken to Little River to a Tory station, and tried for our lives. Captain

The End of Col. Roebuck's Military Career

Patton, Charles Bruce, and two of the Elders were condemned to be hung. The rest of us were sent to jail at Ninety-Six, where we remained till the day before Greene laid siege to the place. A number of us were paroled and started home."

Colonel Roebuck was not paroled, but was sent to a prison ship in Charleston, where he remained until the following August, when he was exchanged and returned home.

As already seen, Draper says that he died in 1788 from the effects of his wounds. Governor Perry says that while in Charleston, "where he was confined for a length of time, and being greatly exposed, he caught cold, which terminated in consumption. He lived only to see the Independence of his country established, and death deprived him of the enjoyment of that liberty for which he fought so long and gallantly."

Col. Roebuck's Death

"Colonel Roebuck was never married and died as he had lived, in his father's home. It is to be regretted that so pure and noble a gentleman left no descendants to inherit his virtues, his name and his fame, but kindred blood of his flows in the veins of many of the most respectable families in Spartanburg."

The Honorable Simpson Bobo was a nephew of Colonel Benjamin Roebuck. The town of Roebuck, on the C. & W. C. Railroad, in Spartanburg County, was named in honor of him.

"It may be asked why such a hero as I have considered Colonel Roebuck to be is not better known in history. The answer is that there were no writers of history in the upper part of South Carolina during the Revolution, and history has ignored the gallant achievements of her brave and courageous sons. Dr. Ramsay, in his history of South Carolina, regrets that no one has furnished him with a detailed account of the movements of Sumter and Pickens, as was done with Marion's Brigade. I recall the names of Pickens, Butler, Roebuck, Thomas and Samuel Earle, and many others who fought so gallantly in the American Revolution. I am forcibly reminded of Gray's most beautiful elegy on a 'Country Church Yard,' 'where many a hero lies buried unknown to fame.'"

Further Tribute by Governor Perry

"Colonel Benjamin Roebuck was an instance of an humble and uneducated man, possessing all the great virtues which can adorn the human character. He was brave amongst the bravest Patriots, magnanimous, amiable and honorable. He was the beau ideal of a soldier and gentleman with his companions in arms. He inspired them with respect and admiration on all occasions and under all circumstances. They had implicit confidence in his courage, prudence and justice. He was modest, unselfish and unambitious. He sought only to serve his country and defend her independence and liberty. This was his sole ambition, and he discharged every duty of life with honor and integrity."

"He sought no popularity or official position. When the latter was given him and he thought he could discharge its duties to the interest of his country, he did not refuse. He shrank from no danger or responsibility in the discharge of his duty. He fought through the whole of the Revolutionary War, commanded a regiment in several important battles, was the idol of his company, and yet his name is not mentioned in history, and his virtues, patriotism and public services are only remembered in tradition."

"I met a great many men who had served under Colonel Roebuck, at the anniversary of The Cowpens, in 1832. They all spoke of him in the same exalted strain as a man, an officer and Patriot."

Govenor Perry was right; for up to the time he wrote, which was more than eighty years ago, no historian had mentioned the name of Roebuck, but since that time it has been done. The first was Lyman C. Drayer, in his "Kings Mountain and Its Heroes," published in 1880. Subsequent historians, Landrum and McCrady, have drawn on Draper, and Roebuck's name is now in history. But it is all due to Saye's "Memoir of McJunkin."

The Rev. James H. Saye was a noted Presbyterian preacher, who resided in Union District, and served the old Fairforest and Cane Creek churches from 1840 to 1860. He married a granddaughter of Major Joseph McJunkin, a noted soldier, who fought all through the Revolution in upper South Carolina. Being greatly interested in Revolutionary history, and having the Major and many other survivors of that memorable struggle to draw on, Mr. Saye gathered a vast amount of the most valuable first-hand information relative to persons and incidents in this part of the country. He wove this invaluable material into a narrative titled, "Memoir of McJunkin," which was published as a serial in *The Watchman and Observer*, of Richmond, Va., in 1847. Mr Saye also had considerable manuscript recollections of both heroes and heroines that was never published. When Mr. Draper was gathering data for his "Kings Mountain and Its Heroes," all of Mr. Saye's invaluable material fell into his hands, and thus, at this late day, the illustrous name of Roebuck is made to adorn the pages of history.

Just twenty-five years ago, the widow of Mr. Saye was still living, and we were fortunate enough to get a complete copy of the "Memoirs" and a part of the manuscripts, which we had republished in *The Piedmont Headlight,* while Colonel T. Larry Gantt was editor.

Anyone wishing to peruse this "Memoir of McJunkin" can find a newspaper copy of it in the Kennedy Library of Spartanburg.

The Life of Colonel Thomas Brandon

THOMAS BRANDON was born in Pennsylvania in 1741, and was of Irish stock. It was probably in 1755 that his parents, with a colony of Irish homeseekers, migrated from their nothern home and settled on Broad River, in what is now Union County, South Carolina. At the breaking out of the Revolutionary War, in 1775, the Spartan regiment was formed, with John Thomas as colonel. Thomas Brandon joined this regiment, took part in its campaigns, and rose to the rank of major. When this regiment was divided, Brandon became colonel, and his command consisted principally of Union County men.

When the news of the fall of Charleston, in May, 1780, reached the up-country, the Whig population was greatly alarmed; for, **Col. Brandon's** besides the ravages of the victorious troops of **Surprise and** Britain, there were numbers of them that were **Defeat** Loyalists at heart, but had played off as non-combatants, that would now show their colors and join the enemy's ranks.

Colonels Brandon and Lyles met on June 4th to plan measures for mutual safety and protection of the country. They agreed to assemble their troops and form a camp near Fairforest Creek, about four miles from the present town of Union. The residence of Christopher Young afterwards stood on the spot. As the place was near the center of Brandon's command, his men first arrived on the ground. He had in his possession a part of the powder formerly entrusted to Colonel Thomas, and considering its preservation of the greatest importance, he directed Joseph Hughes, William Sharp, John Savage, Aquilla Hollingsworth, Samuel Otterman, Benjamin Jolly, and Joseph McJunkin to conceal it with the greatest care in the neighboring forests. They were absent from the camp, engaged in this business, on the night in which Brandon's men were assembling. As some of the parties were coming in, they arrested a "pet" Tory, Adam Steedham by name, and brought him into the camp. He was examined, and soon he was let go, or made his escape. He went directly to the camp of Bloody Bill

Cunningham, which was not far away, and informed him of Brandon's movements.

Cunningham immediately set out to surprise Brandon. He made a charge on his camp soon after sunrise, killed a few men, took some prisoners and dispersed the rest. This defeat took place on the 8th or 10th of June, 1780.

Robert Lusk, Esq., was taken prisoner on this occasion and compelled to disclose the place where the powder was concealed, but the work of hiding had been so effectively done that the Tories found very little of it. The powder was afterwards stealthily carried off to the east side of Broad River, and it constituted the principal supply for Sumter's men at Huck's defeat, Rocky Mount, and Hanging Rock.

Colonels Thomas and Lyles, hearing of Brandon's disaster, provided for the safety of their men.

The men who had been engaged in hiding the powder, hearing of what had happened at Brandon's camp, gathered as many of their friends as possible and retreated to the east side of Broad River. Bullock's Creek Presbyterian Church, in York District, was the place of rendezvous. The Rev. Joseph Alexander was pastor of the church, and having always taken a firm stand for liberty among the people where he labored, the Tories determined on his destruction, hence he was compelled to escape for his life.

On the 12th of June, the refugees came together at the church. Among them were some of the regiments of Colonels Thomas, Lyles and Brandon. The situation, which was exceedingly gloomy, was talked over. The British were victorious, the Tories rising in large numbers, and the cause of liberty desperate The offers of British protection was before them, and numbers were taking them up. What was to be done? What could they do?

Presently a young man called his command together. He recited the facts connected with their present situation. He rehearsed their past toils, sufferings and dangers. He stated at large the reasons for the contest in which they were engaged, and the instances of success and defeat which had attended their efforts in the cause of Independence. He said: "Our cause must now be determined. Shall we join the British, or strive like men for the noble end for which we have done and spent so much? Shall we declare ourselves cowards and traitors, or shall we fight for liberty as long as we have life? As for me, 'Give me liberty or give me death.'" The speaker was John Thomas, Jr., son of John Thomas, of Spartan regiment fame. Some others reiterated the sentiments of Thomas. It was then proposed that those who were in favor of fighting it out, when the question was put, should throw up their hats and clap their hands. The question was put, and every hat flew up, the air resounding with the clapping of hands and shouts of defiance to the armies of Britain and the foes of freedom. It was then proposed that they who needed clothing or desired to see their families could return home, provided they would agree to meet the others at Tuccasegee Ford, on the Catawba River, in North Carolina When the Patriots arrived at that place they had the good fortune to meet Colonel Thomas Sumter. After some consultation, the party said to Sumter: "If we chose you our leader, will you direct our operations?" He replied: "Our interests are the same. With me it's liberty or death." An election was held and Sumter was unanimously chosen general.

Just at this time intelligence was received that the Tories had assembled at Ramseur's Mill, near the present town of Lincolnton, N. C., and that General Rutherford was collecting a force to attack them. There were thirteen hundred of them, under the command of Tory Colonel John Moore. Sumter immediately joined Rutherford, and he and his party wished to proceed at once to the attack, but Rutherford wished to defer it till next day. While Rutherford was halting, a small force, under the command of Captains Falls, McDowell, and Brandon, launched a surprise attack against the Tories at Ramseur's, and Rutherford arrived just in time to see that a complete victory had been won. It is believed that seventy Tories were killed, fifty taken prisoners, and the remainder precipitately fled. Moore was threatened with courtmartial by Cornwallis for cowardice. The victory at Ramseur's completely crushed the Tory element in that part of the State, for they never attempted to organize again during the war.

Colonel Brandon at Ramseur's Mill

The battle at Ramseur's being over, Sumter remained in the vicinity for a few days, and in the meantime he held a court of inquiry to consult as to the course that should be taken. Its members were solemnly pledged to liberate South Carolina, or die in the attempt. Their

Returns to South Carolina

number was so small as to render any important achievement hopeless; and furthermore, they possessed neither arms, provisions, nor any other military stores for the equipment and maintenance of a single regiment for one week, yet they resolved to return to South Carolina. By the aid of General Rutherford, they obtained a quantity of provisions, a few wagons, to which they hitched their own horses, and thus equipped, they set out to wrest their beloved State from the hands of her invaders. Sumter established his headquarters east of the Catawba River, in the territory of the Indians by the same name. Here the whole of July was spent, but not in idleness. His men went out in quest of provisions, ammunition, and arms, and to rally their friends to take a stand for liberty.

For want of current funds, provisions were difficult to obtain, so that their fare often consisted of barley meal, without meat, salt or any other seasoning, and but little of that. All the powder which could be was collected. The good women in the region around gave up their pewter vessels to be molded into bullets, and implements of husbandry were battered into swords. While thus engaged, the Patriots had to maintain the most vigilant care, for the Tories were watching every movement, and often waylaid and fired on them. An instance of this kind came to a small party led by Colonel Brandon, near Bullock's Creek. A captain, by the name of Reed, fell behind the party for some purpose or other, and was met and killed by two Tories Captain Reed's mother, finding out who his murderers were, followed Brandon to North Carolina and besought him to avenge the death of her son. Some of his men volunteered to go with him, and he hunted the Tories and killed them.

The Affair at Stallions

The friends of the murdered Tories, in turn, sought vengeance, and pursued Brandon in considerable force. He retired before them until he could obtain recruits, when he turned to meet his pursuers. A short time before he met their party a Colonel Love fell in with him. Love had encountered the Tories single-handed only a short time before and killed two of them. He made his escape by dodging in a briary old field. Brandon soon learned that the Tories had stopped at the house of a man named Stallions, in York District, to get dinner. Stallions had married a sister of Colonel Love; hence, he was a Tory and she a Whig. Brandon divided his force into two parties, he leading one and Love the other. The house was surrounded. Mrs. Stallions seeing the approach of her brother, ran out and begged him not to fire upon the house. Running back to the house, just as she sprang upon the doorstep, she fell, pierced by a ball shot through the opposite door. The Tories, being attacked on all sides, kept up for some time a fire upon their assailants. It was not long, however, before they raised a flag and surrendered. The Tory loss was two killed, four wounded and twenty-eight prisoners. William Kennedy, an American, was wounded. The prisoners were sent to Charlotte. The victory was gained at a bitter loss to Colonel Love, who mingled his tears with those of his Tory brother-in-law. This affair took place July 12, 1780.

Disagreeing in their notions, Colonel James Williams, and those who desired to go with him, left Sumter in North Carolina and moved in the direction of Ninety-Six. Among those who accompanied Williams were Colonels Thomas Brandon, James Steen, and Major Joseph McJunkin. Williams, therefore, crossed the Catawba and joined Colonel McDowell, who was encamped at Smith's Ford, on Broad River. When Williams joined McDowell at Smith's Ford, Major Patrick Ferguson, with his British Rangers and Loyalists, lay encamped at Fairforest Shoal, in Union District, which was afterward the home of Colonel Brandon. Hearing that there was a large party of Tories at Musgrove's Mill, on the Enoree River, Colonel McDowell detached a part of his force, under Colonels Clarke and Shelby, to unite with Williams for the purpose of surprising them. Secrecy and dispatch were essential to the success of the undertaking. A night march was chosen, and Colonel Brandon, who well knew the country, was the chief pilot. So about an hour before sundown, on August 17, this combined force, consisting of about seven hundred mounted men, left Smith's Ford for Musgrove's. Traveling through the woods until dark, they then fell into the road, and much of the way in a canter, they crossed Gilky and Thickety creeks, Pacolet, Fairforest, Tyger and several smaller streams. Passing within four miles to the right of Ferguson's camp, they reached a point one mile from Musgrove's about daybreak.

Battle of Musgrove's Mill

Helping to secure this memorable victory, Colonel Brandon bore his part of the sufferings endured by the Patriots in getting themselves and their prisoners to a place of safety

Colonel James Williams finally delivered the captives at Hillsboro, where he met Governor Rutledge of South Carolina, who gave Williams a brigadier-general's commission. Sumter and his forces refusing to recognize Williams' leadership, Governor Nash, of North Carolina, gave him permission to raise a company of one hundred men. No one was more active in raising this company than Colonel Thomas Brandon, who had stuck faithfully to Williams in all his difficulties with Sumter and Hill.

Brandon Again in North Carolina

Before Williams, Shelby and Clarke separated in North Carolina, Shelby proposed to raise an army on both sides of the mountains sufficiently strong to meet Ferguson, and the plan was agreed to and the work undertaken. The mountain men soon began to collect. In the meantime, Colonels Hambright, Williams, Lacey and Roebuck were preparing to form a juncture with the mountain men.

A Near Treacherous Act

The following is a digest of a sad occurrence related by Draper, in his "Kings Mountain and Its Heroes," pages 217-220: One day while the Hill-Lacey-Williams party were encamped at the Cherry Mountain, Colonels Williams and Brandon were missed from the camp, and Colonel Hill was informed that they went towards the mountain. When they returned after sunset, Hill inquired where they had been. At first they seemed unwilling to give a satisfactory reply. Hill insisted that they should, like honorable men, impart any information that they might have obtained, as it would be for the good of all. Williams, at length, acknowledged that they had visited the mountain men and found them a fine set of fellows, well armed. Hill then asked where they were to form a juncture with them. "At the Old Iron Works, on Lawson's Fork," was the reply. Hill remarked that that would be marching out of the way; that the avowed purpose of the mountain men was to catch Ferguson before either Cornwallis or Tarleton could come to his relief. After some embarrassment, Williams confessed that deception had been used to direct the mountain men towards Ninety-Six. Hill says, "I then used the freedom to tell him that I plainly saw through his design, which was to get the army into his own settlement, secure his remaining property and plunder the Tories." Manifesting a considerable degree of warmth, Williams said, "That the North Carolinians might fight Ferguson or let it alone, but it was the business of South Carolinians to fight for their own country."

Hill then told him that he would endeavor to thwart his purposes. Though it was night, Colonel Lacey was dispatched at once in order that he might put the mountaineers on "the right scent." Lacey learned from the Whig leaders that Williams and Brandon had informed them that Ferguson had gone towards Ninety-Six, and that they were to form a juncture with the South Carolinians at the Iron Works, on Lawson's Fork. Matters were set right, and "The Cowpens" was the place where the final juncture should be effected the following evening.

We do not know how much truth there is in this, but we do know that Hill was bitter towards Williams, and often harshly assailed his conduct. If it was true, their reason, though not right, is not hard to see They and their home communities had suffered so long and so severely from Tory domination and devastation that further endurance was well-night intolerable. It certainly was not the fear of Ferguson and his hosts, for there was not a cowardly drop of blood in their veins. Braver men and better soldiers did not face British and Tory guns.

When the opportune moment came to strike the decisive blow at Kings Mountain, October 7th, Williams, Brandon, Steen, Roebuck and their associates were there. Speaking of Brandon, Major Thomas Young says: "I was with him in two battles, *i. e.*, Kings Mountain and Cowpens. He commanded a party at the former place, but in consequence of my getting away from my own party, I saw but little of his conduct on that occasion till the battle was nearly over. He took a British officer prisoner, and obtained by it a very noble charger."

At Kings Mountain

On November 20, 1780, General Thomas Sumter won a splendid victory over Tarleton and a part of his force at Blackstocks, in what is now Union County. Tarleton's whole force being near, Sumter retreated across the Pacolet and Broad rivers towards Kings Mountain. Saye, in his "Memoir of Major Joseph McJunkin," says: "After seeing General Sumter out of striking distance from the enemy, the command of Colonel Brandon returned into the vicinity of their own homes, and took post at Love's Ford, on Broad River. This position was well adapted to check the operations of the Tories on the

Col. Brandon Takes Post at Love's Ford

west side of that river, and restrict their intercourse with the British army at Winnsboro." While lying here, says Major McJunkin, a scout was sent over to Sandy River, under Captain Joseph McCool. This party was worsted in a conflict with the Tories in that section, and Daniel McJunkin, the Major's brother, was taken prisoner and carried to Winnsboro. "At my instance," says the Major, "Colonel Brandon sent a flag to Lord Cornwallis, proposing to exchange Colonel Fanning, who was a prisoner with us, for Daniel McJunkin." This proposition was rejected by his lordship, and Daniel was sent forthwith to the jail at Camden. Here he remained till April, when he escaped in company with William Hodge and some others, by cutting the grating out of the window.

Soon after General Greene assumed command of the Southern army at Charlotte, N. C., a part of it was ordered to march into **Colonel Brandon** South Carolina, under General Daniel Morgan. He **Joins General** took post on Pacolet River, at the Grindal Shoals. **Morgan** During his stay at that place, Colonel Brandon and his men rendered General Morgan valuable aid in directing his foraging parties, as they were well acquainted with the country. Morgan being apprised of Tarleton's approach, he broke camp at Grindal and fell back to "Gentleman" Thompson's, now Thickety Station, on January the 15th. Tarleton arrived at the Easterwood Ford, two miles below Pacolet Mills, on the evening of the same day. Colonels Thomas Brandon and Benjamin Roebuck were entrusted by Morgan to watch the movements of Tarleton. On the morning of the 16th, Tarleton crossed the river at Easterwood, and Colonels Brandon and Roebuck, with some others, sat on their horses, counted the men as they passed, and forwarded their report to Morgan. Tarleton proceeded until he reached the camp at Thompson's, which Morgan had vacated the morning before. He remained there until three o'clock, on the morning of the 17th, when he resumed his march towards Cowpens. Up to that hour, he was still watched by Colonels Brandon and Roebuck, but they arrived at Cowpens in time to take their places with their men in the lines of battle.

The front line of "picked riflemen" was composed, in part, of Brandon's men. One of them, John Savage, fired the first shot.

Colonel Brandon commanded a part of the militia and brought Washington to the charge; for, says Major Thomas Young: "In the hottest of the fight, I saw Colonel Brandon coming at full speed to the rear, and waving his sword to Colonel Washington. In a moment the command to charge was given, and I soon found that the British cavalry had charged the American right. We made a most furious charge, and cutting through the cavalry, wheeled, and charged them in the rear." More than one Loyalist was killed by the strong arm of the ubiquitous Brandon, for Major Young furthermore says: "Just as the charge was made upon Tarleton's cavalry, I fell in with Colonel Brandon, who accompanied Washington in the charge. I was just about engaging a British dragoon, when Colonel Brandon darted between us and killed him, and told me to follow him. I did, till he killed two more, and I was with him but a small portion of the time in which the work of destruction and death was going on. I saw him no more after the first part of the onset."

The great victory being won, Morgan moved at once across Broad River, and his famous race into North Carolina had begun. **Brandon's Moves After the Battle of Cowpens** When the army was safely across the Yadkin, Morgan advised a portion of the South Carolina militia to return and defend their homes as best they could. The commands of Colonels Brandon and Thomas thus returned. Brandon formed his camp near the present site of Union, with a view of protecting the Whigs in that, their home region. Soon after his arrival in that section, Colonel Brandon received orders from General Sumter to collect as many men as possible and meet him on the east side of the Congaree River. In obedience to this command, Brandon marched into the vicinity of Granby, but hearing that a superior force of the enemy was maneuvering, with a view of preventing his juncture with Sumter, he deemed it expedient to return towards home. When out of the reach of pursuit, he received intelligence from Colonel Roebuck that he designed to attack a body of Tories in the direction of Ninety-Six.

Brandon immediately detached a part of his force, under the command of Major McJunkin, to co-operate with Roebuck in this enterprise When McJunkin arrived in the region of the contemplated operation, he received the intelligence that Roebuck had already met the enemy and defeated them. McJunkin then fell back with his party to unite again with Brandon. The victory achieved by Roebuck was known as the battle of Mud Lick, fought in Newberry District, on the 2nd of March, 1781.

The 10th, 11th, 12th and 15th of May were made memorable by the fall of the British posts of Camden, Orangeburg, Fort Motte, and Granby, in the order named. Brandon came out under Pickens, when he joined Sumter, and took active part in these operations. When General Pickens was maneuvering between Augusta and Ninety-Six, to prevent the garrison of that place, under Lieutenant-Colonel Cruger, from reinforcing Browne at Augusta, Colonels Brandon and Hayes were hovering on the eastward of Ninety-Six to recruit their forces and intercept supplies from that quarter.

On May 12, General Greene laid siege to Ninety-Six, which lasted for more than a month. In the meantime, Sumter, who was maneuvering lower down, ordered Brandon to join him, but says McCrady, "Colonel Brandon had called at Ninety-Six on his return home, and showing him (Greene) Sumter's orders to bring his men to his aid below, but that for particular reasons, which he (Greene) would afterwards explain, he (Greene) had interfered with that arrangement, and had desired Brandon to join him with all the forces he could collect to expedite the reduction of Ninety-Six. To this Sumter replied, acquiescing in this diversion of his troops, and expressing his gratification that they could be of service to the General."

To say the least of it, the management of the siege was bunglesome, and after thirty-eight days, with heavy losses, Greene gave it up. We are not able to find any further account of services rendered by Brandon, but we are sure that he was faithful and active to the end. But few, if any, in upper South Carolina ever did more to secure Independence than Colonel Thomas Brandon.

Some Post-War Services

After the war, he purchased the tract of land belonging to that noted Loyalist Colonel Fletcher, which was sold under the Confiscation Act. This plantation was at the Fairforest Shoal, now Murphy's Shoal, just five miles south of the present town of Union.

Elected to Jacksonborough Legislature

Independence having been practically won, and feeling the need of a legislative assembly, Governor Rutledge, on the 23rd of November, 1781, wrote letters to the brigadier-generals, sending them writs for the election of members of the senate and house of representatives.

The full number composing this body was to be twenty-eight senators and one hundred and seventy-four representatives, which in due time were elected The State was divided into twenty-eight parishes and districts. The upper, or Spartan District, between Broad and Saluda rivers, elected for senator, Simon Berwick; for representatives, Colonels William Henderson, Thomas Brandon, John Thomas, Jr., and Samuel McJunkin.

Governor Rutledge at first intended to call this assembly to meet in Camden, but the capture of Governor Burke and his council, in North Carolina, warned him of the danger of assembling the body at a place beyond the immediate protection of the army. General Greene, finding the country between the Edisto and Ashley rivers possessed of sufficient military advantages to admit of his covering Jacksonborough, warmly pressed the governor and council to convene at that place, which they did.

Jacksonborough was a small village, on the west bank of the Edisto, where the river was known by the name of Pon Pon. It consisted of a court house, jail, and two or three small houses. It was about thirty-five miles from Charleston. The legislature was accordingly called and convened at Jacksonborough, on the 18th of January, 1782. Thirteen senators and sixty-nine representatives were to constitute a quorum. On the day appointed thirteen senators, just a quorum, and seventy-four representatives appeared. John Lewis Gervais was chosen President of the Senate, and Philip Prioleau, Clerk; Hugh Rutledge, Speaker of the House, and John Berwick, Clerk.

The assembly having organized, Governor Rutledge delivered an address marking out the lines, which were followed by the body, A full synopsis of this address may be found in McCrady, South Carolina, in "The Revolution," Vol. IV, page 563.

Colonel Brandon also served his district as a justice of the court, county ordinary, and general of militia.

Brandon was undoubtedly a man of great physical endurance and prowess, having all the dare-devil bravery and fearlessness **Some Rash** belonging to the Irish stock. While possessing **Deeds** many noble and generous traits, he was a most bitter hater of the Tories, and they seldom obtained mercy at his hands. Mrs. Angelica Nott, wife of Judge Abram Nott, says: "I knew Colonel Brandon well. He was true and valiant, but overbearing and cruel."

Cumbered with many prisoners, the victors of Kings Mountain were returning to the mountains of North Carolina from whence they came. When near Gilbert Town, Colonel Brandon discovering that one of the Tories, who had been carrying a couple of the captured guns, had dodged into a hollow sycamore by the roadside, dragged him from his hiding place and completely hacked him to pieces with his sword.

On another occasion Brandon captured a notorious Tory. The trembling wretch begged so piteously for his life that Brandon's men pleaded with their leader to spare him, but Brandon shot him with his own pistol. It is said that on his death bed Colonel Brandon remarked that this was the only act of his life that his conscience could not get rid of.

Such acts may be considered rather barbarous and unwarranted, but when the many shocking atrocities suffered by the liberty-loving Whigs at the hands of Tories are considered, it was enough to arouse the spirit of revenge in the most considerate breast.

Colonel Brandon passed away February the 5th, 1802, in the sixty-first year of his age, and is buried in the old Union Presbyterian cemetery, near the present Monarch Cotton Mill, where several of his comrades in arms are sleeping their last sleep. His grave is marked.

His Death

Colonel Brandon was twice married. His first wife was Elizabeth McCool, daughter of Adam McCool, who resided at McCool's, now Scaife's Ferry, on Broad River, a short distance below the present Lockhart Manufacturing Company. His second wife was Mrs. Rebecca Harlan, widow of George Harlan. There were seven children—three sons and four daughters, viz.: Thomas, William, James, Mary, Elizabeth, Martha, and Anna.

The Life of Colonel Elijah Clarke

ELIJAH CLARKE was born in 1736, some accounts say in Virginia, others in North Carolina. Which is correct, we do not know. Dr. Landrum, in his "History of Spartanburg County," says: "According to the pages of history, Elijah Clarke was the first settler in the territory afterwards embraced in the county of Spartanburg." Again, "Colonel Elijah Clarke, who afterwards became a noted soldier of the Revolution and an officer of distinction, settled on Pacolet River, at no great distance from the present manufacturing town of Clifton, about the year 1755. In the course of time he was followed by other families, but at the end of said year there were not more than a dozen families residing within the present limits of Spartanburg County.

"For about nine or ten years, Elijah Clarke remained on Pacolet River, spending most of his time doubtless in building houses, opening roads, clearing lands and preparing a future home for himself and family, but the tardy progress of civilization and the many disadvantages by which he was surrounded, caused him, no doubt, to seek another and a more inviting country for his future habitation, and he removed from South Carolina to Georgia in the year 1774, settling in Wilkes County."

Dr. Landrum is most probably correct as to the time of Clarke's settlement in South Carolina, but is in error as to the place. Instead of on Pacolet River, near Clifton, it was near the Grindal Shoals. Mrs. Sarke Sims, whom the writer remembers, is the authority for this. Her father, Henry Fernandis, owned and reared his family on lands embraced in the Clarke grant. The Fernandis and Sims graveyard, near the public highway, just below the mouth of Mill Creek, shows the exact location.

His first appearance in the history of Georgia was in 1776, when as captain of a company he was intrusted with the care of some wagons, loaded with provisions for the army. While crossing a small stream he was attacked by a body of Indians, who, after a severe contest, were put to flight. In an expedition against East Florida he rendered important services.

Begins Military Operations

In the early part of 1779, a Colonel Boyd, at the head of a number of North Carolina Loyalists, attempted to force his way through South Carolina to join Colonel Hamilton, another North Carolina Loyalist commander, who was in Georgia. Andrew Pickens, with three hundred and twenty men, was pursuing Boyd, and had forced him across the Savannah. At the river, Pickens was joined by Dooley and Clarke, with about one hundred dragoons. They gave Pickens command of the whole. They pursued Boyd, and in a few days overtook him on the east bank of Kettle Creek, just as his men had shot down some beeves and were preparing their breakfast. Pickens divided his force into three divisions, Dooley commanding the right and Clarke the left. Boyd was shot down early in the action. After half an hour's fighting, the Whigs drove the enemy across the creek, where they made a short stand. The victory was complete. The Whigs numbered four hundred and twenty, that of the Loyalists more than seven hundred, of which not more than three hundred joined their command at Augusta. White, in his "Historical Collections of Georgia," says: "At the battle of Kettle Creek he (Clarke) increased his military fame."

Distinguishes Himself at Kettle Creek

After the victory at Kettle Creek many Georgia citizens, who had gone to South Carolina for safety, returned with their families and property to Wilkes County, but in a little while were greatly alarmed by the approach of a body of Indians. To Colonel Clarke was committed the great responsibility of remaining on the frontier to guard the fords. This was a trying time. The enemy had devastated the fairest portion of Georgia Clarke's house was pillaged and burned; his family ordered to leave the State. White says: "The love of freedom, a persuasion that Heaven would favor the righteous cause of the Americans, inspired Clarke with hope, and the loss of his property and the indignities offered to the helpless females of his family did not in the least intimidate him, but served him to renewed action."

His House Pillaged and Burned

The fall of Charleston in May, 1780, caused great consternation in South Carolina and Georgia. A council of officers was called to meet near Augusta to decide on what should be done. The governor and some other State officials of Georgia, with Colonels Clarke, Clary,

Promises to Co-operate with Williamson

Colonel Elijah Clarke

Dooley, and several other officers were there General Andrew Williamson, of South Carolina, read the terms of Charleston's capitulation, which provoked much discussion, but no plan was agreed upon. Clarke and Dooley promised Williamson to co-operate in any plan that might be adopted at a future council, either to defend the two States or retreat with him to North Carolina. Though seemingly greatly opposed to it at first, Williamson soon took British protection and went to Charleston

Clarke was not the kind of man to take British protection. He was not to be deterred. He resolved to gather what force he could, march into South Carolina, and join those that were rallying under Sumter. On the 11th of July one hundred and forty-eight men, well mounted and well armed, met at Freeman's Fort and immediately pushed across the Savannah River, into what is now Abbeville County. Here they learned that a force of British and Loyalists were on their front, and Clarke's men concluded that it would be hazardous to continue their advance in the face of superior numbers. They being volunteers and not subject to coercion, Clarke was induced to return to Georgia, suffer his men to disperse, and await a more favorable opportunity for the enterprise.

Clarke Plans to Join Sumter

Colonel John Jones, one of Clarke's command, seriously objected to a retrograde movement, and proposed to lead all who would go with him to the borders of North Carolina and join the American forces in that quarter. Thirty-five men volunteered to go with him. They chose Jones for their leader, and John Freeman for second in command, and solemnly pledged implicit obedience to their orders Benjamin Lawrence, of South Carolina, a superior woodsman and one well acquainted with the country, now joined them and rendered valuable service as their guide. Passing through a dangerous region, they palmed themselves off as a Loyalist party, engaged in the King's service, and under this guise they were, in several instances, furnished with pilots, who directed them on their route.

Colonel Jones Surprises a Tory Party

After passing the headwaters of Tyger River, in the northeastern part of what is now Greenville County, one of these guides informed them that a party of Rebels had, the preceding night, attacked some Loyalists, a short distance in front, and defeated them. This doubtless refers to the Tory repulse by Colonel John Thomas at Cedar Springs. Colonel Jones expressed a desire to be conducted to the camp of those unfortunate Loyalists friends that he might help them in taking revenge on those who had shed the blood of the faithful subjects of the King. About eleven o'clock, on the night of July 13, Jones and his little party were conducted to the Loyalist camp, where about forty men were collected. Leaving the baggage and horses in charge of the others, Colonel Jones selected twenty-two of his followers and resolved to surprise the Tories. Approaching the enemy with guns, swords, and belt-pistols, they were found off their guard and generally asleep. Quickly surrounding them, they fired on the camp, killing one and wounding three, when thirty-two called for quarter and surrendered. The best horses were selected, the usless guns destroyed, and the captives paroled as prisoners of war. Jones' methods and manners of deception were so clever that the Tory pilot did not discover the real character of the men he was directing until it was too late to have even attempted to prevent the surprise and capture of his Loyalist friends. This same pilot was now forced to guide the Americans to Earle's Ford, on North Pacolet River, where a junction was formed the next day with Colonel Charles McDowell.

Draper does not locate the place where Jones made this night attack, but Dr. Landrum says that he has good reasons for believing that it was at Gowen's old fort, on the old Blackstock road, near South Pacolet River.

Colonel Clarke did not long remain in Georgia. When he returned to that State he found some warm and zealous advocates **Clarke Raises** of arousing the Whigs to active resistance to the **Force—Joins** oppressor; for so complete was their domination **Sumter** that while there, Clarke and his associates were compelled to secrete themselves in the woods, where they were privately supplied with food by friends. Such life was not only irksome and almost unendurable, but did not give the least prospect for the accomplishment of anything toward the relief of a down-trodden people. Therefore, the regiment was re-assembled in augmented numbers. There was a general desire that Colonel Clarke should lead them along the eastern slope of the mountains toward North Carolina, where they could unite with others, and thereby render some useful service to their bleeding country. As perilous as the undertaking appeared, it was accomplished without a mishap.

When they neared the region where they expected to find friends, they were joined by Colonel Jones and his force, which, it will be remembered, refused to return to Georgia some time previous. A little later, Clarke was joined by the brave Captain James McCall, with about twenty men from the Ninety-Six region. For want of confidence in the activity of Colonel McDowell, or for some other reason, Clarke pushed on and joined Sumter, who was encamped on or near the Catawba River.

While the events just narrated were taking place, Major Patrick Ferguson, with his King's Rangers, a large and ever-increasing **Tory Depreda-** force of Tories, about fifteen or sixteen hundred, **tions in the** were marching through the Fairforest region in **Up-Country** the up-country. Upon his arrival in the Union District, he stopped for awhile at the Fairforest, now Murphy's Shoal. Later he moved up to the Meadow Woods section, and subsequently he encamped for three weeks on a hill on the old John Winsmith plantation, two miles south of Glenn Springs.

During this period of several weeks, all that region of country was scoured daily by Tories, plundering the people of their cattle, horses, bee-gums, vegetables of all kinds, beds, wearing apparel, and even pulling the rings from the fingers of the women.

The horses of Ferguson's men were turned loose to destroy the growing crops, while foraging parties drove the cattle to camp, for slaughter, usually shooting those down that they did not care to bring in, and leaving them in the woods to rot.

During the period of serious Indian outbreaks, the white inhabitants built stockade forts in different sections for protection against the redskins. These consisted of several small houses, built in a huddle, surrounded by logs stood on end in a deep ditch. These logs were so high and so substantially put in the ground that they could hardly be climbed over or broken through. There were loopholes all around, through which the defenders could thrust their guns and fire on their assailants. The stockade was usually surrounded by strong abatis, and sometimes a deep ditch. One of these was erected a short distance from the north bank of Goucher Creek, about one mile from Goucher Creek Church, in what is now Cherokee County. It was called Fort Anderson, or Thickety Fort.

The most notorious Tory leader and plunderer that ever infested that region was Patrick Moore. With about one hundred of his kind, he took possession of Thickety Fort, and from there his marauding gangs would sally out, plunder the helpless Whig inhabitants, and, usually, wantonly destroy what they did not want, or could not carry off. So thorough was their work that Draper says: "The women and children were often left without clothing, shoes, bread, meat or salt."

Several raids were made on the home of John Nuckolls, who resided on Whig Hill, near Thickety Creek, and was brutally murdered by the Tories at McKown's Mill, on Broad River, in December, 1780. In the summer preceding his murder they made a clean sweep. The only bed left for the infant child was a sheepskin used for a saddle blanket. It was probably at this time when they were shooting stock, breaking up furniture, and ripping open feather beds, when Mrs. Nuckolls began tongue lashing them. One of the dastardly scoundrels struck at her head with a sabre, and throwing up her arm to ward off the blow, received a wound which left a scar that she carried to her grave.

In his absence, the house of Captain Nathaniel Jefferies was visited by one of these plundering parties. They took such articles as they chose, abused Mrs. Jefferies as the meanest of all Rebels, built a fire on the floor, and drove off the cattle and horses.

On another occasion one of these parties plundered the house of Daniel Jackson, who resided in the Irish settlement, near Fairforest Creek. As one fellow was descending, loaded with plunder, Miss Nancy Jackson kicked him down the stairs. This so enraged him that he threatened to send the Hessian troops there the next day. Giving her fright, she ran off, gathered five other girls and went to Mrs Adam Potter's that night. Mrs. Potter lived near the Grindal Shoals, on Pacolet, a distance of nine miles.

The Capture of Thickety Fort

Sumter hearing of the ravages of Ferguson and his associates, directed Colonel Clarke, with his Georgians, together with those in his camp who resided in that region and wished to aid in its protection, to repair to that quarter. Captain William Smith, of Spartanburg, and his company availed themselves of this opportunity. When they arrived at the Cherokee Ford, on Broad River, Clarke and his forces met Colonel McDowell, who had been joined by Colonels Shelby, Andrew Hampton and others.

Shelby, Clarke, Hampton, and Major Charles Robertson were

detached, with six hundred men, to surprise Thickety Fort, which was about twenty miles distant They took up the line of march at sunset, reached and surrounded the post at daybreak the next morning. Colonel Shelby sent in Captain William Cocke to demand an immediate surrender, to which Moore replied that he would defend the place to the last extremity Shelby and Clarke then drew their lines all around, to within musket shot of the fort, with a full determination to make an assault. The "six hundred" made so formidable an appearance that Moore relented, and proposed to surrender on condition that the garrison be paroled, not to serve again during the war, unless exchanged. This was readily agreed to, as the Americans did not care to be encumbered with prisoners. Thus ninety-three Loyalists, with one British sergeant-major, stationed there to discipline them, surrendered without firing a gun. Among the trophies of victory were two hundred and fifty stands of arms, all loaded with ball and buckshot.

The capture of Thickety Fort took place on Sunday morning, July the 30th, 1780, which relieved the suffering country round about of the greatest scourge ever inflicted upon it. Loaded with the spoils of victory, the gallant "six hundred" returned at once to McDowell's camp, near the Cherokee Ford. Draper tells us that among the spoils taken at Kings Mountain was the fragment of a letter, without date or signature, in which this account is given of Thickety Fort, Moore and his surrender of the place: "It had an upper line of loopholes, and was surrounded by a very strong abatis, with only a small wicket to enter by. It had been put in thorough repair at the request of the garrison, which consisted of neighboring militia that had come to the fort, and was defended by eighty men against two or three hundred banditti without cannon, and each man was of the opinion that it was impossible for the Rebels to take it. The officer next in command, and all the others, gave their opinion for defending it, and agreed in their account that Patrick Moore, after proposing a surrender, acquiesced in their opinion, and offered to go and signify as much to the Rebels, but returned with some Rebel officers, whom he put in possession of the gate and place, who were instantly followed by their men, and the fort full of Rebels, to the surprise of the garrison. He plead cowardice, I understand."

At this time all the forces under McDowell could not have exceeded a thousand men. The policy of the Americans was, therefore, to maintain their position near the Cherokee Ford, guard against surprise, and harrass their adversaries until by augmented numbers they could drive them from the country.

Second Battle of Cedar Springs

A few days after the return from Thickety Fort, McDowell again detached Colonels Clarke, Shelby and Graham, with six hundred mounted men, to watch Ferguson's movements, and whenever possible, to cut off his foraging parties. They marched southward, some twenty-five miles, to Brown's Creek, in what is now Union County, where they agreed to assemble; as it was a better position to observe the operations of the enemy than the Cherokee Ford. Only a few of the parties began to collect, when a superior force of their adversaries forced them to retire. They bore off some twenty-five miles, to the upper part of the Fairforest settlement, within the present limits of Spartanburg. It seems that on the way they got their forces together. By watching their opportunity they hoped to gain some decided advantage over their opponents, whom they knew abounded in that quarter. Hearing of the adventure of these bold "Rebel" troopers, Ferguson made several attempts to surprise them, but our frontier heroes were too wily to be caught napping. Clarke, who seems to have been chief in command, together with his officers and men, were constantly on the alert, having no fixed camp, and were hard to find.

On the evening of August the 7th, Clarke and Shelby halted their troops for refreshments, and, if not disturbed, a night's repose, on Fairforest Creek. Draper says that this camp was "nearly two miles west of Cedar Springs, at a point where the old road crossed that stream, leading thence to Wofford's Iron Works, and thence onward to the Cherokee Ford." Dr Landrum not only concurs in this view, but is much more specific in establishing the exact location. Says he: "From this point (Wofford's Iron Works, now Glendale) the road ran in the direction of Georgia. Leaving Cedar Spring about one mile to the left, it ran by the old Anthony Foster place, the late residence of E. H. Bobo, Esq. (now that of Dr. S. T. D. Lancaster), by the home of the late Isham Hurt, by Bethlehem Church, Dr. Miller's old place, Captain David Anderson's, Major Frank L. Anderson's, and on in the direction of Georgia via Simpsonville, in the lower portion of Greenville County. Like the old Blackstock, this is one of the oldest roads in Spartanburg County. It has been known in the neighborhood through which it passes as the 'Old Georgia' or 'Pinkneyville' road. It was at the crossing of this old road, over Fairforest, near Mr. Will Wood's, where the plantations of the late Captain A. Copeland and Captain John Blassingame came together, that Clarke and Shelby, on the 7th of August, stopped for refreshments and to camp for the night, if not disturbed."

Notwithstanding the seeming certainty of the location by Dr. Landrum, Captain N. F. Walker, of Cedar Spring, in an address delivered at the Glendale Park, May 11, 1901, says: "The temporary camp of Shelby and Clarke, on the Fairforest, was unquestionably near or at the old Antioch Ford, which is in a direct line of travel from Musgrove's via Blackstocks, Cedar Spring, and on to the Wofford or Berwick or Buffington Iron Works." He furthermore says: "Draper and some other writers place the crossing of the forces of Clarke and Shelby and pursuers six or eight miles further up Fairforest—almost due west from Cedar Spring. But I think the following evidence will show conclusively that this is a mistake." He then quotes from the diary of Allaire, a British lieutenant: "August 7th—Got to the ground the Rebels were encamped on at 4 o'clock, on Tuesday morning, August 8th. They had intelligence of our move and were likewise alarmed by the firing of a gun in our ranks; they sneaked from their ground about half an hour before we arrived. Tuesday 8th—Learning the Rebel wagons were three miles in front of us, at Cedar Spring, Dunlap, with fourteen mounted men and one hundred and thirty militia, were dispatched to take the wagons. He met three Rebels going to reconnoiter our camp, he pursued, took two of them—the other escaped, giving the Rebels the alarm." Allaire's statement is corroborated by Colonel Isaac Smith, whose father fought in the battle. He says: "On the morning of the battle at Cedar Spring, the American forces under Clarke, having made a stand at that place, sent back three men—Britton Williford, John Losson, and one other—to reconnoiter the movements of the enemy. They passed down the road in the direction of the camp on the Fairforest, from whence they had proceeded in the latter part of the night previous. The British, too, had sent forward three men for a like purpose. They met in a short turn of the road, near where Colonel Smith now lives, and particularly located by an old graveyard, which I have seen often. They were so near each other before either party discovered the other that no chance of escape remained. Losson first discovered the three British men, and momentarily said to his comrades, 'Here they are, boys, every man to his man,' and so they did The same instant and so simultaneous were the reports of the guns of the parties that it was difficult to know which fired first. Five out of six fell, leaving only Williford to tell the tale of destruction.

"The firing was distinctly heard at Cedar Spring, where the Americans were halting. Colonel Smith said he had heard his father repeatedly say he heard the report of the guns distinctly. Williford returned to the lines and reported the occurrence. Williford lived many years in the district and reared a family, and was regarded as a man of character. Poor Losson fell, and a brave man he was reported to be."*

As his father was in the battle, Colonel Smith got his information from him, and he related it to Rev. N. P. Walker, who recorded it, the manuscript being now in possession of his son, Captain N. F. Walker, of Cedar Spring. It will be observed that Colonel Smith repeatedly says that the Americans were at Cedar Spring. Allaire says the same thing. About midway between Cedar Spring and Golightly, on the east side of the public road, is a beautiful old homestead, known as the Zimmerman place.† At or near this place, the ancient road leading from Cedar Spring to the Antioch Ford, on Fairforest, left the present highway, bearing to the left. The old graveyard mentioned by Colonel Smith is yet to be seen a short distance south of the Zimmerman place, which, as Captain Walker says, proves conclusively that the camp was at or near the Antioch Ford instead of higher up. Another thing: the old Georgia road, crossing on Fairforest, was too far out of the way when the Americans were making a hurried return to their command at the Cherokee Ford.

The stop on the evening of August 7th made by Clarke and Shelby on Fairforest was of short duration. Several trusty scouts sent out to make observations returned before day the next morning with the intelligence that the enemy were within half a mile.

*Walker's Manuscript.
†The Zimmerman house has been burned down since the above was written

About the same time, says Drayer, "the report of a gun was heard in the direction of the British party, which was afterward ascertained to have been fired by one of Dunlap's men—one who felt some compunctions of conscience at the idea of surprising and massacring his countrymen, but who, protesting that it was accidental, was not suspected of treachery."

This warning was amply sufficient for the wary Americans, yet, according to Mills and Mrs. Ellet, they had still more. The first battle at Cedar Spring had a heroine in the person of Mrs. Jane Thomas; the second battle had one in the person of Mrs. Mary Dillard. Captain Dillard, a Patriot soldier, lived somewhere near the Enoree River. On their march, some of the Americans stopped at Dillard's home, where his wife entertained them with milk and potatoes. The same evening, Ferguson and Dunlap, with a Tory party, came up. They inquired after Clarke, wishing to know if he had been there, and, if so, how many men did he have and which way he went. She replied that he had been there, but could not guess his numbers, and that he had been gone a long time. She was then ordered to prepare supper for them.

In passing around, while performing this duty, she heard one of the officers tell Ferguson that he had just heard that Clarke was to encamp at the Great (Cedar) Spring that night. It was resolved to surprise and attack them before day. This stirred the anxiety and patriotism of Mrs. Dillard. The meal was hurriedly prepared, and when the officers sat down to the table she slipped out a back way to the stable, where she bridled a young horse and mounted him without a saddle. Though the distance was long and the night would be dark, she determined to go herself. Making all possible speed, about half an hour before day she came in full gallop to one of the videttes, and was immediately conducted to Colonel Clarke, where, in almost breathless haste, she said to him: "Be in readinesss either to fight or run, the enemy will be upon you and they are strong."

With this abundant warning, Clarke and Shelby abruptly broke camp and moved towards the iron works via Cedar Spring. Draper says when something like a mile and a half from the iron works, and about a mile from Cedar Spring, suitable ground was chosen and the men formed for battle, when the spies came running in with the information that the enemy's horse were almost in sight.

The beautiful elevated tract of land lying on either side of the present Cedar Spring, or Glendale "Stop," on the Southern Railway, has, for generations, been known as "The Old Thompson Place." A part of it was cleared and set in peach trees previous to the Revolution, and as at least a part of the affair now under consideration took place there, it is called by some "the peach orchard fight."

But few of the earlier historians pay any attention to this contest at all, and those who do, fail to note that there were two fights at or near the Cedar Spring at different times; hence the fragments and traditions of each are jumbled together in such confusion that a correct account is now impossible. Having studied the materials in hand and gone over the ground at different times, we can only proceed on the assumptions of our best judgment.

From the branch near the spring towards the northeast there is a hill, about one-fourth of a mile from base to summit, and is traversed all the way by the old Cedar Spring and Glendale road. The level crest of this long slope would be the logical place for Clarke and Shelby to make their stand, which they doubtless did. There are some proofs of it. The "peach-tree grave," of which we will have more to say, is there. Many years ago an old gun barrel was picked up there, which was most probably used in the fight. Dr. Winsmith, while delivering an address at Cedar Spring, about seventy years ago, pointed to "that hill" as the place of the contest.

The Line of Battle Formed

Major Dunlap, who was an officer of much energy, soon put in his appearance with a strong force, part Colonial dragoons and part mounted militia, and commenced the conflict. The Whigs were as eager for the fray as the over-confident Britons. Dunlap's mounted volunteer riflemen, it is said, recoiled and gave back at the very first fire from Clarke and Shelby's lines, and it was with difficulty that their commander rallied them. Having succeeded, he placed himself at the head of his dragoons and led them to renew the contest, followed by the mounted riflemen, who were, however, averse to coming into close quarters. Says Draper: "Dunlap's dragoons, with their broad swords, played a prominent part in the action, and from the disproportion of Tories killed over the dragoons, according to the British account, which is doubtful, it would appear that Clarke and Shelby's riflemen must have been busy in picking them off."

It was probably at this time that Colonel Clarke manifested his great bravery and heroism; for, says Governor Swain, of North Carolina, in an article published in the *University Magazine,* in 1861, "It was in the severest part of the action that Colonel Shelby's attention was arrested by the heroic conduct of Colonel Clarke. He often mentioned the circumstance of pausing in the midst of the battle to look with astonishment and admiration at Clarke's fighting." Draper says: "In the fierce hand-to-hand contest, he received two sabre wounds, one on the back of his neck and the other on his head, his stock-buckle saving his life; and he was even for a few minutes a prisoner in charge of two stout Britons, but taking advantage of his strength and activity, he knocked one of them down, when the other quickly fled out of the reach of this famous backwoods Titan. Clarke was every inch a hero, and was indebted to his own good pluck and prowess for his escape from his enemies with only slight wounds and the loss of his hat in the melee." William Smith, of Tennessee, an eye-witness, relates that Clarke received a sword wound in the neck and lost his hat near Wofford's, returning to McDowell's camp bareheaded.

By skilful management and hard fighting for a half hour, Dunlap was beaten back with considerable loss—about fifty prisoners taken, including two officers. Mills says that he was pursued for a mile, but could not be overtaken. About two miles below the battleground, Dunlap and his fugitives were met by Ferguson and his whole force, who together advanced to the scene of action, from which Dunlap had just retreated. Clarke and Shelby were now compelled to make a hasty retreat, not having time to carry the wounded, but they were treated humanely by Ferguson, and left on the field when he retired. As Clarke and Shelby expected, Ferguson pursued them, hoping to recapture the prisoners. The Americans retired slowly, forming frequently on the most advantageous ground to give battle, and thereby so retarded the pursuit, that the prisoners were finally placed beyond recapture. Really it was a running fight from near Cedar Spring all the way back to the Iron Works and beyond.

Draper says: "Three miles northeast of the old iron works they came to Pacolet, just beyond which, skirting its northeast border, rises a steep rocky hill, fifty to sixty feet high, so steep where the road passed up at that day that the men, in some cases, had to help their horses up its difficult ascent. Along the crest of this hill or ridge, Shelby and Clarke displayed their little force, and when Ferguson and his men came in view, evincing a disinclination to pursue any further, the Patriots, from their vantage-ground, bantered and ridiculed them to their hearts' content. But Ferguson, having maintained the chase four or five miles, now abandoned it, with nothing to boast of save his superior numbers." Clifton Mill No 1 stands at the foot of this hill.

As to the numbers engaged in this affair accounts widely differ, but as six hundred Americans were detached, under Clarke and **The Numbers** Shelby, naturally that would be their number. It **Engaged and** is safe to say that Dunlap's detachment was seven **Lost** hundred, and Ferguson's whole force about 1,500. Reports of losses are more confusing, but the American loss was at least four killed and twenty wounded. The British Lieutenant Allaire, in his diary, puts the British loss between twenty and thirty killed and wounded.

It took place on Tuesday, August 8, 1780, but the time of the day is in dispute. Mills says it took place before day, when it was so dark that friend or foe could hardly be distin-**Time and Place** guished. McCall says it occurred in the afternoon. **of the Contest** Governor Perry's traditions convey the idea that it was in the morning or forepart of the day. This is corroborated by Captain William Smith, Allaire, and all the circumstances. The most probable time was between eight and nine o'clock in the morning.

Mills says that the fight took place at the Green Spring—meaning Cedar Spring. Colonel Shelby, one of the chief commanders, says it was at Cedar Spring. Samuel Espy, who was in the action, says the same thing. Colonel William Graham, a prominent officer in the affair, refers to it as "at Wofford's Iron Works." Alexander McFadden, a survivor of the contest, speaks of it as "the Battle of Wofford's Iron Works." McCall, the historian, says the enemy pursued the Americans to "Wofford's Iron Works, where they chose their ground and awaited the attack." William Smith, of Tennessee, another survivor, says, "We had a battle near Wofford's Iron Works" Captain William Smith, of Spartanburg, who was an officer in the fight, and resided near the battleground the most of his long life, says that the contest took place "near the Old Iron Works." The difference in these statements are more apparent than real. Wofford's Iron Works were at the head of the present Glendale pond, on Lawson's Fork. The old road between the works and Cedar Spring was almost a straight line, which would make the distance only a little more than two miles. It is evident that Clarke and Shelby did not take their stand nearer the spring than half a mile, and perhaps farther. If the main fight took place at the old Thompson homestead, it would have been about midway between the two points, and as the Americans fell back to the works fighting, we can easily see why both names were given to the action.

When Clarke and Shelby halted on Fairforest the evening before the battle, Josiah Culbertson, a brave young man, and son-in-law of Colonel John Thomas, was given permission to go to his home for the night, which was not far away. About daylight the next morning, he rode fearlessly into the encampment he had left the evening before, supposing it still to be occupied by his comrades, not knowing that they had decamped and Dunlap had just taken possession of it. Culbertson was equal to the emergency, for seeing everything so different from what it was the evening before, he quickly discovered his mistake, and with extraordinary coolness and presence of mind, he rode slowly out of the encampment with his trusty rifle resting on the pommel of his saddle before him. As he passed along he saw the dragoons getting their horses in readiness and making other preparations, indicating an immediate movement. No particular notice was taken of him in the British camp, as they supposed him to be one of their own men, who had gotten ready for the onward move before his comrades. When out of sight, he dashed off in a gallop in the direction he supposed that Clarke and Shelby had gone and soon overtook them, finding that they had chosen their ground and were ready to receive their enemies.

Incidents in Connection With the Fray

During the engagement this same Josiah Culbertson had a notable personal encounter. Meeting one of Dunlap's dragoons some distance from support, the dragoon arrogantly demanded Culbertson's surrender. The intrepid American replied by whipping his rifle to his shoulder, the fire of which brought the haughty Briton from his horse to the ground. When

The Peach-Tree Grave

the dead were buried next day, this dragoon was thrown into a hole near where he lay, and lightly covered with earth. At the time of his death he had some peaches in his pocket, and from the seed a peach tree grew, and for many years bore successive crops of fruit. An old gentleman, Robert White by name, and born in the eighteenth century, lived to the advanced age of ninety years and resided near the battleground most of his long life. Many years ago he informed Prof. N. F. Walker, of Cedar Spring, that in early life he had not only seen the tree, but had often eaten fruit from it. Professor Walker can yet point out the immediate vicinity of "the peach-tree grave." It is near the brow of the long slope, on the east side, and only a few yards from the old road leading from Cedar Spring to the "Stop" on the railroad. The location of this grave is conclusive proof that at least a part of the battle was fought there, as we have previously tried to show.

We take the following from Walker's manuscript: "Michael Miller, or more generally know as Mike Miller, a German and dragoon in the British army, was taken prisoner in the battle at Cedar Spring by Captain Smith, the father of Colonel Isaac Smith. His horse fell and he was unable to make his escape. When Captain Smith took him prisoner he said he was 'darned glad of it, for he had been trying to get away from them for some time.' He was paroled and went up in the district, married and raised a respectable family. He was the father of Mrs. David Whetstone, Mrs. James Anderson, Sr., Mrs. John Montgomery, Mrs. Theron Earle, and others."

The Capture of Michael Miller

The Rev. James H. Saye wrote his "Memoir of McJunkin" more than eighty years ago. As the following is taken from that Memoir, the reader should bear the date in mind: "A person passing at the present time (about 1840) from the direction of Unionville towards Spartanburg Court House crosses this ancient highway (the old Georgia road) at Thompson's old residence. After passing this, by looking to the left, the eye rests upon a parcel of land extending down a hollow, which was cleared and planted in fruit trees prior to the Revolutionary War. Just where the road now enters a body of woodlands there is yet some traces of a former human habitation. In this orchard two patrol parties met from adverse armies. The party from Dunlap's camp were in the orchard gathering

The Peach Orchard Episode

peaches, when the liberty party fired on them and drove them from the place. In turn they entered the orchard, but the report of their guns brought out a strong detachment from Cedar Spring, and a reinforcement from Shelby. The captain of the patrol, when he saw the enemy approaching, drew up his men under cover of a fence along the ridge, just where the old field and the woodland now meet, and where the traces of an old place of residence are now barely visible. Here he awaited their approach. The onset was furious, but vigorously met. The conflict was maintained against fearful odds until the arrival of reinforcements from Shelby's camp. The scales now turned, and the assailants fell back. The whole force of Shelby and Clarke were soon in battle array, confronted by the whole British advance, numbering six or seven hundred men."

"The onset was renewed with redoubled fury. Here it was that Clarke astonished Shelby by the energy and adroitness with which he dealt his blows. Shelby often said he stopped in the midst of the engagement to see Clarke fight. The liberty men drove back their foes when the whole British army came up. A retreat was now a matter of necessity as well as sound policy. Shelby and Clarke had taken fifty prisoners, most of them British, and some of them officers. These, Ferguson was extremely anxious to retake, and his antagonists by no means willing to lose. Hence, the pursuit was pressed for miles with great vigor, and the retreat managed so skilfully as to render the great superiority of the Royal army of no avail. A kind of running fight was maintained for five miles, until the prisoners were entirely out of reach."

It will readily be seen that this account of the "peach orchard fight," given by Mr. Saye, agrees in several points with the one previously given, one chief difference being the place where the contestants met, although the orchard could have been only a short distance from the brow of the long slope, where we believe they first came together. The meeting of the patrol parties in the orchard could easily have been one of the episodes of the day, the remainder of the account referring to the main action.

A Noted Captain "Captain William Smith was born in Bucks County, Pennsylvania, September 20, 1751, and early settled in what is now Spartanburg County, South Carolina. He served in Captain Joseph Wofford's company, on the Snow Campaign, in 1775, and the next year as lieutenant on Williamson's expedition against the Cherokees. In 1777, he was made a captain in the militia and was stationed in Wood's Fort, on Tyger. In December, 1778, he was ordered to Georgia, serving under General Lincoln, and took part in the battle of Stono, in June, 1779; in the contests as we have seen near Wofford's Iron's Works, Hanging Rock, and Musgrove's Mill, in August, 1780; and subsequently at the battle of Blackstocks, in the siege of Fort Granby, at Guilford Court House, Quinby Bridge, the affair at the Juniper, the capture of some British vessels at Watboo Landing, under Colonel Wade Hampton. In the latter part of the war he ranked as major. After the war, he was chosen county judge, was a member of Congress from 1797 to 1799, and State senator for twenty years. Few men served the public longer or more faithfully in military and civil life than Judge Smith. He died, June 22, 1837, in the eighty-sixth year of his age. His widow survived till October 2, 1842."*

In his writings, Governor Perry says that as late as 1842, as many as twenty graves were still seen that contained the dead who **The Slain and Their Sepulture** fell in this battle. Draper says: "It is questionable, however, if so many on both sides were killed in the action." In this we concur, for as there were only four Americans killed, it is not probable that the Royalists received such careful burial. There is an old tradition which says that some who fell in this action are buried in the graveyard, on the east bank of Lawson's Fork, only a few rods away from the site of the old iron works.

Of the Americans killed we have the names of three, viz.: Major Burwell Smith, Captain John Potts, and Thomas Scott. Major Smith had contributed greatly to the frontier settlements of Georgia, where he had been an active and successful partisan in Indian warfare. His fall was deeply lamented by Colonel Clarke and his associates. A tradition of an old resident in the battle ground region was that an American officer named Potter was shot out of a peach tree at Thompson's place. This doubtless refers to Captain John Potts. Sad the thought, that the last resting place of these noble men who made the "supreme sacrifice" with their blood, and paid the price of our oppressed country's redemption, has long since been forgotten, and now utterly unknown.

---

*Draper's "Kings Mountain and Its Heroes," page 99.

General B. B. Foster, whom the writer well remembers, was born at the old Anthony Foster place, near Cedar Spring (now the residence of Dr. Sam Lancaster), once related to Dr. Landrum that a Mr. John Bagwell told him that the Tories killed at the Thompson place were put in one hole, but buried so shallow that the wolves scratched them out, and that he (Bagwell), with his mother and sister, cut brush and piled on the grave to prevent any further molestation by the wolves.

Major A. J. Wells, a native of Spartanburg, relates the following: "After the war, the widow of a Tory came to the neglected burial place and had the fallen dead disinterred, from which she readily selected the remains of her husband, for he was six and a half feet high, and piously bore them to her distant home for a more Christian interment."

The following was related several years ago to Colonel T. L. Gantt by Squire J. F. Sloan, of Pacolet: "Mr. John Lee, one of our old citizens, stated to him (Sloan) that his father, who lived in our country during the Revolutionary War, passed by the Thompson place, at Glendale Station, a short time after the battle of Cedar Spring. Mr. Lee saw a dog before him with something in its mouth, and on approaching the animal he found it eating the arm bone of a man. This shows that the battle was fought not far from that spot, and the dead were hastily buried in shallow graves."

A long-cherished purpose has at last been accomplished, that of making an honest and painstaking effort to unravel the tangled historical and traditional accounts of the second battle of Cedar Spring or Wofford's Iron Works. How well we have succeeded we leave our readers to say. Some may inquire: why such a long and tedious narration of such trivial affairs? Because they are not trivial. True, in the eyes of modern warfare, they may appear so, but it should be remembered that this was the darkest period that ever overshadowed the Patriot cause in the South, and though trivial it may appear, this stroke put at least one nail in the coffin of British oppression. It shows the undaunted, unflinching and uncompromising heroism and bravery which displayed a determination to conquer or die. Finally, without reflection on anyone, but few, even those who pass over the hallowed ground, know anything about it. Surely, if the blood of the slain Patriots could cry from the ground, would it not say, "Won't you do as much as to think of us?—just a thought as you walk over our dust. We gave all we had, for what we never obtained; but you are the fortunate possessors of the greatest country in the world; the land of the free; civil freedom; freedom of conscience and freedom to worship God. All this we helped to buy for you with the cost of our lives."

When Clarke and Shelby returned to McDowell's camp they were much in need of rest, which they had for a few days But in a short while McDowell removed from the Cherokee Ford and took post on the east bank of Broad River, at Smith's Ford, about ten miles lower down. The affair at Cedar Spring or Wofford's Iron Works did not lessen the British and Tory activities in that region. By the work of faithful scouts, McDowell was kept well posted as to their movements and whereabouts. The term of enlistment of Shelby's regiment being about to expire, he was desirous of more active service before retiring to his home on the Holston.

Battle of Musgrove's Mill

Colonel James Williams, with a small force, having joined McDowell at Smith's Ford, and hearing that a body of two hundred Loyalists were guarding a bad, rocky ford at Musgrove's Mill, on the Enoree River, some forty miles distant, McDowell detached the forces of Clarke and Shelby to go with Williams to attack them at that point. As a detailed account of this battle has been given in the writer's "Life of Colonel James Williams," we will suffice by saying that Colonel Clarke commanded the left wing of the American army in that brilliant contest, and aided materially in conducting the prisoners to a place of safety in North Carolina. Reaching the mountain region, they met and rejoined McDowell's party from Smith's Ford. Colonel Shelby now proposed that an army of volunteers be raised on both sides of the mountain, in sufficient numbers to cope with Ferguson. All the officers and some privates agreed to the propriety and feasibility of the undertaking. It was agreed that the Musgrove prisoners be sent to a place of security, and they were turned over to Colonel Clarke, who, after conducting them for some distance, decided to return to Georgia, transferring the prisoners to Colonel Williams, who safely landed them at Hillsboro.

Colonel Clarke was determined on making an effort to recover a part of his own State. In this undertaking, he was joined by

Clarke Assaults Augusta

Lieutenant James McCall, of South Carolina, who proceeded to the western part of the Ninety-Six district, hoping to raise a joint force on the borders of the two States of at least two thousand men. With this force it was thought that Augusta would capitulate with little or no resistance, as Cornwallis had so greatly reduced the garrison when preparing to meet Gates at Camden, and that Ninety-Six, as a consequence, would probably evacuate. This was a bold and masterly scheme, and if the thousand men could have been found, great success might have been attained. But unfortunately, the Ninety-Six region was a hotbed of Toryism, and after the most strenuous efforts by McCall, instead of five hundred, as had been counted on, he could only induce eigthy men to go with him. With this number, he marched to Soap Creek, forty miles northwest of Augusta, which had been agreed upon as a place of juncture. Clarke had been more successful, his number being three hundred and fifty. Such a force was greatly inadequate, but Clarke refused to relinquish his much cherished undertaking, and resolved to depend on courage and strategem in lieu of numbers.

Clarke's movements were so sudden and unexpected to the enemy that he reached the vicinity of Augusta unobserved and found them unprepared for the attack. On the morning of the 14th of September, he halted near the town and formed his command into three divisions; the right, commanded by McCall, the left by Major Samuel Taylor, and the center by Clarke himself. As they advanced, Taylor fell in with an Indian camp, and under some desultory firing the Indians retreated toward their allies. A mile and a half west of the town there was a trading house, called the White House, and Taylor pressed on, hoping to get possession of it. At this house the Indians joined a company of the King's Rangers, commanded by a Captain Johnson. The firing at this point gave Colonel Browne the first intimation of the Americans' approach. Browne was the commander-in-chief of the British garrison in Augusta. He advanced to Johnson's relief in person, with the main body of his garrison. The center and right divisions, under Clarke and McCall, completely surprised the garrison and forts, which they took possession of without resistance. Seventy prisoners and all the Indians were taken, which were put under guard, and Clarke, with his residue, went to the assistance of Taylor. Upon Clarke's approach, Browne took shelter in the White House, and the American efforts to dislodge him failed. A desultory fire was kept up until night, but the post could not be reduced without artillery. During the night, Browne strengthened his position by throwing up some earthworks around the house, and in other ways making it more impervious to the fire of his assailants.

The next morning the Americans brought two pieces of artillery form the British works, which were placed in a position to bear upon the house, but the carriages not being designed for field service and none to skilfully handle them, they did little service. Captain Martin, of South Carolina, the only artillerist in Clarke's command, was killed soon after the pieces were put in action. A fire with small arms was continued through the day, but with little prospect of success.

On the morning of the 15th, before daylight, the Americans drove the Indians from the river bank, which cut off the enemy's water supply, which greatly added to the sufferings of the wounded. Early in the engagement Browne was shot through both thighs, and in his agony was often heard calling for water and medical aid. The dead men and horses, which lay about the White House, became very offensive. Although the garrison was reinforced by fifty Indians, the sufferings of the wounded, the want of water, and the sickening smell of animal putrefaction, it was supposed that these things would be an inducement to surrender, but Browne was not of the yielding kind. On the 17th, Clarke sent in a summons for surrender in the morning and another in the evening, but his replies were that he determined to defend himself to the last extremity.

As soon as Clarke appeared before Augusta, Browne sent messengers by different routes to Ninety-Six, informing Colonel Cruger of his immediate need of reinforcements. Cruger lost no time, and by forced marches, on the night of the 17th, Clarke's scouts informed him of Cruger's approach, with five hundred British regulars and Royal militia. For sundry reasons, Clarke's small force was further depleted by abandonment, some having gone to visit their families, others laden with captured goods, etc.

The next morning, Cruger, with his force, appeared on the other side of the river. The ranks of Clarke being so depleted, he was compelled to raise the siege, having lost about sixty killed and wounded. Among the killed were Captains Charles Jourdine and William Martin. The wounded Whigs, who could not be moved, were left in the town. Captain Ashby, an officer noted for his bravery and humanity, with twenty-eight others, fell into the hands of the enemy, and suffered the most revolting barbarities. Browne was in the White House in bed on account of his wounds. He had Captain Ashby and twelve other wounded prisoners brought in and hanged on the staircase, so that his eyes might feast on the death struggles of the unfortunate victims. Their bodies were given to the Indians, who mutilated them to their satisfaction, finally throwing them into the river. Other helpless ones were given them, and they glutted their vengeance by roasting them by hot fires and other wanton cruelties.

After the siege was raised, the country was searched by the British, and those who had relations engaged in the American cause were arrested and crowded into prisons, where by inhuman treatment and disease, many of them died. Other who were suspected of intercourse with Clarke's command were hanged without a form of trial. An old gentleman in his seventy-eighth year, because he had two sons, captains, in the Patriot cause, was chained to a cart and dragged forty-two miles in two days. When he attempted to rest his feeble frame by leaning on the cart, the driver was ordered to scourge him with his whip.

Immediately after the siege, Clarke's men dispersed to look after and take leave of their families, to meet again at a time and place appointed. The assemblage met about the last of September, and Clarke found himself at the head of three hundred men, but they were encumbered by four hundred women and children. Owing to the country's devastation and barrenness of sustenance, to leave their families behind under such circumstances meant to abandon them to starvation and the barbarities already described. With this helpless multitude, Colonel Clarke commenced a march of nearly two hundred miles, through a mountainous wilderness, in order to avoid being cut off by the enemy, who were already on their trail. After eleven days, Clarke, who was the Moses on this occasion, with his followers, reached the Watauga and Nolanchucky rivers, on the confines of the States of North Carolina and Tennessee, in a starved and otherwise deplorable condition. Fortunately, they were received with the greatest kindness and hospitality by the inhabitants of that region. McCrady says: "Supplies of clothing, substance and shelter were in no instance withheld from them, nor were these gratuities momentary; they ceased only with the demands upon their bounty, which the occasion called for." Cruger had started in pursuit of Clarke, and had called upon Ferguson, who was on Fairforest, to co-operate, but Cruger finding that Clarke's course would carry him too far from Ninety-Six, he gave up the chase.

In early November, 1780, Lord Cornwallis abandoned Charlotte and fell back to his old headquarters at Winnsboro, and Sumter, having assumed command as brigadier-general, moved his camp, with four hundred and twenty-five men, to Fishdam Ford, on Broad River, twenty-eight miles from Winnsboro.

Joins Sumter at Fishdam

This move on the part of Sumter, says McCrady, "was the result of a plan arranged between himself and General Smallwood. Sumter's nearness to Cornwallis's camp would probably cause his lordship to send a detachment after him, and then Smallwood would strike the main force at Winnsboro. For some reason Smallwood did not keep the engagement, but Sumter commenced his part of the move. On the 7th of November, General Sumter crossed the Broad at Fishdam Ford, from what is now Union, into Chester County." Saye, in his "Memoir of McJunkin," says: "The notions of his (Marion's) barbarism had risen to such a height in the British army that his capture was one of prime importance. To affect this purpose, Cornwallis detached Colonel Tarleton, with the main body of his cavalry, and a select portion of his light infantry, to rush into the Pee Dee country. Apprised of this movement, Sumter took a position at the Fishdam Ford, on Broad River, within less than thirty miles of Winnsboro. In the absence of the British cavalry, he felt safe in his position, thinking that he could elude any force which Cornwallis could send against him. The latter determined to drive him from his quarters or punish him for his audacity. For this, he sent Major Wemys (pronounced Weems) with a force considered adequate to route that under Sumter. Historians generally state that Sumter's camp was on the east side of the river. This is a mistake. His position was west of Broad River, and his camp midway between that stream and a small creek which, flowing from the west, falls into the river near a mile below the ford. Here, says local tradition, was Sumter's camp." As Mr. Saye wrote about eigthy years ago and had Major McJunkin, a Revolutionary soldier, for a guide, we accept his account, especially that relative to the location of Sumter's camp, as authentic.

During the day, before the British assault that night, Colonels Clarke and Twiggs, and Majors Candler and Jackson, of Georgia, with about one hundred men, came to Sumter's camp. In the evening a small party of South Carolinians, under Colonel McCall, joined him. Advancing on Sumter's camp, Colonel Wemys obtained for his guide a young Loyalist, by the name of Sealy, who had been discharged from confinement by Sumter the day before, and thereby knew his exact position, even that of his tent, which stood on the side of the main road crossing the encampment. Wemys' well-informed guide enabled him to reach the American post sooner than he expected. A delay till daybreak—which was the time set for the attack—he thought Sumter would discover his presence and perhaps make an attempt to escape, so Wemys determined to make the assault without loss of time. While there is quite a difference in it and other historical accounts, we prefer to reproduce that given by Mr. Saye.

"Again, says 'Local Tradition,' on the night of the 12th of November the fires were kindled in Sumter's camp at dark, and the soldiers began to divest themselves in various ways, apparently as devoid of care as a company of wagoners occupying the same spot for the night would be at the present day. No special pains were taken by the general to have guards placed. But one individual in the camp was oppressed by anxious solicitude. That man was Colonel Thomas Taylor, of Congaree. He had been out with his command during a part of the previous day, towards Tyger River. In his excursions he had heard of the approach of the party under Wemys, and from his intelligence of their movements conjectured their purpose. He went to Sumter and remonstrated in regard to the state of things in his camp. Sumter gave him to understand that he feared no danger, and felt prepared for any probable result Taylor's apprehensions were not allayed by the security of his commander. He determined to take measures to guard against surprise, and to this Sumter gave his hearty assent. Taylor conjectured that if the enemy came that night his approach would be along the road leading from the mouth of Tyger, and hence must cross the creek at the ford to reach Sumter's position. He placed himself at the head of his own men, marched them across the creek, built up large fires of durable material, sent out a patrol party in the direction of the enemy, examined a way for a safe retreat for his party down the creek, and took all other precautions deemed proper in the circumstances. He withdrew his men from the fires, some distance in the direction of the main army, and directed them what to do in case of alarm."

"They slept on their arms until midnight, when they were aroused by the fire of their sentinels. The patrol party had missed the enemy, and hence no alarm was given till the sentinels fired. The British judging from the extent of Taylor's fires that the main body occupied that position and that no advance guard had been placed, immediately charged down the hill with the expectation of falling upon Sumter's men in confusion. They crowded around the blazing fires in search of their victims. Taylor's men were ready, and delivered their fires at this juncture. The enemy fell back, but were again brought to the charge, but were again repulsed, and fled in consternation, leaving their bleeding commander to the mercy of their foes. It is said that when Taylor's men delivered their first fire, a scene of confusion resulted in Sumter's camp utterly beyond description. The soldiers and officers ran hither and thither, whooping and yelling like maniacs. Some got ready for action and joined in it, while others ran clear off, and did not join Sumter again for weeks. Hence this action was denominated in the region round about as Sumter's second defeat, though the rout of the enemy was completed, and the American loss was nothing." The British loss was twenty-three killed and wounded, Colonel Wemys being among the latter.

The precaution and strategy exercised by Colonel Taylor, which saved Sumter from destruction, is all credited, by McCrady, to Colonel Richard Winn, but Mr. Saye, living in that community, and being well acquainted with numbers of the survivors of the Revolution, we believe his account to be trustworthy, and that it was Thomas Taylor, not Richard Winn, who saved the night.

The coming of the morning light revealed the fact that the enemy had precipitately fled after the second encounter with Taylor's men. Colonel Wemys was found on the ground, shot through both thighs. He had recently returned from an expedition against the Whigs, on the Black and Pee Dee rivers, where he had acted under the orders of Cornwallis. While there he committed many atrocious deeds. The most revolting of these was the execution of Adam Cusack. Cusack was an uncompromising Whig, who would neither give a parole as a prisoner of war, nor take British protection; therefore, he was much hated by the enemies of his country. He was charged with refusing to transport some British officers over a ferry, and also with having shot at them across the river, is one account; another has it that he had shot at a negro servant of a Tory officer. He was taken prisoner soon afterward, and for this offense he was tried by a courtmartial, and on a negro's evidence he was condemned. His wife and children prostrated themselves before Wemys, as he sat on horseback, pleading for a pardon, but instead of heeding their piteous cries, he would have ridden over them had not one of his officers prevented the foul act. From this scene he proceeded to superintend the execution of the unfortunate man. He was carried to a spot, not far from the present village of Society Hill, and there hanged. Notwithstanding this dastardly deed, and having accounts in his pocket of several houses burned at his command, he received every consideration as a prisoner of war at the hands of Sumter.

It will be remembered that one Sealy, a young Loyalist, who had just been released by Sumter, guided Wemys to Sumter's camp. He wore homespun clothing, like that of the Americans, and in directing a party to Sumter's tent, his identity was mistaken, so he received a sabre blow from one of his own men, which ended his life. He thus met the fate that he deserved.

A British surgeon, who was sent to Fishdam under a flag to care for the wounded, declared that when he returned to Winnsboro that he had never seen so much injury done by so few troops in so short a time since he had been in America. Tarleton admits a British loss of nearly twenty officers and men killed and wounded.

The affair of Fishdam aroused Cornwallis to action. Tarleton, who was at that time in pursuit of Marion, was hastily called by him to intercept Sumter, who had immediately removed from his post, on Broad River, to the Padget's Creek section of what is now Union County. Here, it appears, that Sumter and Colonel Clarke planned a concerted move against Ninety-Six. By his rapid movements,

The Affair of Blackstocks

Tarleton came near striking them, but being apprised of his approach, in the nick of time, they changed their course, and after a close race they halted at Blackstocks long enough to defeat the advance of Tarleton's army.

Being wounded at Blackstocks, Sumter retreated toward Kings Mountain, with Tarleton in pursuit. Colonel Clarke and Lieutenant-Colonel McCall determined to press on in the movement against Ninety-Six. Since the fall of Charleston, this section had been little disturbed by the war. The British post at Ninety-Six, under Colonel Cruger, was the only one that had not been assaulted by the Patriot forces. One reason for this was probably because it was such a strong Loyalists' region. There was one section, however, more friendly to the cause of freedom—Long Cane. To this neighborhood Clarke and McCall turned their attention for recruits.

The Battle of Long Cane— Clarke Wounded

After resting a few days in the vicinity of Wofford's Iron Works, they advanced in early December by an upper route towards Long Cane, and on the way were joined by Colonel Benjamin Few, of Georgia, with some refugees from that State. Colonel Few assumed the command. The position chosen for their encampment was favorable for their increase of numbers, and the prospect was flattering that in a short time they would be sufficiently strong to confine the British within their stronghold. Cruger was aware of the consequences which would result from permitting Few to remain unmolested, so determined to attack his camp, and hoped that he might surprise him On Sunday, December 10th, Cruger dispatched Lieutenant-Colonel Allen, with two hundred regular troops, two hundred Loyalists and fifty dragoons. The next day, Allen halted within three miles of Few's camp before he was aware of the approach Clarke, McCall, and Major Lindsay were ordered by Few to meet the enemy, commence the action and sustain it until the main body could be brought up. They advanced about a mile and a half, where they dismounted, and tied their horses within one hundred yards of the enemy's front, which was composed of Loyal militia, and attacked them at once, the action becoming lively. The regular troops had just formed when the firing commenced. In about ten minutes the Loyal militia retreated; some of them fled, and the remainder formed in the rear of the regular troops. Clarke sent an express to Few to hurry up with the main body, and with his troops advanced on the regulars and delivered a fire, which wounded some of them. At this juncture, Colonel Clarke received a wound in his shoulder, which was at first supposed to be mortal, and he was carried from the field.

The advance on such superior numbers proved disastrous to the Americans. Allen met them with a fire and the bayonet. About this time McCall was wounded and his horse killed. The horse falling on him, McCall narrowly escaped with his life. Major Lindsay was also wounded. All their leaders having fallen, the Americans retreated, and were charged by the enemy's dragoons. Major Lindsay, who had received three wounds, was sabered upon his head and arms, and one of his hands cut off as he lay upon the ground. Fourteen Americans were killed, and several others, helpless because of wounds, were slain on the ground where they lay. Thus the atrocities committed by Tarleton at the Waxhaws were repeated on a small scale.

Instead of Few coming to Clarke and McCall's rescue as he had proposed, when the remains of their commands returned to his camp they found the main body under orders to move off, Few not having informed them of his intentions. Such conduct was wholly unjustifiable.

Having recovered from his wounds, Colonel Clarke joined General Pickens, who receiving intelligence that Major Dunlap had **Clarke Captures** been detached from Ninety-Six with seventy-five **Dunlap at** British dragoons for foraging purposes, Pickens at **Beattie's Mill** once detached Clarke and McCall to attack him. On the 24th of March they came up with Dunlap at Beattie's Mill, on Little River, in what is now Abbeville County. Dunlap being surprised, he retired into the mill and some outhouses, but these were too open for defense against Clarke's riflemen. Knowing his odious reputation among the Whigs, Dunlap resolved to sell his life dearly, so he resisted for several hours, until thirty-four of his men were killed and himself and several others wounded, when he held out a flag and surrendered. The prisoners taken were forty-two, including the wounded.

His activities were suspended for a while on account of smallpox, but were resumed on his recovery. He took part in the siege **Further** of Augusta, engaged in several expeditions against **Activities** the Indians, the final one being that of General Pickens against the Cherokees, which resulted in their subjugation and treaty, by which considerable lands were ceded to the State of Georgia.

Some time after the war he was made a major-general in the militia of Georgia, and engaged in several battles with the Indians, the principal one of which was Jack's Creek, fought in 1787, in which he defeated the Creeks.

Becomes a Major-General

In 17—, Clarke attempted a settlement on the Indian side of the Oconee River, and also crossed the St. Mary's to the Florida side, and drove in the Spanish post. This displeased the United States government, and also that of the State, which brought proceedings against him. He was given a hearing before a court, consisting of four justices of the peace, which released him from custody. This emboldened him to further operations. Forts were erected, houses built within the forts, and a town laid off. He was chosen major-general and placed at the head of the enterprise, a committee of safety was appointed and everything wore the appearance of a permanent settlement.

Trouble With the U. S. Government

Upon hearing this, Governor Matthews sent a force of militia, under Generals Twiggs and Irwin, to induce Clarke to move, which he refused to do. Further pressure was brought to bear on him, but not until a force of dragoons came and began arrangements to cut off his supplies, in the meantime promising Clarke that if he would evacuate the post, himself, men and property should be protected, would he give it up. The militia took posession of the works and set fire to the fort, when Clarke abandoned the enterprise.*

General Elijah Clarke died December 15, 1799, aged about sixty-three years. He was buried at Woodburn, Georgia, his adopted State.

His Demise

"Mrs. Hannah Clarke, relict of Major-General Elijah Clarke, died in this (Wilkes) County, on the 26th day of August, 1827, aged ninety years. Mrs. Clarke had attended her husband through many interesting periods of the American Revolution, and had often experienced some of the distressing vicissitudes of war. She once had her

Mrs. Hannah Clarke

---

*White's "Historical Collections of Georgia"

house burnt, with all its contents, during the absence of her husband, by a pillaging party of British and Tories, who ravaged that part of the country in which she then resided, and was turned out to seek shelter as she could, with a family of several children then in her charge. She was afterwards robbed of the horse on which she was riding to meet her wounded husband, near the North Carolina line. During part of the campaigns in which General Clarke was engaged she accompanied him, and on one occasion in attempting to remove from a place of danger near which an engagement was soon expected, she had her horse shot under her, while two children were on his back with her. She was at the siege of Augusta, and present when the garrison, under Browne, capitulated, and many of the prisoners, then and at other times taken by her husband, experienced her benevolence and hospitality. She lived to behold and rejoice in the prosperity and happiness of that country which she had frequently seen desolated by cruelty and bloodshed, and in the enjoyment of the esteem and affection of a large circle of friends. She attained a good old age, and at last after a short struggle was liberated from all earthly cares, and entered into that rest which remaineth for the people of God. Her remains were interred at Woodburn, near the resting place of her husband, who had twenty-eight years before closed a life of patriotic exertion in the cause of his country."*

General Clarke Honored

Woodburn was the name General Clarke gave his country home, a custom of the times. It is in Lincoln County, about fourteen miles from Lincolnton, and within two miles of the Savannah River Early historians say that General Clarke was a resident of Wilkes County, which was true at one time, but in 1796, when Lincoln was formed, a part of Wilkes was cut off, which automatically cut him out of Wilkes and put him in Lincoln.

After General Clarke had slept in his tomb for one hundred and twenty-five years, the Elijah Clarke Chapter of the D. A. R.'s, of Athens, Ga., and the Hannah Clarke Chapter, of Quitman, Ga, erected a suitable monument to the graves of the noted hero and heroine. The unveiling took place with elaborate ceremonies, May 14th, 1924. The monument bears the following inscription:

*White's "Historical Collections of Georgia," page 682

Erected to the Memory of General Elijah Clarke, 1736-1799, Revolutionary Soldier and Patriot, and his wife, Hannah Arrington, by the Elijah Clarke Chapter, Athens, Georgia, and Hannah Clarke Chapter, Quitman, Georgia, Daughters of the American Revolution, 1924.

Clarke County, Georgia, in which Athens is situated, was named in honor of General Clarke.

The Life of Lieutenant-Colonel William Farr

IT IS QUITE singular that a soldier and officer of ability should fight all through the war for Independence and his name not for once be mentioned in history. Such is the case with Lieutenant-Colonel William Farr. Had it not been for an occasional glimpse given of him by Saye, in his "Memoir of McJunkin," and the efforts of D. A. Thomas, a great-grandson, his name, like so many others in that memorable struggle, would have been unheard of by this and succeeding generations. It affords us great pleasure to bring to the attention of the public some things in the career of this forgotten hero.

William Farr was born in Virginia, about 1729. Nothing is known of his early life, education, etc. As expressed by a writer, "The first clear light to dawn upon his manhood finds him settled in Mecklenburg County, North Carolina, and here it was, doubtless, that the natural fire of his love of liberty was kindled to a flame preparatory to the performance of a noble duty for his country's good." As to how long he remained here, we do not know; but some time previous to the Revolution, in company with two brothers, he removed to South Carolina and settled on Broad River, not far from Fishdam, in what is now Union County.

William Farr first married a widow Jeter, whose maiden name was Black. By this marriage there were three sons, viz.: William Black Farr, Richard Farr, James Farr, and one daughter, Harriet, who married Daniel McElduff, a Revolutionary soldier. Losing his first wife, on October 4, 1779, he married Elizabeth Taliavo Stribling, by whom there were four sons, John Pulaski Farr, Titus Green Farr, Robert Goodloe Farr, Harper Farr, and one daughter, Frances, who married David Anderson Thomas, of Chester District.

Hostilities having begun between the mother country and the Colonies, the afterwards famous Spartan regiment was formed about the end of August, 1775, and John Thomas, Sr., was made colonel We do not know whether William Farr was present at the organization or not, but he soon belonged to it, and was captain of a company.

Beginning of His Military Career

The first session of the Continental Congress convened in Philadelphia, in October, 1774. This body finishing its business, the **The Snow** members from South Carolina returned home and **Campaign** gave the people an account of its proceedings, which pleased the lovers of liberty. To strengthen the action of Congress, a Provincial Congress was assembled in South Carolina. Delegates were elected from every parish and district in the Colony. The first meeting was held in January, 1775. The actions of the Continental Congress were approved and a council of safety appointed. The business of this council was to look after and protect the interests of independence. We must not infer from the foregoing that all the people in the province rallied to the standard of the Congress and the Council of Safety. Far from it. There were many, in every part of the country, that remained loyal to England. The great activities of the Liberty men aroused the Loyalists; agents were sent out by the Royal Governor to gather the friends of the King, and to organize them for the defensive and offensive. Such a state of affairs could not long avoid the clash of arms. The first of these was the besieging of Colonel Williamson at Ninety-Six, in November, 1775. In this affair, the Loyalists rather got the best of it. This partial success emboldened them to continue their opposition to the Provincial Government. But the Council of Safety, acting under the authority of Congress, determined to quell the Loyalists at any cost. Accordingly, before Williamson's partial capitulation at Ninety-Six, in obedience to the order of the Congress, Colonel Richard Richardson, with about one thousand men, was marching from towards Charleston in the direction of the country between the Broad and Saluda rivers.

On November 27, 1775, he pitched his camp on the banks of the Congaree, where he remained three days. Here he was reinforced to about fifteen hundred men. Reaching the Dutch Fork, between the Broad and Saluda, he encamped at McLauren's Store. Here he was joined by the Spartan regiment, under Colonel John Thomas, Sr., and with them came Captain William Farr. Richardson's forces now amounted to about twenty-five hundred. Winter was on, and many of the men were thinly clad and ill-provided for, considering the severity of the weather; but they had set out to put down the King's men, and nothing could deter them from it. Detachments were sent out, and post after post of the enemy were broken, until they were practically driven from the country. On Christmas Day, 1775, the whole army was encamped at Hollingsworth Mill, on Rabun Creek. A heavy snow began to fall, and continued without intermission for thirty hours. The ground was covered two feet deep. The army had no tents, and their clothes and shoes were terribly worn. For a week they did not set foot on the ground, only when they cleared away little places to build their fires for cooking and warming purposes. This terrible snow and the sufferings which it brought on gave it the name of "The Snow Campaign." But the purposes of these suffering Patriots were for the time accomplished, and we are quite sure that none did their duty more faithfully and endured their sufferings more stoically than did Captain Farr. This was his first actual military service.

In 1776, William Farr volunteered as a captain in the State militia of South Carolina, and in that capacity he remained until 1777, when the Spartan regiment was divided and a second Spartan regiment formed, with Thomas Brandon as colonel. Farr was a part of the time captain of horse, and part of the time captain of foot in the second regiment.

It is said that Farr was with General Lincoln at the battle of Stono, June 20, 1779. The fall of Charleston, in May, 1780, brought consternation to the Patriot ranks. Many fled to North Carolina for safety, and others, who did not want to leave their families, took British protection. It looked for a time as if all was lost.

On June 8 or 10, after Charleston's fall, Colonel Brandon's command, to which which Captain Farr belonged, was surprised at his camp on Fairforest, about four miles from Union, and literally broken up. Captain Farr fled to North Carolina, and, it is said, participated in the battle of Ramseur's Mill. While there he joined Sumter, and subsequently fought at Rocky Mount and Hanging Rock.

Flees to North Carolina

Colonels Williams, Brandon, Steen and some others returned to South Carolina about the middle of August, and on the 18th took part in the brilliant engagement at Musgrove's Mill. Captain Farr accompanied his command under Colonel Brandon and did his bit in that affair (For a detailed account of this battle see pages 74-81.)

At Musgrove's

We consider the following legend as worthy of mention: Colonel Farr had a faithful slave, "Lemerick" by name, who often accompanied him on his campaigns as an attendant or body servant. Lemerick lived long after the Colonel passed away, and was lavish in the narrations of his former master's prowess in war One of his stories was that "Everybody said Colonel Shelby whipped the British at Musgrove's Mill, but that was not right, for old Master had them whipped before Colonel Shelby got there."

The Whigs were so greatly elated over their success that they determined to press on to Ninety-Six at once, but just as they were in the act of mounting, a messenger came from McDowell informing them of General Gates' calamity at Camden. Nothing could be done only to beat a hasty retreat to North Carolina. After a continuous march, accompanied by the greatest hardship and suffering, they succeeded in delivering their prisoners at Hillsboro.

There is a family tradition that Farr was at Kings Mountain, which we think probable, because Brandon's command, to which he belonged, was there, but we have no way of verifying it. It appears that about this period Farr rose in rank quite rapidly, for we find him major, and before Blackstocks, lieutenant-colonel

Colonel Farr at Blackstocks

After Sumter's victory at Fishdam, on Broad River, on the night of November 9, he moved in the direction of Ninety-Six. When at Padgett's Creek, some miles southwest from Union, a number of Georgia militia joined Sumter. At this time Joseph McJunkin was appointed major. Saye, in his "Memoir of McJunkin," says: "This was probably done to fill a vacancy occasioned by the death of Lieutenant-Colonel James Steen." Major William Farr, subsequent to this, is called lieutenant-colonel in Major McJunkin's written narrative. Hence, the writer concludes that Farr succeeded Steen, and McJunkin ranked next to Farr in Brandon's regiment.

Sumter's march toward Ninety-Six was interrupted by the intelligence that Colonel Tarleton was following him by forced marches, with the intention of falling upon him. He turned northward, which put the Enoree River in his front. Sumter had barely passed this stream with his main body when Tarleton's advance obstructed the passage of his rear guard. He pushed on, however, and was gaining ground on his pursuer. Apprehensive that his flying foe would succeed in crossing Tyger River without hindrance, which was only a few miles in advance, Tarleton left his artillery and such of his infantry as he was unable to put on horseback, and pressed forward with all possible speed. Sumter succeeded in reaching the Tyger at Blackstock's house and ford, where he took a strong position, with the view of allowing his weary troops to take refreshment.

His main body occupied the hill on which Blackstock's house stood. This was a large tobacco house, built of logs, long and narrow, consisting of two apartments eighteen feet square, with a space of eighteen feet between. The rear guard was left some distance behind on the road. Just here it will be interesting to hear a commanding officer speak. We take the following from Major McJunkin's personal narrative: "Sumter having stopped to take some refreshments, and the troops having made up fires, prepared the dough and rolled it around sticks and set it before the fires in order to bake. I, being officer of the day, was informed of Tarleton's near approach, and immediately sent word to Sumter, who ordered that we should come up to the building where he was, which we did, leaving our dough on the sticks for the British. Then Sumter said: 'Boys, who will bring on the action?' and Colonel Farr and myself stepped out and asked who would go with us, when our heroes stepped out until Sumter said there was enough. Then Sumter said: 'Go on, boys, and if you are not strong enough, retreat, and fight as you retreat.'"

When Tarleton arrived and saw Sumter's strong position, he decided that he would just guard his opponent and hold him there until the balance of his forces should come up. But Sumter was not made up of the stuff to submit to such bondage. He immediately formed his lines, and the party mentioned by Major McJunkin went forward to the attack. The action commenced with great spirit, but the assaulting party had to gradually yield to superior numbers, when Tarleton made a general charge, with the view of driving Sumter from his advantageous position. He was repulsed in this first onset with heavy loss. A second charge was made, but with no better success. He then withdrew his whole force and left the field.

The numbers of the respective parties engaged are variously estimated. Tarleton's was thought to have been about four hundred, and Sumter's about the same, including one hundred and fifty Georgians, under Colonel Twiggs. It is said that the British loss in killed and wounded was near two hundred, and that of the Americans about one-sixth of that amount. Among the wounded was General Sumter, who received a bullet in the breast, which disabled him for service several months. The command now devolved on Colonel Twiggs. Although it was near sundown when the enemy quit the field, it was deemed expedient to retreat that night. A litter was constructed upon which General Sumter was carried, between two horses.

The retreat was continued the next day towards Kings Mountain by the way of Grindal Ford, on Pacolet. Tarleton's whole force having come up, in the morning he returned to the battlefield to find that his prey had flown. After hanging John Johnson, a good Whig, he began the pursuit of Sumter, and followed as far as Grindal. While in that vicinity, he encamped for a night at the house of Jack Beckham, a noted scout, who lived about two miles eastward from Jonesville, on Sandy Run Creek. Mrs. Beckham first saw Tarleton while standing in the yard ordering his men to catch her poultry for supper. She spoke civilly to him and hastened to prepare supper for him and his suite, as if they had been honored guests. When about to leave in the morning, he gave the house up to pillage and ordered it burned, but because of the earnest remonstrances of Mrs. Beckham he recalled the order.

William Hodge, a good Whig, lived near the Pacolet, about two miles above Grindal Shoals. Leaving Beckham's, Tarleton, with his whole army, came up to Hodge's house a little after sunrise. His provisions and provender were seized, his stock shot down, and his houses and fences burned to the ground. Hodge was made a prisoner, and Tarleton told Mrs. Hodge that her husband would be hanged to the first crooked tree on the road. Instead of hanging him, he was sent to jail in Camden, where he came near starving to death. After remaining there about four months, Hodge, with Daniel McJunkin and some others, succeeded in cutting the grating out of the prison window and made their escape.

It appears that at Grindal Shoals Tarleton gave up the pursuit of Sumter and rejoined Cornwallis at Winnsboro.

The affair at Blackstocks took place November, 1780.

LIEUTENANT-COLONEL WILLIAM FARR   191

Sumter being incapacitated by his wound received at Blackstocks, his forces were broken up into squads in order that they might better obtain subsistence, and for lack of a leader in whom they had implicit confidence When General Morgan arrived at the Grindal Shoals in December, the hopes of the partisan leaders were revived and they soon flocked to Morgan's standard. Among these were Colonels Thomas Brandon and William Farr, with a number of the Second Spartan regiment. Tarleton being sent out with special instructions that he "push Morgan to the utmost," he fell back from the Grindal Shoals to The Cowpens, where, on the morning of January 17, 1781, he prepared to give Tarleton battle.

Colonel Farr Gave Permission for the First Shot

Three lines were formed across the plains. The first and main line consisted of about three hundred and ninety Maryland regulars and one hundred and fifty Virginia militia, commanded by Lieutenant-Colonel Howard. One hundred and fifty yards in front of Howard's line a second one was formed, consisting of about three hundred and fifty volunteer militia, commanded by General Andrew Pickens. One hundred and fifty yards in front of Pickens' line was a corps of sixty or seventy picked riflemen, scattered in loose order along the whole front. Colonel William Farr and a part of his command was in the front line.

When Tarleton reached The Cowpens shortly after sunrise, he found Morgan in perfect readiness to receive him. He at once proceeded to form his lines of battle, and being in readiness the British advanced in a sort of trot, uttering a loud halloa. As the British halloaed, Morgan was heard to say: "Boys, they give us the British halloa; give them the Indian halloa," and, galloping along the lines, he cheered the men and told them not to fire until they could see the whites of their eyes. Every officer was crying, "Don't fire!" for, says Major Thomas Young, "it was a hard matter for us to keep from it." As the Redcoats streamed along, a column marched up before the front line, led by a gaily dressed officer, on horseback. This fellow seemed to be rather busy, and made himself obnoxiously conspicuous in the eyes of the patriotic Americans. Word passed along the line, "Who can bring him down?" John Savage looked Colonel Farr full in the face and read "Yes" in his eyes. So Savage darted a few paces in front, laid his rifle against a sapling, a blue gas streamed above his head, a sharp crack of a rifle broke the solemn stillness of the moment, and the result was that a horse without a rider wheeled from the front of the advancing column. Thus it will be seen that the first shot fired at the battle of Cowpens was by the order of Colonel William Farr, and one of his men, John Savage, fired it. A few moments later the contest was on, and in about an hour's time the glorious victory at The Cowpens was won.

Referring to these facts, a writer says: "The high honor conferred in the colonelcy of so splendid a regiment was nobly sustained by Colonel Farr, than whom and his men no voices were more entitled to join in the vociferous shouts of that glorious victory after the work was done."

It appears that after the battle of Cowpens Colonel Farr joined Pickens' command, and with his forces engaged in that campaign fighting and driving the Indians, who sided with the British, across the mountains, and had reached the Hiawassa River, in Tennessee, when peace was declared in 1782. Thus it will be seen that after many others had ceased to fight, Colonel Farr was still on the job.

Once when the Whigs had been driven from the west side of Broad River, Colonel Farr and some of his associates were en-
Some Personal camped on the east side. Farr hearing that his wife
Incidents was sick, determined to visit her and look after her condition. Major Joseph McJunkin, Captain William Giles, Adam Skain, Thomas Wood, and probably some others volunteered to accompany him. They crossed Broad River at night, and cautiously approached the house and found it full of Tories. Farr and Giles went to one door, while McJunkin, Skain and Wood went to the other. McJunkin knocked at his door, and the Tories rushed to the other one to make their escape The first one to put out his head was killed by Farr with his sword. Then he and his friends rushed into the house and captured the lot. His friends then told him that they would look after the prisoners. Major McJunkin is quoted as saying that the prisoners were taken off, disposed of, and were never heard of afterward. The friends of Farr soon returned to the house, where he made such provision for his family as the short time permitted, and the whole party returned to the east side of the river before daylight.

Another account before us differs somewhat from the above. It is as follows: "A party of Tories visited the home of Colonel

Farr during his absence and were committing such depredations that the facts were quickly made known to him, whereupon Colonel Farr, Adam Skain, Thomas Wood, William Giles and others banded together and cautiously approached and surrounded the house. The Tories detecting the situation, began to flee from the house, but at the door Colonel Farr killed one with his sword, and the party burning with indignation, their hearts filled with the sentiment,

>Lay the proud ursurpers low,
>Tyrants fall in every fire.
>Liberty's in every blow.
>Forward! let us do or die—

marched in hot pursuit. The pursuers soon returned, but uttered not a word. This band of Tories was never heard of again."

On another occasion, while encamped on Little Brown's Creek, on the old Pinckneyville and Union road, information reached Colonel Farr that some Tories were committing their usual depredations on Broad River. With a squad of his men he at once started in pursuit, and encountered the marauding Tories with their booty in the Savage neighborhood, near Manus' old field. The Whigs completely routed them, killing quite a number and recaptured and returned the stolen property. Until recently the Tory graves were pointed out by a few old people, which gave silent testimony to the splendid soldiership of Colonel William Farr and his chosen comrades.

Some Post-War Services Colonel Farr held several positions of honor and trust after the war. He was a member of the Jacksonborough legislature, and in after life always referred to one of his colleagues as "Gizzards." The reason why, we know not.

Freedom having been won, the Colonies becoming States, and the State government machinery put in working order, in 1789 the Circuit Court districts in South Carolina were seven in number, viz.: Beaufort, Charleston, Orangeburg, Camden, Cheraw and Ninety-Six. In 1791 it became necessary to make two additional districts, and thus Washington and Pinckney were added. The legislature selected three men, viz.: Colonel William Farr, of Union; Colonel Edward Lacey, of Chester, and Bayliss Earle, of Spartanburg, to select a location for the court house, jail, etc., for Pinckney. The place selected was on the south side of Pacolet and Broad rivers, near their confluence. The name Pinckney was given in honor of Charles C. Pinckney. The courts were held here until the year 1800, when the present districts were arranged. The hanging ground was about one mile from the village, and it is known that one horse thief was hanged there. The old jail and some other ruins still remain.

When this district was first formed, each county had several judges who constituted the County Court, having jurisdiction in certain cases. These judges were known as "Justices of the Quorum," and were distinct from the "Justices of the Peace," whose subordinate functions could also be performed by these judges. Finally, this form of jurisprudence was merged into the District Court. Colonel Farr was at one time a member of this court. It is said that he was once sheriff of the district, but of this we are not certain.

We quote the following: "Colonel Farr died in 1794, and was buried in the graveyard on the Scaife place, about thirteen miles from Union Court House. Brave and kind, patient under hardships, magnanimous in victory to the defeated, this great man deserves to be remembered. The snows of nearly a century (now more than a century and a quarter) have fallen upon his grave, but the integrity of his personal character, his fidelity to fixed principles, his unconquerable and undying consecration to right and to his country are still kept alive in the light of those vestal fires of liberty before which he bowed in the earliest spring. To this almost forgotten hero, let us inscribe Gray's beautiful words:

His Demise

> " 'On some fond breast the parting soul relies,
> Some pious drops the closing eye requires,
> E'en from the tomb the voice of Nature cries,
> E'en in our ashes live their wonted fires.' "

Major Joseph McJunkin, a fellow soldier with him, said: "Colonel Farr was a true Patriot, was a brave, energetic, hard-fighting soldier, and a virulent hater of Tories."

Though his ashes lie in an unmarked grave, may his name linger in the memory of every lover of liberty.

The Life of Colonel Joseph Hughes

ABOUT one hundred and seventy years ago two brothers, Thomas and William Hughes by name, left the shores of the Old Dominion, turning their faces toward the New World. They were born in Wales, were well educated, and surveyors by profession. Stopping for a time in the region now crossed by Mason's and Dixon's line, Thomas Hughes married Miss Ann Jolly (some say Martha Tucker Jolly), of Virginia, and William married Miss Mary Gill Leonard, of Maryland.

Not long after their marriage they, with some others, emigrated to South Carolina. Mrs. Thomas Hughes having relatives at Georgetown, their intention was to settle there. Reaching Carolina, they crossed the Broad River and encamped on the west side of that stream, in what is now Union County. While here some of the emigrants who accompanied them became ill, which compelled them to remain all the winter. They were so favorably impressed with the climate and surroundings, Mrs. William Hughes especially being charmed with the appearance of the country, which reminded her of Maryland, they decided to settle where they were, and began work preparatory to establishing permanent homes. The brothers made surveys, and with the consent of the British government they appropriated a large tract of land, extending fourteen miles up and down on each side of Broad River, which embraced the present famous Lockhart Shoals. This settlement must have been made some time subsequent to 1753, because it was not until that year that the Indians ceded the upper section of South Carolina to England.

When they came from Virginia, the Hughes brothers brought with them ten negro slaves each, and with these they commenced to clear land, and by springtime they had prepared sufficient ground to plant their crops. The soil being very fertile, they obtained fine yields of wheat, corn and other grains. They built a saw mill to saw lumber for their houses, and later erected corn and flour mills. The machinery for these mills was ordered from England and shipped to Charleston, from which place it was hauled to its destination by ox teams, the time required for the trip being about three weeks. The site upon which they were erected is now occupied by the present Lockhart Cotton Mills. The Hughes employed a miller by the name of John Lockhart, and he and his wife, Polly, lived on the hill overlooking the shoals. William Hughes named them after his miller—*Lockhart Shoals.*

Being active and energetic, success crowned the efforts of these sturdy pioneers, who did everything they could to advance their enterprises. They built comfortable two-story houses, with cellars underneath; also negro houses and outbuildings.

At length, others came from Virginia and North Carolina and joined the settlement established by the Hughes; among whom were the names of Smith, Addis, Cook, McLunny, Albertson, Culbertson, Harrison and others; some buying land from the Hughes, and to others it was given them for neighbors. The carpenter who built the Hughes houses was an Englishman by the name of Polson, and was given several acres of land, which was owned in recent times by Miss Mary Emma Foster.

The first Masonic lodge ever organized on Broad River, and most probably the first in upper South Carolina, was organized in William Hughes' house.

Joseph Hughes, the subject this sketch, was born in Chester District, in October, 1760 or 1761, and was the eldest son of Thomas Hughes and Ann, his wife. As already seen, his parents resided on the Union side of Broad River, but at the time of his birth they had removed temporarily to Chester, on account of Indian troubles.

For some time after war broke out between England and the Colonies, the contest was waged principally in the North, but the **Revolutionary War Begins** Royal Government was by no means inactive in the South. British Indian agents and other emissaries were busily engaged in exciting the Red Men to line up against the whites. Chief among these were Alexander Cameron, John Stewart, and Richard Paris. Their efforts were successful to the extent that in 1775 Colonel Richard Richardson waged a campaign and apparently subjugated the insurgents between the Broad and Saluda rivers. Peace was not, however, to remain very long, for new and greater dangers awaited the frontier settlements in upper South Carolina. In the early part of 1776, Cameron assembled four hundred warriors, and by every possible argument and intrigue succeeded in inducing them to array themselves against the friends of liberty. Fearing this, they sent their agents to confer with the Indians, hoping to get them either to side with them or remain neutral, but finding the Red Men already against them, the agents had to flee for their lives. An alliance was formed between British, Tories and Indians, and in accordance with their plans, on the 20th of June began the work of death and destruction.

The following is an instance of the shocking barbarities imposed upon the helpless inhabitants. A Captain McCall, who had long been, treacherously, taken prisoner, to impress him with the dreadful fate that awaited him, was frequently taken to the place of execution to witness the horrible tortures. In his journal, McCall tells of the execution of a boy twelve years of age, the details of which are blood-curdling. Light-wood splinters, eighteen inches in length, were sharpened at one end and split fine at the other, so when set on fire the blaze would not be extinguished when thrown through the air. The victim was then stripped naked and suspended by the arms between two posts, three feet from the ground. The lightwood splinters were then hurled, so that the sharp end would pierce the flesh, while the other end continued to burn. Thus three of the most cruel methods of death were united in one—crucifixion, piercing the flesh, and burning. This continued for two hours before death relieved the poor boy's sufferings Such were some of the agonies inflicted on the early pioneers. The crackling of flames, the shrieks of the dying, and the wails of the bereft rent the air all through the up-country. Says McCrady: "Several hundred men, women and children of the helpless inhabitants of the frontiers fell a sacrifice to the tomahawk and the scalping knife."

This state of things caused the greatest possible consternation. The people were almost destitute of arms and ammunition, and the men would not assemble until they had placed their families in comparative safety. Some crowded into the little stockade forts, and others fled as far as Orangeburg.

General Williamson lost no time in arousing the suffering inhabitants to the defense. Having embodied a number of men in May, Williamson formed a camp on Fairforest Creek, in the vicinity of the residence of Colonel John Thomas, within the present limits of Spartanburg County. Owing to the demoralized condition of the country, his

Hughes Begins His War Record

army increased very slowly, the number being only four hundred and fifty at the middle of July. At that time the inhabitants of the Saluda section had taken refuge in an old fort called Lyndley's, and were attacked by a force of Loyalists and Indians. Williamson arriving in time, the assault was repulsed. A hundred rangers, as a convoy of wagons, with arms, ammunition, stores, etc., were sent to Williamson, and being reinforced by Colonel Jack's regiment, of Georgia, his force was then eleven hundred and fifty men.

It was, probably, at this time that Joseph Hughes enlisted in the regular service. We take the following from his pension application: "He entered the service in the militia of South Carolina at the commencement of the war, between fourteen and fifteen years of age, and attached himself to, and was enrolled of Captain Joseph Jolly's company roll at Seneca Town, on Seneca River, having gone to that place with a detachment for provisions. From that place he marched under Captain Jolly, of Colonel John Thomas' regiment, General Williamson's Brigade; soon after his arrival to the middle settlement of the Cherokee Indians, and thence down to the Tennessee valleys, destroying and burning all the towns we found."

Williamson being heavily reinforced, he, with a detachment of three hundred men, advanced upon the Indians at Oconee Creek. Being apprised of his approach, the savages were waiting for him in ambush. Suddenly and unexpectedly he found himself under a dreadful fire, his horse shot from under him, an officer slain by his side, and his forces thrown into disorder. Colonel Samuel Hammond, who was with him, succeeded in rallying the confused forces, and by a well-ordered charge retrieved the day. Williamson then proceeded across the Smoky Mountains and advanced into the heart of the Indian country. A junction being formed with Colonel Rutherford, of North Carolina, Williamson assumed command of the whole. Passing into a narrow defile, surrounded by mountains, another ambush awaited him. Twelve hundred Indians secreted in the encircling mountains poured a deadly fire into his ranks, but a bayonet charge put the enemy to flight. Williamson continued his work of devastation, burning villages and destroying crops. The whole country east of the Appalachian Mountains being laid waste, the conquered Indians sued for peace. In the treaty following, the territory comprising the present counties of Greenville, Anderson, and Pickens were ceded to the whites.

This expedition was in the latter part of 1776, and Hughes says, as well as he recollected, from the time he joined the army on Seneca till he was discharged was about fourteen weeks. Soon after his return he spent some time in the Georgia expedition without being in any engagement.

After the disastrous expedition of General Lee against Florida in 1776, the British had erected a fort at St. Mary's River, from **The Florida Expedition** which they frequently raided the southern parts of Georgia. To stop this, General Robert Howe, with a large force, resumed the invasion in 1778, but with no better success than that of Lee. In this expedition the South Carolina militia were under Colonel Andrew Williamson and Colonel Stephen Bull. Hughes says that he thinks that Colonel Brandon commanded Thomas' regiment; is not positive whether Captain Jolly or Captain Palmer commanded the company that he was in, but believes that Palmer did. McCrady says: "The route of the expedition lay through a country so barren that not a berry was to be found, nor a bud to be seen. . . . A malarial region, intense heat, bad water, insufficient shelter, and salt meat so imparied the health of Howe's troops that the hospital returns showed one-half of the men upon the sick list. Through lack of forage, horses perished, and those which remained were so enfeebled that they were incapable of transporting the artillery and wagons. The soldiers were dispirited and distracted. The command was rent by factions, and Howe proved incompetent to deal with its discordant element."

This is corroborated by Hughes, who says: "This expedition was in 1778, and lasted from early in the spring until late in the fall. The army suffered much from heat, hunger and thirst, and had no engagement except a skirmish on the river Santillee with an infamous Tory (commonly known as Burntfoot Brown) and his party."

After the return from the Florida expedition, Hughes was stationed at Augusta for three months. The next important service that he rendered was under General Lincoln, who **At Augusta and Charleston** commanded the expedition against Stono, in South Carolina, the engagement taking place June 20, 1779. Hughes had this to say about it: "He was in that engagement, and a desperate one it was. His regiment was commanded by Brandon, then a colonel, and his company by Captain Palmer.

Many were killed in this engagement, and neither side had the advantage; not much good was, however, done for our cause."

Some time after the affair at Stono, Hughes was sent to Charleston and was stationed for two months at Ten-Mile Branch, under Lieutenant-Colonel Steen, who was in command of Brandon's regiment at that place. At the expiration of this time the troops were discharged, and it appears that they returned home. At length he was called out to the defense of Charleston, but by the time Brandon's regiment reached the Congaree, news came that that place had fallen. That was in May, 1780.

About this time he received from Governor John Rutledge a commission of first lieutenant in Captain Benjamin Jolly's company, **Becomes a Lieutenant** in Colonel Brandon's regiment, which was the second division of the Spartan. This commission was lost when Hughes' house was burned in the year 1788 or 1789.

The fall of Charleston produced so much consternation and fear in the up-country that the determined ones were put to the severest test. Not only were the British advancing and the **Helps to Hide the Powder** Tories uprising, but many Whigs, both officers and privates, considering their cause hopeless, were taking British protection and receiving paroles as prisoners of war.

Under these disturbing conditions, Colonels Brandon, Thomas and Lyles met on the 4th of June to consider measures for the mutual protection and safety of their homes and communities. They agreed to assemble their forces at a point on Fairforest Creek about four miles south from the present site of Union. As the place was near the center of where Brandon's command resided, his men arrived first. He had in his possession a part of the powder formerly entrusted to Colonel Thomas, and its safe keeping was considered a matter of the greatest importance. Hence, Brandon directed Joseph Hughes and some others to conceal it in the woods with the greatest possible care. While away on this mission Brandon's camp was surprised and his troops dispersed by Bloody Bill Cunningham, who had been apprised by an escaped Tory of Brandon's position and number. Although a captive Whig was forced to tell where the powder was secreted, the work was so skillfully done that the enemy found but little of it. The remainder was afterward carried safely over Broad River and furnished the principal supply for Sumter's troops at Huck's defeat.

Hughes and his comrades, hearing what had happened at Brandon's camp during their absence, collected as many of their friends **Rocky Mount and Hanging Rock** as possible and retreated over Broad River to Bulluck's Creek Church, in York District. Parts of the regiments of Brandon, Lyles, Thomas and a few others came together, talked their situation over, some public addresses were delivered, and then the matter was put to a vote as to whether they would give it up or fight it out. Every man voted to fight, adopting the slogan, "Give me liberty, or give me death!"

Soon after this decision they proceeded to the Tuscaseegee Ford, where they joined Colonel Thomas Sumter, and after some exchange of views Sumter was elected General. His first move was against the Tories at Ramseur's Mill, in North Carolina, "but," says Hughes, "before we arrived the Rowan militia of North Carolina had defeated them." Continuing with Sumter, Hughes took part in the engagements at Rocky Mount and Hanging Rock.

Returning to North Carolina after the battle of Hanging Rock, Sumter met Colonel James Williams, who had decided to return to **At Musgrove's Mill** the Ninety-Six District, in South Carolina. Such of Brandon's and Steen's regiments as desired it, joined Williams, who immediately repaired to Smith's Ford, on Broad River. Colonel Charles McDowell, who was lying at the Cherokee Ford, a few miles above, detached a small force under Colonels Shelby and Clarke to join Williams in an expedition against the Tories at Musgrove's Mill, on the Enoree River. Lieutenant Joseph Hughes being one who desired to return to South Carolina with Williams, took part in the brilliant affair at Musgrove's.

After the contest at Kings Mountain had raged about an hour, the British lost their leader, Major Patrick Ferguson, and being surrounded **Hughes at Kings Mountain** and "hemmed like ducks in a coop," they hung out the white flag in token of surrender. For some reasons, it was with difficulty that the Americans were restrained from firing after the British and Tories were crying for quarter. At length order was restored and the mountaineers closed in and surrounded their prisoners. Colonel Campbell then proposed "three huzzas for liberty," which was readily acceded to, and the welkin rang with the shouts of victory.

According to Draper in his "Kings Mountain and Its Heroes," "an occurrence now transpired that for a few moments changed the whole scene in that quarter, and threatened, for a brief period, the most tragic consequences." A British account relates that "a small party of the loyal militia returning from foraging, unacquainted with the surrender, happening to fire on the rebels, the prisoners were immediately threatened with death if the firing should be repeated." It may have been a volley from this party or some other Tories who were enraged because proper respect had not been paid to their flag. At any rate, there was firing done, which, says Draper, "mortally wounded Colonel Williams, who was riding towards the British encampment." Colonel Campbell, being nearby when this unfortunate affair occurred, doubtless reasoned that if the fire was from an outside party it was the advance of Tarleton's expected relief; or, if from the surrendered Tories, it was a bold attempt to shoot down the Whig leaders and escape. Acting on the spur of the moment, he ordered the men of Williams' and Brandon's commands to fire on the enemy, which was instantly obeyed with deadly effect. Hughes says: "Was at Kings Mountain. General Williams, of South Carolina, was killed after the British raised their flag to surrender by a fire from some Tories. Colonel Campbell then ordered a fire on the Tories, and we killed near a hundred of them after the surrender of the British, and could hardly be restrained from killing the whole of them."

When the victors at Kings Mountain hastened to North Carolina for the security of themselves and their prisoners, it appears that Hughes did not go with them, but returned to his home vicinity, where he and a few adventurous spirits like himself harrassed the Tories whenever and wherever they could find an opportunity.

When General Morgan came into South Carolina near the end of the year 1780, Hughes with his associates were ready to join Morgan, and when that daring feat took place at Hammond's Store, he was there to do his part.

We take the following from Draper's "Kings Mountain and Its Heroes": "Though yet a Lieutenant, he (Hughes) commanded his company at Cowpens. He was not only a man of great personal strength, but of remarkable fleetness on foot. As his men, with others, broke at The Cowpens and fled before Tarleton's cavalry, and though receiving a sabre cut across his right hand, yet with his drawn sword he would outrun his men and passing them, face about and com-

Hughes' Heroic Conduct at Cowpens

mand them to stand, striking right and left to enforce obedience to orders, often repeating with a loud voice: 'You d—d cowards, halt and fight—there is more danger in running than in fighting, and if you don't stop and fight, you will all be killed.' But most of them were for awhile too demoralized to realize the situation or obey the commands of their officers. As they would scamper off, Hughes would renewedly pursue, and once more gaining their front, would repeat his tactics to bring them to their duty. At length the company was induced to make a stand on the brow of a slope some distance from the battle line behind a clump of young pines that partially concealed and protected them from Tarleton's cavalry. Others now joined them for self-protection. Their guns were quickly loaded and they were themselves again. Morgan galloped up and spoke words of encouragement to them. The next moment the British cavalry were at them, but the Whigs reserved their fire till the enemy were so near that it was terribly effective, emptying many a British saddle. Then the survivors recoiled. Now Colonel Washington gave them a charge—the battle was restored when Howard and his Marylanders with the bayonet swept the field. Such is the account related by Christopher Brandon to Daniel Wallace. Tarleton acknowledges that an unexpected fire from the Americans, which came about as they were retreating, stopped the British and threw them into confusion, when a panic ensued and then a general flight. It was a high and worthy compliment from his old commander, Colonel Brandon, who declared that at The Cowpens *"Hughes saved the fate of the day."*

Major Thomas Young, a fellow soldier with Hughes, relates the following: "He was at The Cowpens and when the charge was made upon the militia by Tarleton's cavalry, the flint came off Hughes' gun; a dragoon struck at him several times and cut the barrel of his gun. Hughes dodged around a tree several times, till he got a chance to club his gun, which he threw and struck the dragoon and nearly dismounted him; the fellow then left him." A similar, if not the same incident, is narrated by William Sims: "In time of the retreat of the militia, Joseph Hughes was hotly pursued by two British dragoons. His gun was not charged, and he made the best defense he could by parrying their blows with his rifle and dodging around a tree. When they overtook him, John Savage was in the act of priming his rifle. As soon as he got ready, he shot down one of the dragoons, and Hughes struck the other with the butt of his gun and nearly dismounted him. As soon as the fellow could command the reins, he put spurs to his horse and fled." Sims furthermore says: "I have heard John Savage say that Hughes looked like a mad bull in the time of the battle of Cowpens. He was large, strong and active, and would be ahead; he sweated and foamed at the mouth."

As a deserved recognition of his incalculable and invaluable services rendered, early in 1781 he was promoted Captain when he was **Promoted to the Captaincy** scarcely twenty years of age. He was at the Battle of Eutaw Springs, fought in August, 1781, and led his company with his usual daring and characteristic bravery. He says: "This was the severest engagement I ever was in."

This was the last general engagement that Captain Hughes took part in, although he remained in the service until the close of the war, being engaged in several skirmishes with Tories, but none of note.

Though a mere boy, Hughes was of a reckless and dare-devil character rarely possessed by any man. In the summer of 1780, **Some Dare-Devil Adventures of Hughes** Major Patrick Ferguson, with his hordes of British and Tories, were moving slowly through the Fairforest settlements, camping as long as three weeks in one place. The Whig families were defenseless, as a number of officers and privates had taken British protection, and those in arms had fled to North Carolina and elsewhere, thereby leaving them on the mercy of Ferguson's foraging parties and bands of Tory plunderers. But these marauding bands were not entirely unmolested. Their conduct was more than the fiery Hughes could tolerate, for by this time there were several boys who were able to bear arms; hence, they organized a company called the "Hughes Guerrillas," adopting for their motto, "We do and dare; in God we trust."

Besides the Hughes', there were other choice spirits such as "Old Squire" Kennedy, William Kennedy, his son, William Sharp, Thomas Young, Joseph McJunkin, Christopher **A Sort of "Invisible Empire"** Brandon and others, who determined to embarrass Ferguson's operations and those of his Tory allies. They formed a sort of "Invisible Empire." They would appear as suddenly and unexpectedly as if dropped from the skies, strike terror and death to their enemies, then disappear as quickly as they came; but to return when the prey appeared and repeat their tactics again and again.

Before proceeding, it will be well to get a glimpse of their leader. He is thus described: "William Kennedy stood conspicuous. He **William Kennedy** was of French Huguenot descent, the race to which Marion belonged. He was tall, handsome and athletic. His perception was quick, his sagacity equal to any emergency, and his ability sufficient for a great commander. But he persistently refused to accept any office, choosing rather to serve as a common soldier. He was regarded as the best shot with his rifle of any person in all that region. Whether on foot or horseback, at half-speed or a stand, he was never known to miss his aim. His rifle had a peculiar crack when it fired, which his acquaintances could recognize, and when its well-known report was heard it was a common remark, 'There is another Tory less!'

"Although he held no commission, yet the men of the neighborhood acknowledged him as their leader when danger was nigh, and their feet were ever in the stirrup at his bidding. His efforts were often called into requisition by the plundering excursions of the Tories sent out under the auspices of Ferguson, Dunlap and their subordinate officers. He and his comrades often saved their settlement from being overrun by these scouting parties. The crack of Kennedy's rifle was sure to be heard whenever a Tory was found, and it was the well-known signal for his friends to hasten to his assistance. He seemed almost to snuff the battle from afar; and the flush of determination would suffuse his manly countenance whenever he had reason to believe the enemy were near."*

On one occasion a British and Tory scouting party came into the settlement and began their accustomed work of plundering the **A Characteristic** women and children, taking all they had, both to **Adventure** eat and wear. Christopher Brandon and two of his companions, to use the language of the times, were "outlyers," not being able to stay at home on account of the danger of being massacred. One of Kennedy's runners notified them that there was an enterprise on foot. They mounted their horses and hastened to the place of rendezvous. Traveling an unfrequented cowpath through dense woods, they stopped at a small branch to

---
*Draper's "Kings Mountain and Its Heroes," page 129

let their horses drink. While thus halted, the crack of a rifle scattered the brains of one of Brandon's companions on his clothes and in his face, the same ball grazing his cheek, while the dead body of the unfortunate man tumbled into the brook beneath. Putting spurs to their horses, the two survivors received a volley from more than a dozen rifles fired by an unseen enemy, hidden behind the trees, but fortunately they escaped unhurt. The Tory party had heard the approach of the horses of Brandon and his comrades and laid in wait for them.

Arriving at the place of meeting, they found some fifteen or twenty assembled under their bold leader, Kennedy, and were ready for hot pursuit. A few minutes before sunset they overtook the Tory band. They were engaged in plundering a house a short distance from the public road. The cries of the woman and her children attracted the attention of the Whig pursuers. The Tory sentinel fired when Kennedy and his party came near, which alarmed the robbers. They immediately dashed out, mounted their horses and fled. Each one selecting his man, the Whigs gave chase at full speed. Kennedy directed Brandon, who was young and inexperienced, to keep near him and fire only when told to do so.

A man named Neal was the Tory leader, and he was the one singled out and pursued by Kennedy. Neal fled through an open field towards the woods, some distance away. Kennedy kept the road, running nearly parallel with the fugitive, till he reached an open space in the hedge-row of bushes that had partially obstructed the view, when he suddenly cried out: "Whoa!" His horse being well trained, stopped suddenly, and quick as thought the crack of Kennedy's rifle brought Neal tumbling to the ground. When Kennedy and Brandon reached him, he was stone dead, having been shot through the body. The distance of Kennedy's fire was one hundred and forty yards. More than half the Tory party was killed. Relating this adventure in his old age, Brandon said: "Not one prisoner was taken, for it occurred but seldom—our rifles usually saved us that trouble." The Tory booty was re-taken and all restored to the distressed woman and children.*

The celebrated "Fairforest Shoal" (now Murphy's) was on Fairforest Creek, five miles south of the present site of Union. On

---

*Draper's "Kings Mountain and Its Heroes"

"Another Tory Less" the heights overlooking this shoal was an old stockade fort or block-house. Many tragic incidents occurred there and in its vicinity. A Tory, whose name is now unknown, had with his band done much mischief in that region, his greatest crime being the killing of one of William Kennedy's dearest friends. To Kennedy this was unpardonable, and he determined to have revenge. Learning that the culprit was in striking distance, he called his friends together and went in search of him. The two parties met some two or three miles from the block-house and a severe contest followed. The Tories were routed, and the leader, the prize sought by Kennedy, fled. Kennedy, accompanied by Hughes, Sharp, McJunkin and others, pursued. The chase was one of life or death. The fleeing Tory came to a bank of the Fairforest at a point on a high bluff, where it was some twenty or thirty yards to the opposite bank and the water quite deep. Being hemmed by his pursuers, the Tory hesitated not a moment, but put spurs to his horse and plunged over the precipice into the stream below. It was a fearful leap, but Kennedy and his party followed, and on the opposite bank they bagged their game.

Getting their powder wet in the *melee,* they resolved to take their captive below the block-house and hang him. When they arrived there, the officer in command would not permit him to be disposed of in that manner, but ordered him to be taken to Colonel Brandon's camp to be tried by court-martial. Kennedy was placed at the head of the guard, but the Tory begged that Kennedy might not be permitted to go; for he feared that he would kill him on the way. His request was not heeded, however, and they had not gone very far before the prisoner made a dash for liberty; but Kennedy's unerring rifle soon stopped his flight. His remains were brought back to the foot of the hill near the block-house and there buried, where his grave was pointed out for many years afterward.*

Early one morning, Hughes left his hiding place as an honorable "out-lyer" for the purpose of paying a brief visit to his father's home on the west side of Broad River. Apprehensive of his danger, he approached the house cautiously on horse-back, and when within a few steps of it, three Tories sprang out of the door and with their

Hughes' Narrow Escape at Home

---

*Draper's "Kings Mountain and Its Heroes"

guns presented, shouted with great exultation: "You d—d rebel, you are our prisoner!"

"You are d—d liars!" defiantly yelled Hughes, and in an instant he spurred his horse to full speed. As he cleared the gate at a single bound all three of the Tories fired, but missed their mark, and he made his escape without a single scratch. These Tories had been in wait for him all night and had just entered the house to get their breakfast when Hughes rode up. Naturally they were much crestfallen after having taken so much pains to secure such a plucky enemy of King George, and then to be so completely foiled in their purpose.

In one of the many encounters with Tories, Hughes had a lock of hair cut from his head, Captain Samuel Otterson slightly wounded on his chin, while a third person received a cut across the cheek—all by the same ball.

Loses a Lock of Hair

Hearing that a Tory party, with considerable booty, was concealed in a dense thicket on Sandy River, in Chester District, Hughes, in company with Colonels Brandon, Casey, Majors Young, Jolly and some others, went to attack them. Says one of the party: "We got there early in the day, and it was not long before we had possession of the place." Major Thomas Young says: "During this skirmish I witnessed rather an amusing scene between Colonel Hughes and a Tory. Hughes had dismounted to get a chance to shoot at some fellows through the bushes, when a Tory sprang upon his horse and dashed away. Hughes discovered it in time, fired and put a ball through the hind-tree of the saddle and the fellow's thigh. The Tory fell and Hughes got his horse."

At Sandy River

A short time after the battle of Kings Mountain, Hughes, with six or eight others, were lurking in the thickets along Brown's Creek for the purpose of obtaining intelligence of both friends and foes William Sharp, William Giles, John Savage and Charles Crane are said to have been in the party. Late one afternoon they captured a "pet" Tory, who was a Whig or Loyalist, as occasion demanded, and from him they learned that a large party of Tories, some two hundred and fifty strong, intended to camp that night at a schoolhouse near Hollingsworth's Mill, on Brown's Creek. The house was on a high hill, which was covered with thick woods. Hughes and his party de-

The Affair at Hollingsworth's Mill

cided to give them a scare, and arranged their plans accordingly. Putting a rope around the Tory's neck they carried him with them, and shortly after dark they cautiously approached the enemy's camp, spread themselves out around the hill some distance from each other, with the understanding that they should advance until hailed by the sentinel, lie down until they fired, then rise up rush towards the camp, firing one at a time, and shouting at the top of their voices.

As the daring Whigs moved noiselessly up the hill, the Tory campfires threw a glaring light towards the overspreading canopy of the heavens, and lit up the forest far and near. All was joy and gladness in the camp, for the unsuspecting Tories were dancing, carousing, and going on at a great rate. The jovial song and the merry laugh told the listening ears of the approaching Whigs that good cheer abounded among the friends of King George. But hark! In a moment, in the twinkling of an eye, the scene changed. The sentinel hails, then he fires, and bang, bang, go the Whig's rifles as they discharge their missiles of death, accompanied by frightful screams and yells on every side. Terror-stricken, the Tories rushed pell-mell down the hill, crying "mercy! mercy!" at every bound. Hughes and his victorious party came into the camp one after another, and found fires burning, guns stacked, horses hitched, wagons standing around, and cooking utensils, with hats, caps and articles of clothing scattered about in the wildest confusion, but not a man was to be seen. No sound was heard except the gentle stamp of the tethered horses and the distant footfalls of the fleeing Tories, which grew fainter at each successive bound. They kept watch over the spoils until the gray twilight streaked the eastern sky, momentarily expecting the return of the party, but no one came. The sun rose and mounted high above the hills, and still no report from the deserters. The question then arose as to what should be done with the wagons, horses, guns, ammunition and baggage The decision was to cut a road down the hill to a secluded spot, some distance from the camp, to which place the booty was all safely transported, and watch was kept for several days.

At length one of the guard saw a party of fifteen rapidly approaching on horseback. He notified the others and a brief consultation was held. Their conclusion was that it was the advance guard of an army, coming to re-take the spoils, but they resolved to test the matter. They accordingly advanced and hailed the party, while their horses were drinking from the creek. The only response was a rapid and confused flight. They fired upon the fleeing foe, when a single horse fell, and his rider was speedily captured. The report before us says, "From him they learned that his party was just from Kings Mountain, and escaping as best they could from their assailants. Having gotten off from that scene of carnage, they were pushing on with no other object than personal safety."*

According to this last paragraph, the daring feat at Hollingsworth's was on while the battle of Kings Mountain was being fought. This is unquestionably a mistake, for the proof is positive that Hughes, Giles and Sharp were in that memorable engagement. The only satisfactory explanation is that Hughes and his party did not go with the mountain men when they fell back to North Carolina, but immediately returned to their home vicinity to continue their work of harrassing the Tories and embarrass them in every way possible. It will be remembered that a party of Loyalists arrived at Kings Mountain after the British had surrendered, fired, and then scampered off. This party, or some other from the same place, could have lingered on the way sufficiently long for the achievement at Hollingsworth's to have taken place.

Seldom, if ever, was a more daring feat undertaken with greater results attained than that pulled off by Hughes and his half-dozen associates at Hollingsworth's Mill; for no one ever appearing to molest them, they went out and gathered as many of their friends as they could, among whom they divided their spoils, which they appropriated to their own use and enjoyment.

The Burning of Thomas Hughes' House William Hughes resided on the west side of Broad River, probably below the Lockhart Shoals, and his brother Thomas, a short distance lower down. Learning that the "Guerrilas" were on the other side of the river, the Tories seized the opportunity to burn the houses of these two men. They burned the house of Thomas Hughes about ten o'clock at night. Mrs. Hughes was in bed, with a two weeks' old infant. She was driven from the house with the other children, and compelled to take refuge in a negro cabin. The bed on which she lay was ripped open and the feathers strewn over the yard. They took what provisions they wanted and destroyed the balance;

---

*Saye's "Memoir of McJunkin."

COLONEL JOSEPH HUGHES 211

then proceeded up the river with the intention of burning William Hughes' house, but stopped on the way to cook some of their stolen rations and rest until just before daylight, when they expected to proceed with their fiendish destruction.

Learning that the Tories were in the vicinity on a rampage, Mrs. William Hughes went in great haste to notify her kindred and friends on the other side of the river. Leaving her children in the care of a faithful slave called "Old Hector," she went to the river and rowed across, about twelve o'clock at night, apprised the soldiers of the Tory movement and returned in safety to her home. With the assistance of the negroes and children that were large enough to help, she went to work burying and hiding clothing, dishes, and everything that the Tories would be apt to carry off.

In the meantime, the men aroused on the other side of the river got busy. Grasping their arms, they mounted their horses and hastened after the marauders, whom they soon came up with in their temporary camp, and opened fire—completly surprising them. Some were feasting on the stolen provisions, some were asleep, while others were playing cards and exulting over the destruction they had wrought. There were fifty men in the Tory party, but so complete was their surprise, they left everything, and fled in every direction. Some had the presence of mind to mount their horses, while others were left standing. Some few were killed. One Tory, by the name of Love, was so closely pursued that he plunged into the river and attempted to ford the stream. While thus making his way one of the Hughes men took aim and fired, killing him instantly. From that time until now that part of Broad River has been known as *Love's Ford* Thus by the heroism of a brave woman the house of William Hughes was saved and a Tory party broken up.

So bitter were the Tory feelings against the Hughes' that Thomas was murdered by them after peace had been declared. One morning, just at daybreak, Thomas Hughes, assisted by "Cupid," one of his slaves, was calling his hogs in front of his gate, when a party of Tories passing by shot him, the ball passing through his head. Joseph, his eldest son, and the subject of this sketch, immediately mounted his faithful charger, "Rattling Jack," which had carried him through the war, and went in pursuit. He killed six of the Tories, the last one

The Murder of Thomas Hughes

of that number being named Steadman, who was killed near Cross Keys, in the western part of Union District.

Hughes pursued him so closely that the Tory dismounted, left his horse, and fled through the fields and woods on foot. He attempted to cross over a very high rail fence, called a "stake and rider fence." Just as he leaped the top rail, a bullet from Hughes' trusty rifle, directed by his eagle eye, penetrated the Tory's spine. Hughes rode up hastily, examined the body, and being satisfied that life was extinct, he remounted "Rattling Jack," and turned his face homeward to console his mother, brothers and sisters. Selecting a spot on his plantation, they buried the body of the staunch old Whig there, the place now being known as "the old Hughes burying ground." His grave is not marked, but it is said it can be identified.

William Hughes, uncle of Colonel Joseph, and his son John lost their lives in the siege of Ninety-Six.

William Hughes, Jr., son of William, Sr., was sent with an important message from Ninety-Six to another post. He was overtaken by a squad of Whig soldiers, who were operating there, but were strangers in the locality. These soldiers mistook young Hughes for a Hessian soldier and were about to shoot or hang him, when another party of Whigs rode up and identified him, and he was saved. From that time he acquired the name of "Hessian Hughes," and his numerous nieces and nephews ever spoke of him as "Uncle Hessian."

"Uncle Hessian"

Richard Hughes was said to be a brother of Thomas and William. During the war, he buried some money and other valuables The Tories hearing about it, came and demanded the booty. Hughes refused to tell them where it was. The Tories hung him up and cut him down, but he refused to divulge the secret. This was done the third time, when his daughter, who was frantic, told them, and they left him and went and got the stuff. He lived about a week, and then died from the effects of the hanging. The place where the hanging occurred is still known as "Hughes' Hill." Tradition says that when the "Hill" was cleared by Elisha Porter, Esq., nearly a century ago, all the iron belonging to an army gun of that period were found by Porter's sons.

The Hanging of Richard Hughes

We take the following from recollections narrated by William

Sims, who was a lad of eight or ten summers at the time the stirring events he mentions took place: "A party consisting of eight persons were on a scout. They were John Jolly, William Sharp, William Giles, Old Richard Hughes, his son John Hughes, James Johnson, an Irishman, Charles Crane, and a man named Allbritton. They stopped at old Leighton's, near Fairforest, not far above the mouth. Leighton was of doubtful politics, inclined, however, to the strongest side. The house was in the midst of the plantation, and passed by a lane. At the time the scouts stopped a hundred Tories were lying on the other side of the creek. Leighton is believed to have sent them word. In a short time the Tories came and formed across the lane on each side of the house. Two of them then came near the house and fired on the Whigs. Sharp and Giles mounted their horses and charged through the lines and made good their retreat. Jolly and Crane attempted to run off through the field. Crane succeeded, but Jolly was shot through and killed immediately. I saw him the next morning early; my mother heard the firing and went up in the morning; she sent word to Jolly's wife, and got him buried."

The Affair at Leighton's

"The four Whigs that remained in the house kept up a fire till night, when they were forced to capitulate. They were carried to Ninety-Six and put in jail, where old Hughes and his son both died. The others returned. Several Tories were killed and wounded in this engagement."*

Thus it will be seen that the Hughes' suffered very bitterly during and even after the Revolution, the family being largely exterminated; but by the time of the Civil War they had become quite numerous, and several of them gave their lives for the Lost Cause.

Soon after the war was over the youthful hero set sail on the matrimonial sea—one not disturbed by the storms of Tory devastation nor the mutterings of British oppression—seeking a quiet home in bright and sunny climes, where only the gentle zephyrs of liberty—sweet liberty—rustled among the trees of hill and dale, which liberty he had helped to purchase at such a tremendous cost.

Gets Married

---

*It will be seen that two Richard Hughes have been mentioned—one hung on Hughes' Hill, and the other dying at Ninety-Six At this late day it is impossible to give an explanation

Joseph Hughes married Sarah Brown,† and settled on his father's farm, on Broad River, where he remained until 1825. Naturally, we would suppose that he went about his home building with the same energy and unflinching courage that he exhibited when facing danger and death at the hands of enemies in time of war.

He lost his house by fire in 1788 or 1789, and with it his army official commissions and many other valuable papers and records. He was sheriff of Union District at that time, but how long he held that office we do not know.

Says Draper: "For more than twenty of the closing years of his life he was an elder of the Presbyterian Church, and the rough and almost tiger-like partisan became as humble and submissive as a lamb."

Becomes a Soldier of the Cross

The church of which Hughes first became a member having played such a prominent part in the early history of Union District, it deserves special notice. Among the first settlers in that section were the Brandons, Bogans, Jollys, Kennedys, and McJunkins. A little later came the Cunninghams, Hughes, Savages, Youngs, Vances, and Wilsons. The country being an uninhabited wild, these adventurers lived in tents until they could build cabins. Several of these were truly pious, and frequently met on the Lord's Day for religious services. That they might have better facilities, they selected a site near the center of their settlements and erected a house of worship. It was on Big Brown's Creek, about three miles from Union, near the road now leading from that place towards Mt. Tabor. The name given it was Brown's Creek, but being built for the use of both Presbyterians and Episcopalians, it was called "The Union Church." The worshipers and attendants there being almost, if not entirely, uncompromising Whigs, two houses were burnt during the Revolution by Tories, we presume.

The hallowed recollections and sacred memories that clustered around "The Union Church" must have been deeply engraved on the hearts of these fearless defenders of the Faith and of their country; for when the rights of self-government were obtained and when court districts were adopted and laid off by the State, the one in which "Union Church" was situated was named for it. Hence, Union, and Union County.

---

†Gabriel Brown was a captain in the Whig ranks and resided at, or near, the mouth of Brown's Creek. The creek was named after him. Sarah, the bride of Joseph Hughes, may have been his daughter.

Some time after the war the Presbyterians alone erected a house of worship about two miles east of Union, near the present Monarch Cotton Mills, and the original name, Brown's Creek, was retained. It was of this church that Colonel Joseph Hughes became a member and elder. Samuel McJunkin, Joseph McJunkin, William Kennedy, Thomas Kennedy, Christopher Brandon and John Savage, all Revolutionary Patriots of the first water, also served this church as elders.

Dr. Howe, in his "History of the Presbyterian Church in South Carolina," pays the following tribute to Hughes: "Colonel Joseph Hughes was also in the war, and won distinction on the battlefield. He was a large and powerful man; was greatly beloved by his associates for his generosity and noble daring."

Hughes resided on his father's farm, on Broad River, until 1825, when he removed to Greene County, Alabama, and settled near the line between Greene and Pickens; and in the fall of 1829 he moved across the line to Pickens, where he remained until his death, which took place in September 1834, in the seventy-fourth year of his age.

Removed to Alabama

We close this narrative by further tribute of Lyman C. Draper: "He rose to the rank of colonel in the militia. He was tall and commanding in his appearance, jovial and affable in conversation; yet his early military training rendered him to the last stern and rigid in discipline. In all that makes up the man, he was a noble specimen of the Revolutionary hero."

The Life of Major Joseph McJunkin

COPIES of Major McJunkin's personal recollections and a memoir of him, written by his grandson-in-law, the Rev. James H. Saye, being in our possession, gives us ample first-hand material for an extended narrative. Living in what is now Union County, and marrying in what is now Spartanburg, McJunkin mentions the names of many individuals who lived in, and relates many thrilling events which took place in that section. This is very fortunate for lovers of history and adventure; because only a few of the most noted individuals and the greater conflicts are mentioned by historians. There are but few spots in all this up-country that have not been the scene of greater or lesser struggles in the cause of freedom. Much of the soil that we now tread upon has drank the blood of friend or foe, and beneath the sod lie the bones of each.

The Rev. James H. Saye begins his "Memoir" as follows: "It is proposed by the writer to give in the following pages a detailed statement of the personal exploits of Major Joseph McJunkin in the Revolutionary War in this country, together with remarks and observations concerning his contemporaries, and the interesting events of which they were, in the hand of Providence, the instrumental cause."

Joseph McJunkin was born on the 22nd day of June, 1755, near Carlisle, in the State of Pennsylvania. His father, Samuel McJunkin, Esq., was a native of Ireland. His mother, whose maiden name was Bogan, was a native of Pennsylvania. His ancestry was wholly Scotch and Scotch-Irish. At the time of his birth the frontiers of Pennsylvania and Virginia were in a state of consternation. War was on between France and England, and the Indians sided with the French. The defeat of Braddock, the English general, had occurred about the time of McJunkin's birth. The Indian tribes, bordering on the white settlements, were in a state of hostility before that disastrous event, and its occurrence opened the way for them to fall upon the defenseless pale-faces. Large numbers fled, leaving home and property, and sought refuge in the interior. The prospects for the subjugation of the Indians were

216

gloomy, and until that was effected the refugees dared not return to their homes along the frontier. Hence, they looked elsewhere for places where they might dwell in safety.

A short time before these events, James Glen, the English governor of South Carolina, had by treaty purchased from the Indians a large section of territory in the upper part of the Province, the soil of which was fertile and the climate salubrious. Says Mr. Saye: "The country from the Pee Dee to the Savannah, in all the up-country, was measurably void of inhabitants, smiling in all the richness of virgin beauty. Game was abundant. 'The range' was as good as heart could wish. The rich valleys of the Catawba, Broad, Saluda, and Savannah rivers, with their numerous tributaries, offered all the husbandman could ask. Under these circumstances, a large number of the exiles in Pennsylvania and Virginia, with their friends, sought homes in the sunny plains of the South. For here the Red Man was a peaceful neighbor, and gladly exchanged his peltries and furs for the products of civilized men."

Among the emigrants who came to South Carolina was Samuel McJunkin. He stopped on Tinker Creek, in what is now Union County, December 24, 1755. A number of his friends and relatives settled in the same section about the same time. Among these were the Brandons, Bogans, Youngs, Steens, Jollys, Kennedy and others. These were all Scotch-Irish. In fact, a goodly number of the early settlers in upper South Carolina were of the same stock. In matters of religion they were principally strong adherents of the Presbyterian faith. Being remote from the older settlements, these pious people did not enjoy the privileges of church services nor the regular preaching of the Gospel by a stated minister, but these disadvantages did not deter them from the performance of their religious duties. Mr. Saye says: "The Presbyterian population, in a large section of the country roundabout, were dependent upon ministers of the Gospel at a distance for supplies. These supplies were ordered at meetings of Presbytery, when pastors, with the consent of their congregations, agreed to spend a certain number of weeks in traveling for the supply of destitute churches and neighborhoods. They also sent out missionaries, when men of suitable qualifications could be obtained. Pious people often met in those days on the Sabbath, sang and prayed together, read the Scriptures, sermons, etc. Family religion was diligently attended to. Children and servants were instructed in the doctrines and duties of religion. A rigid discipline was maintained in the family, and especially so in regard to proper observance of the Sabbath."

"The earliest recollections of Major McJunkin were in regard to things which occurred during his father's absence from home for the protection of the frontier. His mother prayed with him and her other children during his father's absence, and these prayers were the first things of which he had any recollection. So that although our hero received but little of the benefits of the services of the schoolmaster and minister during the period of minority, yet the foundation of a religious education was laid deep in his nature. These instructions had an abiding influence, and doubtless had much to do in the actions of his subsequent life."

Although these strict religionists and lovers of freedom had fled from their Pennsylvania and Virginia habitations to the havens of Carolina for peace and safety, they did not enjoy these boons very long. Serious Indian troubles arose, and they had to shoulder their guns in defense of their homes and families. This was the reason for Samuel McJunkin being away in little Joseph's early childhood, and that all the family duties and religious training devolved upon the mother.

When trouble arose between the Colonies and the mother country, the tyrannical spirit manifested by the latter caused public **Troubles Begin** meetings to be held all over the country, the result **with the** of which was the assembling of the Continental **Mother Country** Congress, in Philadelphia, October, 1774.

To give strength to the acts of this Congress, the people of South Carolina determined to convene a Provincial Congress, or what we would now call a State Convention. Delegates to attend this Congress were elected from every parish and district in the Province. This body held its first meeting January 11, 1775. The acts of the Continental Congress were approved, and a General Committee and a Council of Safety appointed. The powers of the General Committee were judicial; those of the Council of Safety, executive. Says McCrady: "This council was vested with supreme power over the army, the militia, and all military affairs; in fact, they were the executive government of the colony. To this council was delegated authority to grant commissions, suspend officers, order courtmartials, direct, regulate, maintain and order the army and all military establishments, and of drawing on the treasury for all purposes of public service."

At this time the English government had the Province divided into, what was called, regimental districts, the chief executive of which was some military official, whose duties were to look after the interests of the Crown. The upper district embraced all of the territory between the Broad and Saluda rivers, and was presided over by Colonel Thomas Fletcher (Drayton, in his "Memoirs," calls him Fletchall), who resided on Fairforest, at what is now known as the Murphy Shoals, five miles south of Union. It was said that at the beginning of the Revolution a majority of the people within the bounds of Fletcher's district were Loyalists, and that it was due to his influence. He was popular among the people, had many friends, and when a commission was tendered him by the Republican party in the Province he refused it, and exerted his influence among the people to induce them to continue their allegiance to the Crown. At this time Samuel McJunkin, his relatives and friends were prominent in the Liberty party.

Knowing the situation in Fletcher's district, the Council of Safety deemed it wise to send an embassy into the territory and explain to the people the grounds of dispute with the mother country, and induce as many as possible to enlist in the cause of liberty. Consequently, in the summer of 1775, William Henry Drayton, the Rev. William Tennant and the Rev. Josiah Hart were sent to the up-country. When passing through what is now Laurens, Spartanburg, Union and Chester, these venerable gentlemen were accompanied by Joseph McJunkin, who served them as guide. According to McJunkin, they called public meetings and addressed the people principally on the following topics: (1) "The Constitution of a Roman Catholic Colony in Canada," (2) "The Tax on Tea," (3) "The Stamp Act," (4) "The Imposition of Church Rates by the British Government, Without Allowing the Right of Representation in the British Parliament." McJunkin continues: "They also showed to the people that they of right ought to possess the power of self-government; that as British subjects this power was secured by law, and that they never should surrender their birthright."

This consideration was enforced by touching allusions to the privations and sufferings of the first settlers in this country for the sake of civil and religious liberty. These topics were discussed in a calm, persuasive and Christian-like manner, and had the effect of arousing many of the people to a proper appreciation of the rights of man. Finally, these gentlemen entered into a treaty or stipulation with that part of the population not disposed to resist the measures of the Crown by force of arms that they should remain peaceably at home.

The work of Messrs. Drayton, Tennant and Hart aroused Colonel Fletcher to action. He employed a man by the name of Joseph Robinson and used him as a mouthpiece in addressing public assemblies, and to counteract in any way possible the influence of the ambassadors of liberty. Robinson was a young man of classical education and respectable talents. He had been educated in Virginia for the Presbyterian ministry, but rendered himself peculiarly odious to that denomination by an attempt to obtain orders in the established church in that Province by fraud for one Cotton, an illiterate and abandoned wretch. The nature of the transaction was reported to the proper authorities, and Cotton and Robinson fled the country. McJunkin describes him as "a runaway from Virginia, a man of talent, but utterly void of correct principles."

This man Robinson was sent by Fletcher to Charleston to confer with Lord William Campbell, the Royal governor, as to the best means of keeping the people quiet and loyal. Campbell gave Robinson a number of pamphlets called "cutters," which were carried to Fletcher for distribution among the people. The scope of the teachings in these "cutters" was to show the sin of resisting the laws and policy of the Lord's annointed, the evils which would result, and to offer encouragement to support the measures of the British Crown. Fletcher called public meetings at different places and put Robinson up to address the people in behalf of those measures which he desired to see triumphant. One of these gatherings took place at a meeting house called Dining Creek. The crowd was too large to be accommodated in the building, so Robinson mounted a large rock in the woods and delivered his oration. He read one of the "cutters" and commented upon its contents. He alluded to the case of Saul and David to show the miseries which result from rebellion. He heaped abusive epithets upon the Continental Congress, George Washington, and the principles they advocated. He asserted that when they had involved the people in inextricable difficulties the d——d rascals would run away to the Indian Islands, Spaniards, etc. When this sentence was uttered Samuel McJunkin remarked: "I wonder where Preachers Joe Robinson and Cotton will then be?"

This inquiry by the elder McJunkin so overwhelmed him with a sense of shame that he abruptly descended from his rostrum and went off. As he was going he was heard to say: "I would have carried my point if it had not been for that d——d old Irish Presbyterian, but he has defeated me."

Fletcher, however, continued his efforts to quiet the misgivings of the people as to the measures of the Royal government, and persuading them to believe that their best interests and loyalty were identical. Being poular and influential, his success was considerable.

Major McJunkin begins his personal narrative with the following dream: "I saw a great collection of people, apparently much **A Notable Dream** agitated. They were at a house, and in the yard was a beautiful tree with many branches.. A great storm arose, with the appearance of the blackness of darkness, and raged so that everything appeared likely to be torn to pieces. Finally the tree was spilt to pieces, which greatly distressed the people, who, after the storm abated, raised the pieces from the ground and fastened them together with cords, hoping it would grow together again and flourish.

"At the same time there was this uncommon appearance. a sun arose in the West at the clearing up of the storm, the common sun shining at the same time, but the little sun which arose in the West shone with such brilliancy as to obscure the common luminary of day."

As the Major makes no comment on the dream, we leave it to our readers to put their own interpretation upon it.

In the fall of 1775, Robert Cunningham, a popular man, residing in what is now Laurens County, publicly declared that he would not **McJunkin Begins His Military Career** be bound by the treaty made with a portion of the people by Drayton, Tennant and Hart. He was, therefore, arrested and sent to Charleston. His brother, Patrick Cunningham, raised a body of men and went in pursuit to rescue him, but was too late to accomplish that object.

The Cherokee Indians, not having received their usual supplies, were in a very bad humor. To quiet them, the Council of Safety sent out a quantity of ammunition. This was captured by Cunningham and his party. They also formed an alliance with the Cherokees. This intelligence spreading through the country, a party of Whigs assembled under Major Williamson and pursued the Tories, but failed to restore peace.

In the month of November, the Provincial Congress raised an army for the purpose of subduing the Tories and to reduce the Indians to peace, as they were committing depredations along the frontiers. General Richard Richardson was appointed commander-in-chief of this expedition. John Thomas, Sr., who resided on Fairforest Creek, just above the mouth of Kelso's Creek, was ordered by Richardson to raise a regiment and meet him at Granby. This he succeeded in doing without having to draft a single man. The name was the Spartan Regiment, and John Thomas was colonel. This event marked an epoch in this up-country, for no body of men, equal in number, ever played a more important part in the drama of the Revolution and in subsequent events than did those composing the Spartan Regiment. The region roundabout soon took the name of Spartan District; hence the origin of Spartanburg.

Among the companies in Thomas' Regiment was one commanded by Captain Thomas Brandon. Joseph McJunkin, the subject of this sketch, had enlisted in Brandon's company, and thus began real military service.

Colonel Thomas immediately proceeded to Granby, where he met General Richardson. The army then moved to Weaver's Ferry, on the Saluda, and encamped. While there two of Fletcher's emissaries, Benjamin Wofford and Betty Scruggs, made their appearance They were on their return from Charleston, where they had been to carry some dispatches to the British governor. They were very merry and took close notice of things without seeming to do so. Some of the soldiers knew them and reported to Colonel Thomas, who had them arrested. Wofford was first searched, but nothing was found. Betty was then taken into a camp and her outer garment, called a Joseph, was taken off. The captain succeeded in finding a bundle of papers in a bag under her skirt, which fully apprised General Richardson of the intended movements of the Tories and their plan of union with the British governor.

Being thus informed, Richardson proceeded, through what is

now Lexington District, to a place in Laurens called Liberty Hill. Here he was joined by Governor Martin, of North Carolina. While at that place, Richardson, being informed of Fletcher's measures, sent out a party of horsemen to arrest him. He was found on his own plantation, and with two of his captains, John Mayfield and James ─────, was secreted inside of a large hollow in a sycamore tree. They were carried to Richardson's camp, and after examination were sent as prisoners to Charleston.

The next move of the now combined armies was to Hollingsworth's Mill, on Rabun's Creek, at which place they arrived December 24, 1775. The next day snow began to fall, and continued without intermission for thirty-six hours. The ground was covered two feet deep. The army had no tents, and their clothes and shoes were terribly worn. For a week or more they did not set foot on the ground, only when they cleared away places to build their fires for cooking and warming purposes. This terrible snow and the sufferings which it brought on gave it the name of "The Snow Campaign." While at Hollingsworth's a party was sent to a Tory camp, on Reedy River, twelve miles away. The Indians and Tories ran off without making much resistance. On the return of the party the campaign broke up, the purposes of the suffering Patriots, for the time, being accomplished.

Richardson, in a letter to the Council of Safety, dated January 2, 1776, says: "The people are now more convinced than ever of their being wrong. The lenient measures have had a good effect; the spirit and power is gone from them. And I am sure, if not interrupted by designing men, that the country which I had it in my power to lay waste, and which the people expected, will be happy, and peace and tranquility take the place of ruin and discord. On the rivers, had I burned, plundered and destroyed, ten thousand women and children must have been left to perish, a thought shocking to humanity."

Richardson's optimistic hopes were not of long duration, for the "designing men" soon got busy and a storm of greater fury than ever burst upon the country.

About March, 1776, Colonel Fletcher, by some means, was released from imprisonment in Charleston, and he returned to the **Indian** back-country, where he again used all his powers **Massacres** to arouse the Tories to action. The Indians were also enlisted One Alexander Cameron, a deputy superintendent among the Cherokees, a desperately bad man and emissary of King George, assembled four hundred warriors together, and by the use of every possible intrigue and argument induced them to take up arms against the friends of liberty. Hence, there was a combination or alliance formed by British, Tories and Indians. Fletcher and Cameron were aided in their work by John Stewart and Richard Paris, agents of the British government.

In accordance with previous arrangements, on the 20th of June the Indians began the work of death among the Whig families along the frontiers from North Carolina into Georgia. It was at this period that the Hampton, the Hannon, the Bishop and other massacres took place within the present limits of Spartanburg. In order that the homes of the Tories might be known and thereby rendered immune to the tomahawk and scalping knife, they peeled poles, wrapped them with white cloth, erected them before their houses and sat under them. These were called passovers. All who had passovers and sat under them were passed by unhurt, except one instance, that of Captain James Ford, who lived on the Enoree, at a place called the Canebrake He and his wife were killed under their passover, and his daughters taken captive by the Indians.

Apprehensive of the Indian outbreak, in May a party of Whigs had assembled under General William Williamson, and were encamped on Fairforest, near the residence of Colonel John Thomas. Messengers were sent out by Williamson to find out the intentions of the Indians, and they were killed by them. Hearing of the massacres and wanton killing of their friends, they went in pursuit of the murderers. The Indians were overtaken at Paris', an Indian agent who lived on the present site of Greenville. The Indians, with a few Tories, fled, but a number of prisoners were taken. Among the captives were the daughters of Captain Ford, previously mentioned.

After remaining a few days at Paris' and recruiting, Williamson continued the pursuit until he reached the nearest towns on the Seneca and Tugaloo. At one of these towns he came up with a party, which had an old lady prisoner by the name of High. She was killed by the Indians. When they found that they would be compelled to give way, they stripped her body and left it naked. Her nephew, Edward Hampton, was one of the party, and when he first saw her, supposing it to be the body of his aunt, he took off his hunting shirt and went back and covered the body, and afterwards buried it with as much decency as circumstances would admit.

Joseph McJunkin was in this expedition, and belonged to Captain Joseph Jolly's company in the Spartan Regiment. Continuing the campaign, McJunkin says: "After this we rendezvoused at a place called Seneca Town, upon the Seneca River, and some of us were permitted to go home for clothing, etc. After being refitted, we started to the middle settlement, on the French Broad. After passing through several towns, we went by a part of the North Carolina army, whose main body, as they supposed, had gone to attack the Indians in the valley towns. On the 22nd of September, just after passing this body of soldiers, the Indians had laid an ambuscade for the main North Carolina army, as they supposed." The Rev. James H. Saye thus describes what followed: "The Indians were posted on the crest and sides of a mountain in the form of a horseshoe. Williamson's advance defiled through the gorge, which might be called the heel, and were suffered to approach the part which may be called the toe. In an instant, in front, in rear, on the right and on the left the war-whoop sounded. The war-whoop was answered by a shout of defiance, and the rifles of the Indians answered by an aim equally deadly. The whites were pressed into a circle by their foes, and hence the battle was called 'The Ring Fight.' As soon as the firing was heard the main army pressed to the rescue. Before their arrival, the advance had to contend with fearful odds."

"It was not only a woodsman's fight from tree to tree, but often from hand-to-hand Among these Major Ross, of York District, had a hard scuffle with an Indian, in which the nerve of the white man prevailed over the dexterity of the red. On the arrival of the main army, the Indians were charged on all sides and driven from their chosen position. A large quantity of parched corn, dressed deerskins and moccasins were left on the ground. Among the slain a number of Creek Indians were discovered. In this action Colonels Thomas Neal, of York District; John Thomas, of Spartanburg; John Lyles, of Newberry; and Thomas Sumter participated. The latter, who commanded the regulars, particulary distinguished himself. Major Andrew Pickens also gave manifestations of those qualities which subsequently elevated him in the estimation of his fellow soldiers."

The next day Williamson, with his forces, proceeded to the valley towns, on a stream called Hiwassee, where a great quantity of corn and other provisions were destroyed. Some was thrown into the river and floated down, a part of which lodged in fish traps, and was afterwards found and preserved by the Indians. After spending a few days at these towns, the army crossed the Hiwassee and turned up another river called Lowassee, upon the banks of which were situated some other towns of great beauty. This stream flowed nearly from south to north. After ascending this river some distance, Williamson met the North Carolina army, and the two encamped near each other for one night.

Proceeding onward, Williamson crossed the head waters of the Chattahoochee River and passed a beautiful fenced town called Chota. Here intelligence was received that a force of Indians was encamped at a place called "Frogtown," some twenty miles distant. Colonel Thomas Sumter, with a party, was detached for the purpose of surprising them. Joseph McJunkin was one of the party. In obedience to the order, Sumter set out and the men passed over a fearful precipice, the width of the passage not exceeding fourteen inches. When they arrived at the place nobody was found except a few miserable old squaws. After burning and destroying "Frogtown" the party returned in the darkness of the night, not being able to discover the narrowness of their passage traveled over some time before. Williamson then returned to the Keowee towns, where a treaty was made with the Indians, in which they ceded their lands east of the Oconee Mountains, and bound themselves to live in peace. The territory thus acquired by the whites in South Carolina embraced what are now the counties of Greenville, Anderson and Pickens. A heavy penalty was exacted from the Indians for their alliance with the British and Tories. In some of the battles waged on this campaign, white men were taken disguised as Indians and using the same methods of warfare. Of course they were Loyalists.

Williamson's army disbanded at Seneca Town, with the understanding that the frontiers should be properly guarded. A line of posts was established form North Carolina to Georgia. McJunkin says: "In this campaign a number of Loyalists served in our army in consequence of the treachery of the Indians in the affair of Captain Ford. The Loyalists remained with us in defense of the frontier until the fall of Charleston, when they registered themselves subjects of his Britanic majesty."

In May, 1777, McJunkin received a captain's commission and took the command of a company in the Spartan Regiment, and was ordered to the frontiers by Colonel Thomas for duty He accordingly took command of Jamieson's Fort, on South Pacolet River, in the vicinity of Hogback Mountain, where he remained for three months. After this he spent the balance of the year scouting. His biographer says: "This service, in the circumstances of the country, required him to traverse the country beyond the forts established along the frontiers, to watch the movements of the Indians and bring in the intelligence to the commanding officer of his regiment. This service in all cases is dangerous and difficult when demanded by the necessities of war, is peculiarly hazardous when the enemy to be watched is sagacious, treacherous and cruel as were the Cherokees in 1777. This important trust was, however, well executed by Captain McJunkin, whether employed in watching the Red Men of the wilderness, or the white men who united their strength with the foes of their country and fell like beasts of prey upon the persons and property of their fellow citizens."

In the spring of 1778, the Spartan Regiment was divided, and the Second Spartan was formed, with Thomas Brandon as colonel. This regiment was composed principally of men living in what is now Union County. Captain McJunkin was transferred to the Second Spartan. In the month of June, 1778, McJunkin was ordered to lead his company to Bacon's Bridge, on the Ashley River. Shortly after arriving there, orders were received to disband the army. On his return he was again ordered to the frontier and took command at Wood's, or Thompson's Station, the place bearing both names. This fort (for such it was) stood near Beaver Dam Creek, between the Middle and South Tyger rivers, not far from McMakin's Bridge. It being near the boundary line between the whites and Indians, the fort was doubtless built by the early settlers for protection against the savages. Captain McJunkin remained at that place until February, 1779.

Amid the storms of warfare and savage butchery, the brave soldier found time to wage another contest and capture a prize of an entirely different kind and character—the heart of a noble and patriotic young woman—in whose veins flowed heroic blood. Hence, on the 9th day of March, 1779, Captain McJunkin was married to Miss Ann, the second daughter of John and Jane Thomas. John Thomas was the first colonel of the famous Spartan Regiment, and his wife, Jane, was the heroine of the first battle of Cedar Spring A writer says: "And though his choice was made in times that tried men's souls, he certainly never had cause, if reports be true, to regret it. His wife was worthy to be reckoned among the generation that won the independence of this nation."

Gets Married

On the first of November, 1779, Captain McJunkin was ordered by Colonel Brandon to go to Charlestown, where he remained for four months. While there he fell under the command of Lieutenant-Colonel James Steen, who was stationed at a place called the "Ten-Mile Spring." At the end of February, 1780, he, with his company, returned home. Charlestown fell in May following, and when the news reached the up-country the Whig population was greatly alarmed. Their consternation was all the more aggravated by the reports of the ravages of British victors and the insolence of the Loyalists, who now no longer disguised their devotion to the Royal cause. A large number of these had up to this time maintained a strict neutrality under the pretense of being non-combatants. They now no longer doubted the success of England, and in order to veil their past inactivities became quite despotic, as though they had ever been the champions of Britain.

Continues to Do Military Duty

On the fourth of June, Colonels Brandon, Thomas and Lyles met to consider means for mutual safety and protection of the country. They agreed to assemble their troops and form a camp near Fairforest Creek, about four miles from the present site of Union, on the road to Adam's Ford, on Tyger River. As the place was near the center of Brandon's command, his men were the first to arrive on the ground. He had in his possession a part of the powder formerly intrusted to Colonel Thomas, and its preservation being considered of the greatest importance, Brandon directed Joseph Hughes, William Sharp, John Savage, Aquilla Hollingsworth, Samuel Otterman, Benjamin Jolly and Joseph McJunkin to conceal it, which they did in the greatest care, in hollow logs in the neighboring forests.

While the above named party were away secreting the powder, Brandon's men in assembling had brought, as a prisoner, Adam Steedham, one of the kind then called a "pet Tory." Steedham escaped during the night, and apprised "Bloody" Bill Cunningham, who was not far away, of Brandon's position. Cunningham immediately set out to surprise Brandon, and made a charge on his camp soon after sunrise, killed a few men, took some prisoners, and dispersed the balance. Among the slain was a brother of Joseph McJunkin, and a youth by the name of John Young. This unfortunate affair took place on the 8th or 10th of June, 1780.

Robert Lusk, Esq., was taken prisoner by Cunningham and compelled to disclose the place where the powder was concealed. The work of hiding had been so effectually done that the Tories found but very little of it. This powder was afterwards stealthily carried over to the east side of Broad River and furnished the principal supply for Sumter's men at Huck's Defeat, Rocky Mount and Hanging Rock.

Colonels Thomas and Lyles hearing of Brandon's disaster before reaching him, made provision for the safety of their men. The party who had been engaged in hiding the powder, learning very soon of what had happened at Brandon's camp, collected as many of their friends as possible and retreated over Broad River to Bullock's Creek Church, in York District, which had been appointed as a place of rendezvous for faithful Patriots.

On the 12th of June, the refugees came together at the church. Among them were some of the regiments of Thomas, Lyles and Brandon, and a few who had fled from Georgia. Never was the cause of Independence in upper South Carolina seemingly in more desperate straits. An exceedingly dark cloud of gloom stretched itself across the Patriot skies. Says McJunkin: "Here we were in a sad case. Charleston was in the hands of the British, Brandon recently defeated, the enemy in force were spreading over the country, and we, like a flock of sheep without a leader, were assembled, and a few refugees from Georgia."

The situation described by McJunkin was disheartening in the extreme, but other still darker clouds having arisen, the tensity became sufficient to break any except wills and hearts of steel. Fully persuaded that the cause was hopeless, many loyal Patriots, including some distinguished leaders, had taken British protection and were paroled as prisoners of war. Patrick Ferguson, an efficient British officer, was sent up from Charleston, with a large force to subjugate the remainder.

Such were the conditions that confronted the little band of heroes at Bullock's Creek. What would they do? What could they do? At length a young man called his command together. He stated the facts connected with their present situation, he recounted their past toils, sufferings and dangers; he gave the reasons for the contest in which they had been engaged, and the instances of success and defeat which had attended their efforts in the cause of Independence. He said: "Our cause must now be determined. Shall we join the British, or strive like men for the noble end for which we have done and spent so much? Shall we declare ourselves cowards and traitors, or shall we fight for liberty as long as we have life? As for me, 'Give me liberty or give me death.'"

The speaker was John Thomas, son of Colonel John Thomas, Sr. Captain Joseph McJunkin followed Thomas, and addressed the assemblage, reiterating the same sentiments. The question was put: "All who are in favor of fighting the matter out throw up your hats and clap your hands." Every hat flew up, and the air resounded with the clapping of hands and shouts of defiance to the armies of Britain and the foes of liberty.

The Patriots then agreed to a resolution, allowing anyone to return home for additional clothing or any other necessity, provided he would agree to meet his companions at Tuccaseegee Ford, on the east side of the Catawba River. Captain McJunkin and most of the party set out at once for that place. Major Samuel Morrow, of Spartanburg, was one to meet Colonel Thomas Sumter.

After some consultation and various efforts to collect their scattered comrades, the party said to Sumter: "If we choose you our leader, will you direct our operations?" He replied: "I am under the same promise with you, our interests are identical, with me it is liberty or death." An election was held and Sumter was unanimously chosen general. The next day a report reached Sumter that there was a considerable number of Tories assembling at Ramseur's

Mill, in North Carolina. Says McJunkin: "We started before day, but did not reach the place until the battle was nearly over. The gallant Whigs of the neighborhood had assembled, under their own officers, and drove the Tories from the country with great slaughter."

The battle being over, Sumter remained in the vicinity of Ramseur's for a few days. While there he held a court of inquiry to consult as to the course of future operations. Captain McJunkin was a member of this court. His biographer inquires, "Let the reader now attempt to appreciate the magnitude of the questions coming legitimately under the consideration of this court. Its members were solemnly pledged to liberate South Carolina or die in the attempt. Their number is so small as to render any important achievement hopeless. Aside from this, they possess neither arms, provisions, nor any other military stores adequate for the equipment and substance for a single regiment for one week. Yet they resolved to return to South Carolina and repel force by force." McJunkin says: "Some said if we stick together the Tory will fly before us. Sumter said they are backed by men accustomed to fighting, and if we would gain liberty we must contend like men, and now is the time to strive like soldiers."

"We now prepared some wagons and hitched our horses to them, and some of us acted as wagoners. We went into the Catawba nation and encamped on a hill, which we called Poor Hill, as a memorial of our fare in that region. When we went over into North Carolina to half buy and half beg provisions, the inhabitants asked us why we did not stay at home and defend ourselves there. We got some barley and made batter. We put it into a kind of crock, dug a hole in the ground, set the crock in it and covered it over with hot ashes and embers, and cooked it without salt, beef or bacon, and it tasted mighty sweet."

Such is the picture drawn by one who took part in it, of the conditions, means and resources of Sumter's little band of half-clad and half-starved men when they turned toward their homes to face the tremendous odds which opposed them, their slogan being, "Give me liberty or give me death." Was there ever greater patriotism and bravery manifested on earth?

Sumter established his camp on Clem's Creek, in what is now Lancaster County, just below the North Carolina line. Here he was joined by a detachment of Whig volunteers, under Colonels Hill, Neal, Richard Hampton, Elijah Clarke, and Captain Samuel Hammond.

In the meantime, one Captain Huck had been sent out by the British Colonel Turnbull, and was committing the most horrible **Huck's Defeat** barbarities in York District—pillaging, burning and murdering. Huck was a Philadelphia lawyer, who had gone to the British in New York and joined Tarleton, when he was ordered to the South. The Rev. John Simpson was the minister in charge of Upper and Lower Fishing Creek Presbyterian churches. He was an ardent Whig, and was regarded as the head of the party who had broken up the Tory nests at Beckham's Old Field and at Mobley's Meeting House. On Sunday morning, June 11th, Huck and his party went to the church, where they expected to find the pastor and his congregation, determined, as was believed at that time, to burn both church and people. Fortunately, on Friday before, Simpson had shouldered his rifle and took the field. On the way to the church, Huck's party, with great atrocity, murdered William Strong, an inoffensive and pious young man, who was at the time of the assault reading his Bible. Mrs. Simpson, the pastor's wife, while sitting at her breakfast table, heard the report of the gun which killed young Strong, and thus she was warned of the enemy's approach. Seeing them coming, Mrs. Simpson, with her four children, fled, and hid themselves in an orchard. The marauders took away every valuable they wanted, destroyed the balance, and set fire to the house, which was soon burned down, including a valuable collection of books and important manuscripts, which were in Mr. Simpson's library.

Huck then advanced to Hill's Iron Works, in the Clay Hill section of York. These works were of the greatest importance to the Whigs, for it was there that Colonel Hill was casting cannon, cannon balls, and other ordnance for their use. The farmers for forty or fifty miles around were dependent on them for the manufacture of their agricultural implements. Huck destroyed everything that he could not carry off. He burned the furnace, the forge, grist and saw mills, all the buildings, even the negro huts, and carried off about ninety negroes.

William and Robert Hill, young sons of Colonel Hill, attempted to defend the works when they learned that the British were approaching. Dragging a small cannon, called a swivel, to an eminence which overlooked the road by which the enemy was expected to come, they meant to defy the friends of King George, but were surprised from the rear, and captured. The youths were afterwards released. It is said that the gun is now in the possession of W. D. Grist, editor of *The Yorkville Enquirer.*

From the iron works, Huck retired to White's Mill, on Fishing Creek, in what is now Chester County, about six miles below the York County line. Here he remained for a time committing his usual depredations among the inoffensive inhabitants of that region. Some time previous Huck had, in a public address, used the most blasphemous language, saying "that God Almighty had become a Rebel, but that if there were twenty gods on that side they would all be conquered." He also swore that if the Rebels were as thick as trees and Jesus Christ himself were to command them, he would defeat them. When his doings and words of blasphemy were reported in Sumter's camp, the Irish Presbyterians could stand it no longer. They demanded that they be led against that vile man— Huck. Consequently about three hundred and fifty men were detached, under Colonels Bratton, Neel, and Lacey, to destroy the defiant blasphemer. He had left White's, and when overtaken by the Whigs was at the home of Colonel Bratton. Dismounting, they tied their horses and counted their men. Ninety had fallen off, leaving not more than two hundred and sixty, but they determined to attack the enemy before daylight. Finding that Huck had moved about a quarter of a mile to Williamson's plantation, the attack was delayed for a few hours. After making sufficient observations of the enemy's position, a consultation was held and it was agreed that the men should be divided into two parties—one to be led by Colonels Bratton and Neel, the other by Colonel Lacey—the parties to approach from different directions. Evidently Huck had not considered himself in any danger. His men were carelessly posted, no pickets were advanced, no patrols sent out, and the soldiers not on duty were asleep in their tents.

Just as the morning began to dawn, the Whigs advanced in silence, cut off the troopers from their tethered horses, and opened fire about seventy-five paces from where the enemy were lying. A fence along the lane gave the Patriots some little protection and afforded good rest for their rifles. Three times the British charged with their bayonets, but were forced to fall back because of the destructive fire of the Americans. Apparently considering the matter so small, the over-confident and God-defying Huck did not at first get out of bed; but at last, aroused to his danger, he hurriedly arose, and without his coat, mounted a horse, and while trying to rally his men, he was shot, and fell dead. Word was then passed along the Whig lines, "Boys, take the fence, and every man his own commander." No sooner said than done; the fence was leaped and a rush upon the enemy, who, after a vain resistance, threw down their arms and fled in great confusion. Some few fell on their knees and begged for quarter, which was granted, with but one exception. The Whigs mounted their horses and pursued the flying Loyalists for thirteen or fourteen miles, wreaking vengeance and retaliating heavily for their cruelties and atrocities. The contest raged about an hour. The Whigs loss was one man killed. His name was Campbell. The British loss was between thirty and forty killed and about fifty wounded.

Some things happened simultaneously with the attack on Huck that deserves to be mentioned. One was that some prisoners recently captured were on their knees begging for life when the assault commenced, which saved them. Another was the release of two stalwart Patriots—James McClure and Edward Martin, who, during the action, were tied in a corn crib awaiting their execution the next morning. But the most noted of all was that Colonel Bratton, whose house was near, had engaged a devoutly pious old gentleman to stay with his family during his absence in the army. He did this for the double purpose of protection and his religious influence. The family were engaged in their devotions. A chapter had been read, and all were on their knees. The old man was offering fervent supplications to the throne of Grace. He offered an earnest petition for the destruction of that vile man—Captain Huck. No sooner had the petition been expressed than the family were startled by the crash of arms and the results noted above followed.

McCrady says that "Huck was killed by one of two brothers, John or Thomas Campbell, who both were foremost in the action." Major McJunkin says: "Several men claimed the honor of killing him, but one John Carol's claim seemed to be the best sustained by the circumstances" Whether it was John Campbell, John Carol, or someone else, the defiant blasphemer met his just deserts, and, like Judas, went to his own place. While the work of Huck's destruction was going on, Sumter was preparing to assault the enemy at Rocky Mount. It was made, but proved unsuccessful. He then marched to Hanging Rock.

We will give our readers the privilege of reading McJunkin's account of this affair. "We marched all night the 6th of August. The battle commenced the 7th. It was found by the guides that we were close to the place an hour or two before day. A whispered order came along the line that any one might sit down, with arms in hand to be ready. I and a fellow soldier sat down by a pine, and both slept a little, and when we awoke he said to me in a confident tone: 'This day I shall die.' When orders were given to march he went cheerfully, but fell in the first fire of the enemy. His name was Mitchell High, of Fairforest."

The Battle of Hanging Rock

"The battle commenced at nearly sunrise. The Tory line was said to be 1,400 strong, commanded by Colonel Brion, while we were not five hundred, and some of us were left to take care of our horses, and the British were about four hundred strong, encamped on the Camden road, about two hundred yards from the Tory camp, who were to the south of the Hanging Rock Creek, forming something like a half-moon or workman's square. Our line was divided into three divisions—right, center, and left. The left was commanded by Colonel Steen, who went up between the Tory and British lines. The other two divisions were commanded by Colonels James Liles, Samuel Watson, and Ervin, of North Carolina, who was before this time called Granny Ervin, and who afterwards was spoken very highly of on account of his good conduct that day. All led by General Sumter, who had given orders not to fire a gun until we passed between the British and Tory lines to the extremity. The battle being thus commenced, the British sent out a party commanded by one McCullough, commenced what was then called street firing upon Steen's command. General Sumter, with the center and third divisions coming round at the same time, began to cut off their flank, so of that detachment not one got back, but were all killed or taken. Their commander, McCollough, falling near the Tory camp, surrendered, and begging for water, one of Steen's captains (myself) got a canteen out of the Tory camp, who were all by this time fled, and gave him to drink. Then turning our whole force on the British line, pursued them off the ground, when some prisoners informed us that Colonel Turnbull, with four hundred British soldiers, lay last night four miles off, which caused our General (Sumter), on seeing a troop of British horse coming in sight to say, 'Boys, it is not good to pursue a victory too far,' and we returned to the Tory camp, when the British line rallied and raised a whoop. General Sumter, on hearing them, said, 'Boys, can't we raise a whoop of victory?' when the air was rent with the cry of victory Then taking up the line of march and having gone about a mile, the British sent a flag to get leave to bury their dead, which was granted Myself, one of Colonel Steen's captains, being in the rear, having charge of the prisoners, said to General Sumter: 'You have, through the divine hand of Providence, achieved a great victory today,' and he answered, 'We have won a great victory, but it will scarcely ever be heard of because we are nothing but a little handful of raw militia. But if we had been commanded by a Continental officer it would have sounded loud to our honor.'"

"After marching until about two o'clock, we halted to take some refreshments, having marched all night and had a hard fight this morning, and having taken none for twenty-four hours, you may be sure we felt somewhat in need of refreshments. We then took up our march till night and took up camp. On the morning, we began to march again, toward Charlotte, in North Carolina. About this time we got very scarce of lead, and the ladies, or heroic females, being stimulated by the barbarous conduct of the Tories and two British officers, Huck and Tarleton, gave us their dishes, spoons, tankards, etc., to cast into balls, and we used them instead of lead."

On this march, Sumter was joined by Colonel James Williams, and also received instructions from General Gates to co-operate with him in the contemplated attack on the British forces at Camden.

Disagreeing in their notions, Williams preferring to return towards Ninety-Six rather than a march down the Wateree, took that direction. Such of Sumter's force as desired it joined Williams. Among these were Captains Steen and McJunkin. Mr. Saye says: "Colonel Williams, having separated from Sumter, turned his face toward the British post at Ninety-Six. He was probably induced to take

Returns to South Carolina

this course from several considerations. He resided but a short distance from that place, and his friends were suffering from the domination of the British and Tories. General McDowell had advanced with a considerable force into the northern portion of the State. The Northern army, under Gates, was advancing towards Camden. The recent spirited conflicts in which the command of Sumter had been engaged had rekindled the spirit of liberty and taught the militia that it was possible for them to conquer a foe superior to themselves in number and equipments."

Williams, therefore, advanced southward and took post near Smith's Ford, on Broad River, about the 16th of August, where, according to McJunkin, he lay for one day. General McDowell was encamped at the Cherokee Ford, a few miles above. Hearing that a body of some five or six hundred Loyalists had assembled at Musgrove's Mill, on the Enoree River, some forty miles distant, McDowell detached a part of his command, under Colonels Clarke and Shelby, to unite with Williams for the purpose of surprising them. Says McJunkin: "On the evening of the 18th of August, took up our line of march to Musgrove's Mill, on the Enoree River. On our march we were overtaken by Frances Jones, who informed us of the defeat of General Gates and Sumter's defeat. Continuing our march, and leaving Colonel Ferguson a little to our right, we reached the Tory camp, three hundred strong, forty miles from Smith's Ford, at the dawn of the day, and commenced the fight, killed a great many and took many prisoners, and marched forty miles to North Tyger River. The reason of our rapid march to North Tyger was this: The Tory prisoners told us that there were four hundred British soldiers, under the command of Colonel Innes, encamped just over the river, and knowing that Colonel Ferguson, whom we had just passed a little to our right, must also have heard the firing, and not knowing but that they would break in upon us (who were only about one hundred and fifty strong) and serve us worse than we did the Tories. We got our water as we passed the brooks, and hunger was so great that we pulled green corn and ate as we marched."

As we have given details of this glorious and heartening victory in other articles, we desist in this case and submit the following, which sheds much light on the conflict and the horrors of the times. Saye, in his "Memoir of McJunkin," says: "The writer has been told by Richard Thompson, Esq., of Fairforest, that he passed through the battle ground at Musgrove's a few days after it occurred He was then a lad of twelve or fourteen, and going in company with his mother to visit his father, John Thompson, who was a prisoner with the British at Ninety-Six. He stated that there were marks of the battle for two miles along the road, on the east side of the river, and that he made this observation in regard to the shooting of the different parties. The marks of the balls shot by the Whigs on the trees were generally from three to five feet above the ground, while their antagonists had shot entirely above the heads of the Whigs. On his arrival at Ninety-Six, he learned from his father and other prisoners of his acquaintance that the fugitives from the battle had reported that the Whigs amounted to five thousand; that the garrison was in such a state of consternation that they would probably have fled if the Whigs had showed themselves. He further remarked that the prisoners at that garrison were treated in a barbarous manner. They were crowded into the jail, notwithstanding the warmth of the season; food of an unpalatable and unhealthy kind alone was furnished, and very inadequate in quantity. There was no attention to the cleanliness. Colonel Thompson was handcuffed, in addition to other hardships unbecoming his rank as an officer and his standing as a citizen. Mr. Thompson was released about the first of November, got home to his family and died Christmas, of disease contracted during his imprisonment."

Shortly after the battle of Musgrove's, Captain McJunkin was stricken with fever, which disabled him for service until November; consequently he had no share in the stirring events which took place in September and October, including the mighty victory won at Kings Mountain.

On the 8th of November, Sumter was lying on the west side of Broad River, at Fishdam. The British Major Wemys attempted a **Takes the Field** night surprise, and attacked Sumter's camp at one **Again and Is** o'clock on the morning of the 9th, but being on his **Appointed Major** guard he won the victory and made Major Wemys a prisoner, being severely wounded. Soon after this affair, Sumter took up a line of march towards Ninety-Six. McJunkin, having now sufficiently recovered, took the field again and assembled as many of his command as possible and joined Sumter at Padgett's Creek, in

Union District. Says Mr. Saye: "At the same time a number of the militia from Georgia effected a junction with Sumter. McJunkin was then appointed major, and received a commission as such. This was probably done to fill a vacancy occasioned by the death of Lieutenant-Colonel James Steen. Major William Farr, subsequent to this, is called lieutenant-colonel in Major McJunkin's written narrative. Hence, the writer concludes that Farr succeeded Steen, and McJunkin ranked next to Farr, in Brandon's Regiment. Steen was killed some time previous to this in Rowan County, North Carolina, attempting to arrest some Tories."

Sumter's march toward Ninety-Six was interrupted by the intelligence that Colonel Tarleton was following him by forced marches, **At Blackstock's** with the intention of falling upon him. He then turned northward, which put the Enoree River in his front. Passing that stream with the main body, Tarleton's advance had gotten so near as to obstruct the passage of the Whig rear guard. Sumter, however, pushed on with all possible speed, and gained ground on his pursuers. Apprehensive that his flying foe would succeed in crossing the Tyger without hindrance, Tarleton left his artillery and such of his infantry as he was unable to mount, and pressed forward at double quick. Sumter, reaching the margin of the river, posted his main body in a strong position on the hill, where the Blackstock house was situated. The rear guard was some distance behind, and the men composing it commenced to prepare their dinner. Fires were built, and the dough was rolled around sticks and set up before the fire to bake. At that stage of their preparations Tarleton's forces came in sight.

Major McJunkin, who was officer of the day, immediately notified Sumter that the enemy was in sight. After viewing Sumter's position, Tarleton concluded to hold him under guard until the balance of his forces could come up, but Sumter was not the kind of metal to submit to such bondage. He drew up his forces and called for volunteers to advance and commence the action. Colonel Farr and Major McJunkin were the first to step out. When a sufficient number had responded, General Sumter gave orders to advance, commence the attack, and, if necessary, fall back. The assaulting party began a spirited onset, but gradually yielded to superior numbers, until Tarleton made a general charge, hoping to drive his adversary from his advantageous position. He was repulsed with a heavy loss. He tried again, with no better success. He then drew off his whole force and left the field.

The British loss in killed and wounded amounted to near two hundred. That of Sumter's was about one-sixth of that number. Among the wounded was General Sumter, who received a bullet in the breast, which disabled him for service for several months. The command now devolved on Colonel Twiggs, of Georgia. Although it was near sundown when the enemy quit the field, it was deemed expedient to retreat that night. Accordingly a litter was constructed, upon which General Sumter was carried, between two horses. Some of the militia got as far that night as twelve miles from the scene of action. The retreat was continued the next day toward Kings Mountain. While on this retreat a party of Whigs encamped on Gilkie's Creek. A "pet" Tory lived nearby, and some of them told him that they would press him into service and take him along with them the next morning. To escape that disaster, he took a chisel that night and cut off one of his toes.

The next morning after the battle, Tarleton returned to the field, and finding his opponent gone he wreaked his vengeance by hanging John Johnson, a good Whig, who had been captured the day before. Some time in the summer Mr. Johnson had taken British protection, as many others had done, and when forced to fight he chose to fight for liberty. He resided in the vicinity of Hamilton's Ford, on Tyger River, where some of his descendants were found many years afterwards.

Speaking of conditions at this time Major McJunkin says: "Now, nothwithstanding that Sumter had been somewhat victorious in the last two engagements, the prospect of successful engagements still appeared gloomy indeed, for we had just lost one of our bravest colonels (Williams), and our gamecock (General Sumter) now wounded, and the Tories prowling about, robbing and burning our very few followers' houses, etc., and hunting them like partridges, and murdering and hanging them wherever they could catch them. Yet, notwithstanding all this gloom, we did not entirely despair of success at last, for we had been victorious at Musgrove's, Kings Mountain, Fishdam and Blackstock, and even the fair sex—our mothers, wives, and sweethearts—stimulated us to persevere, and above all we had reasons to believe that the Great Ruler of all events was on our side."

Continuing, Major McJunkin gives as a sample of what the faithful Whigs had to suffer at the hands of those villainous scoundrels, thieves and murderers—the Tories. "A Tory colonel of North Carolina, whose name was Moore (Patrick), having heard that Sumter was wounded, came on with a band of Tories to my father's house (Samuel McJunkin, Esq.), there being no one but females at home, staid all night, was joined by some of the South Carolina Tories, among whom was one Bill Hainsworth, and on going off in the morning began to pillage and take all they could of provisions, bed clothes, wearing clothes, etc., and after they had taken nearly all that they could, this Bill Hainsworth, seeing a bed quilt, took it, and started to put it on his horse, when my sister Jane seized it, and they began to pull, she no doubt pulling with all her might, for they had left nothing to cover the family from the cold of night; some of the Tories crying, 'Well done, woman!' and some 'Well done, Bill!' till he slipped in some filth by the garden, where the Tories had beastly went the night before, when she put one foot on him and pulled it away from him. Their colonel having sworn during the scuffle that if she could get it away from him she could have it, and seeing her take it and his back well bedaubed, told her to take it in the house and sit down on it."

After seeing General Sumter out of striking distance from the enemy, Colonel Brandon, with his command, returned into the vicinity of their homes and took post at Love's Ford, on Broad River. This position was well adapted to check the operations of the Tories, on the west side of the river, and to restrict their intercourse with the British army at Winnsboro. While lying here, says McJunkin, a scout was sent over to Sandy River, in Chester District, under Captain Joseph McCool. The Tories being numerous in that section, McCool was worsted in the contest. Daniel McJunkin, a brother to the major, was taken prisoner, and carried off to Winnsboro. At my request, says the Major, Colonel Brandon sent a messenger, under a flag of truce, to Cornwallis, proposing to exchange Colonel Fanning, a noted Tory, who was a prisoner of Brandon's, for Daniel McJunkin. The proposition was rejected, and Daniel was sent to Camden, where he remained until the following April, when he and William Hodge, of Grindal Shoals, succeeded in cutting the grating in a window and made their escape.

In December, a part of the Continental army, now under General Greene, was detached, and sent into South Carolina under the command of General Daniel Morgan. Morgan reached the Grindal Shoals, on Pacolet River, where he took post on Christmas Day. The principal object of this expedition was to enable the Whigs in that section of the State to embody, for, since the affair at Blackstock, the army, then under the command of General Sumter, had been dispersed in small squads in order to acquire something to subsist on, and for the want of a leader in whose ability they had confidence.

The coming of Morgan was the signal for the gathering of the partisan bands. He was soon joined by a body of militia from North Carolina, commanded by Major Joseph McDowell. The regiments of Colonels Brandon and Thomas took post near Morgan's camp. A part of General Pickens' Brigade, under Major McCall, joined his standard. A party of Georgians, under Majors Jackson and Cunningham, also came up.

Such a gathering made things look some better for the suffering Whig inhabitants in that section. A grave situation, however, confronted the patriotic Americans. They must have provisions and means of sustenance, for they had little of either, and to add to the gravity of the situation they were in a country that had been devastated by plundering Tories until little or nothing could be obtained. Miss Angelica Mitchell, who lived in sight of Morgan's camp, said: "We lived at that time generally without bread, meat, or salt—on roasting ears. When we killed a beef a pint of salt, with hickory ashes, preserved it. We went without shoes, and sewed woolen rags around our feet. I have done that many times." But Morgan's army must have supplies or go elsewhere; hence his foraging parties were sent abroad to glean whatever they could find. Being well acquainted with the surrounding communities, these expeditions were greatly aided by portions of the commands of Colonels Brandon, Thomas, Farr, Roebuck, and Majors Joseph McJunkin and Henry White.

There being a nest of Tories on Little River, in Laurens District, they advanced as near as Fairforest Creek to embarrass these oper-

The Affair at Hammond's Store ations. Morgan immediately detached Colonels Washington and McCall, with two hundred mounted militia and seventy-five cavalrymen, who fell on the Tories at a place called Hammond's Store, and destroyed them.

Cornwallis, with an army of three thousand men, still flushed with the victory at Camden, lay at Winnsboro, and Tarleton, with eleven hundred more, was at Strother, just above Alston, on Broad River; so Morgan could not hope to remain undisturbed very long, and in this he was not disappointed. On the 1st of January, 1781, Cornwallis ordered Tarleton to move towards Ninety-Six, with special orders that he push Morgan "to the utmost." After moving westward, about twenty miles, he found that Ninety-Six was safe. He then proposed to Cornwallis that they make a joint movement against Morgan, which was acceded to. So, on January 12th, Tarleton resumed his march, and on the evening of the 15th he reached Easterwood Ford, on the Pacolet.

When Colonel Washington was returning from Hammond's Store to Grindal Shoals, he passed near where General Andrew Pickens was encamped, in the Plumber settlement, between Fairforset Creek and Tyger River. Major McJunkin obtained leave to stop at Pickens' camp, and while there the intelligence of Tarleton's advance on Morgan was received. No time was to be lost. Feeling that it was unsafe to send a written message, Pickens chose Major McJunkin to bear the information verbally, and selecting James Park for a companion, they set out about dark for Morgan's camp. It was a perilous journey, the night was intensely dark and the streams very high because of excessive rainfall. After swimming Fairforest Mill Creek and Pacolet, he reached the northern bank of that stream, where he was hailed by the sentinel and kept in the edge of the river until the corporal of the guard could come, when he was conducted to General Morgan's tent. Major McJunkin informed him that "Benny Tarleton was coming to give him a blast"—that he had promised Lords Rawdon and Cornwallis on leaving Winnsboro that he would have the "Old Wagoner," *i. e.*, Morgan, to dine with them in a few days.

Morgan sent a hurried message that night to Colonel Washington, who was at Wofford's Iron Works, to meet him the next evening at the place where Thickety Station, on the Southern Railway now is, which was done. Resuming his march the next morning, The Cowpens was reached about sundown that evening, when hurried preparations were made to meet Tarleton's expected assault.

As we have described this battle in other articles, we will not repeat it here. The heretofore unrelated incident told by Major McJunkin is worthy of mention.

"On the second night before the battle of Cowpens," says Major McJunkin, "my mess in sleeping consisted of Colonel Glenn, of Newberry, and Major Jackson, of Georgia. Colonel Glenn, after having slept, said that he had a dream. He was asked to tell it. He said he had just dreamed he had a dreadful conflict with a very large and terrible-looking snake. That at striking at the snake with his sword he had cut it in two. That the head had escaped, but the tail lay powerless at his feet. He then asked Major Jackson if he could interpret the dream. 'I do not profess to be a construer of dreams,' said the Major, 'but I suppose the party to which you belong and the enemy now pursuing, as a great serpent, will have a battle. That the snake, Tarleton, will suffer a partial defeat, lose a considerable portion of his force, but, at the head, effect his escape in safety from the scene of the conflict.'" Knowing what happened at Cowpens two days later, who will not say that that dream was a prophetic revelation, which was literally fulfilled?

It will be remembered that for unknown reasons Cornwallis had not co-operated with Tarleton in the movement against Morgan as he had agreed to do, but remained in camp, near Bullock's Creek Church, in York District. When Tarleton arrived at his camp after the conflict, he related his defeat, with the loss of one whole regiment and many of his cavalry. This so enraged his lordship that he swore that he would retake them at all hazards, at the same time leaning so hard on his sword that he broke it. This was told to Major McJunkin by his father, who was a prisoner with Cornwallis at the time.

Just how far McJunkin accompanied Morgan into North Carolina, and how long he remained, we do not know; but as early as March 1st we find him again on his native heath. Colonel Roebuck won his brilliant victory at Mud Lick, March 2nd. Receiving this intelligence, McJunkin started on his return to Brandon's headquarters. On the night of the same day, while away from the main body of his command, accompanied by a single soldier (Lawson by name) doing scout duty, he had an encounter with some Tories and was shot in his right arm, which practically disabled him for the balance of the war. The details are as follows:

"On his return, he and Lawson, one of his men, scouting at a distance from the rest of the party, rode up towards a house at night. At the gate they were confronted by three Tories. Fight or die was the only alternative. He and Lawson presented their rifles at two. Lawson's gun fired clear and killed his man. The Major's gun fired also, but was a mere squib, and produced no other effect than to set fire to his adversary's shirt. As Lawson's antagonist fell, he jumped down, picked up his gun and shot down the other Tory, and passed his sword through his body. The Major's fire so disconcerted his adversary that he missed him. The Major charged, sword in hand, and his adversary fled. His flight on horseback soon caused his shirt to burn like a candle. This light so disconcerted McJunkin's horse that he could not make him charge the fugitive. After running him a mile, to get a blow at him he ran his horse alongside. At that instant the flying Tory drew a pistol, fired, and the ball struck and broke McJunkin's sword arm. His sword, luckily, was fastened to his wrist by a leather string. As his arm fell powerless by his side, he caught the sword in his left hand and drew it off his sword arm, and with a back-handed blow, as their horses ran side by side, he killed his man. Lawson's second man recovered, notwithstanding he was shot and run through with a sword."

"Notwithstanding the severity and inconvenience of this wound, Major McJunkin rejoined his men and continued his march to Brandon's camp that night. Here his pains became so excruciating that some of his soldiers cut the ball out of his arm with a dull razor. For safety, during the period necessary for his recovery, he was carried by a party of his men into an unfrequented part of the country, lying on Brown's Creek, and his wants cared for in the midst of a dense thicket. The appearance of his wounded arm beginning to indicate great danger, one of his fellow soldiers, by great exertions and personal danger, succeeded in bringing Dr. Ross to his place of concealment. The name of this soldier was David Brown. Under the treatment of Dr. Ross his wound began to heal and the prospect of recovery to grow bright. But here a new danger appeared. The Tories, learning the place of his retreat, were making arrangements to march upon his party. To avoid this difficulty, he was carried by his men across Broad River, into the vicinity of the Rev. Dr. Joseph Alexander," whose house, says

Major McJunkin, was a real lazaretto for the sick and wounded of our army."

"Here he took the smallpox in the natural way. His mother came over to wait upon him, took the disease and died. Here he remained, however, until partially recovered, both of his wound and disease On the 7th of May, he returned to his father's house. The Tories hearing that night of his arrival, a party came the next morning and made him prisoner. The party was commanded by one Bud Anderson. This party, immediately after his capture, set out towards the iron works, on Lawson's Fork. These works have sometimes been called Wofford's, at others Berwick's. On this march other prisoners were taken, some of whom were killed on their knees begging for quarter. Being arrived at or near the works, a kind of trial was gone through to decide what should be done with him. The sentence of the court was that he should be hanged in five minutes from the reading of the verdict. A rope was tied around his neck, he was set upon some kind of scaffolding, under the limb of a tree, and the rope fastened to it. At this moment a party was seen approaching on horseback at full speed. The commander of those having him in charge ordered the execution stopped till the object of the approaching party was ascertained. One of them came up and whispered something in the ear of the leader. The leader ordered the execution suspended for the present, and for the whole party to mount. They hurried away, and after beating about the country for a short time, set off in the direction of the British garrison at Ninety-Six. The motive of the delay of his execution was the approach of a party of Whigs, as he afterwards learned. While in the custody of this party of Tories, no epithets were too abusive or insulting to be applied to him with the greatest freedom and frequency. When they arrived within a mile of the British post, the party halted some time for consultation or some other purpose. While here he lay on the ground with his wounded arm resting on his forehead."

"Another party of Tories came up, their leader believed to have been the famous William Cunningham. As soon as he cast eyes on Major McJunkin, he rushed upon him with his sword drawn. Just as the Major expected to receive its descending point, he suddenly wheeled off and said, 'I was mistaken in the man.' Thence he was carried into Ninety-Six. A courtmartial was summoned to investigate his case. The forms observed were somewhat honorable. He was charged with killing one of his Majesty's subjects, the man that broke his arm. He showed them his arm, told them where they met the Tories and where the man was killed, and asked if it was possible for a man whose sword arm was broken to pursue a man a mile and kill him. General Cunningham, the president of the court, said it was impossible, and the whole court concurred. He was, therefore, acquitted of the one charge, but sentenced to close confinement as a prisoner of war. He remained in jail at this place from that time, about the 12th or 14th of May, till a few days before General Greene lay siege to the place, the 23rd of the same month. He was paroled with some others and allowed to return home. When they arrived at the ferry, on the Saluda River, they heard of a skirmish that had recently occurred up that river, and soon a detachment of Greene's army came in sight. The paroled prisoners were taken by this party to General Greene. Upon consultation and advice from Colonel Brandon, they turned back with Greene's army and remained with them until near the time the siege was raised. They then got opportunity and returned to their several homes."

To those who believe in the overruling of and the protecting hand of Divine Providence, was there ever a clearer case than this? Shot, smallpox, rope around his neck fastened to a limb, sword uplifted, ready to descend, tried by a blood-thirsty courtmartial; yet, in all these, just at the moment when his life apparently would be snuffed out, there was an interference as sudden as that which stayed the uplifted hand of Abraham over the bounded and prostrate form of Isaac, and his life was spared.

McJunkin, being thus disabled, he had no share in the remaining events of the war, except to participate in such measures as were necessary to protect the person and property of the Whig population from the aggressions of the Tories until peace was declared.

About the close of the great struggle in which he played such a conspicuous part, he bought a tract of land in the vicinity of his **His Post-War Career** father's house, and applied himself industriously and energetically as long as physical strength would permit. He and his wife reared a large family, and both lived to an old age. He united with the Presbyterian Church at Brown's Creek, of which he was many years a ruling elder.

There was a Quaker meeting house in the Major's vicinity and they moved off and sold their place of worship to a citizen, who contemplated moving the building to his plantation and making a barn out of it. Before the removal began, Majors McJunkin and Otterson, James Dugan, William Hobson and some others bought it for a place of worship for themselves. Religious services were begun there by the Rev. Daniel Gray, and this was the beginning of Cane Creek Presbyterian Church, which afterwards became large and influential.

His biographer, the Rev. James H. Saye, says: "Through life he was a peaceable, industrious, enterprising man; a public-spirited citizen; a friend to science, and a devoted Christian."

Tributes to Major McJunkin

Colonel R. J. Gage says that "Major Joseph McJunkin was one of that band of sturdy Irish Presbyterians who came from Pennsylvania and settled in Union before the Revolutionary War. He was a tall man, over six feet in height, and when young, was remarkably strong, active and adventurous. He was a man of acute intellect, gifted with remarkably close observation and wonderful memory. He was a conspicuous leader in the Revolution, and it was astonishing as to the accuracy with which he described the scenes of that eventful period."

In 1842, an anniversary celebration was held on The Cowpens battle ground. The only survivor of the contest on the ground that day was Major McJunkin. "Boys," he said, "my dear sons, I call you all. It has been sixty-one years since I stood right here upon this field, with my rifle in my hand fighting for my rights—for your rights, too, my sons, and you must preserve them too. Old Morgan had picked out eleven of us who were to fire as a signal for opening the ball, and placed us in front several paces. He walked behind and through the ranks everywhere, all the time cracking jokes and encouraging the men, and said, 'Boys, squinney well, and don't touch a trigger until you see the whites of their eyes,' and many a Briton fell before the execution of that order. Now, the sun was just rising when the enemy swept along the road. They halted and began taking off their knapsacks and all useless accoutrements, and at the command they advanced upon us at a slow, steady march. It was a beautiful line, and their uniforms and shining muskets glis-

Major McJunkin at Cowpens Again

tened in the sunlight. When they came near enough for us to distinguish plainly their faces, we picked out our man and let fly. Then a sheet of flame soon followed. After the second fire, our orders were to fall back behind Howard's Continentals and form again. The Britons thought we were running, and rushed forward just in time to receive the deadly fire of Howard's Continentals. Then Billy Washington's cavalry, on our left, charged upon their right, upon Tarleton's Legion. The whole line was thrown into confusion, a general rout took place, and the day was ours before we knew it. Oh, it was a glorious day for us!" And the old man's eyes filled with tears as memory carried him back. "But, Major," someone asked, "what could have given such a sudden turn to the battle?" "Why, my son, look here," pointing to the bark on the trees, "look at those scars—all of them are on the British side—they shot too high. We made our marks on the men; we outshot them."

The collection of books found in Major McJunkin's library was a very creditable one, and indicates the character of his mind.

His Library Jefferson's Notes, Newton's Letters, Carnors on Life, Fordyce's Advice, Gibbon's Roman Empire, Witherspoon's Works, Davis' Sermons, Prideoux's Connections, Doddridge's Family Exposition, Newton on the Prophecies, Josephus' Works, Swift's Works, Chaaptal's Chemistry, Encyclopedia, Pope's Works, Duane's Military Library, Zimmerman on Solitude, Junius' Letters, Buffon's Natural History.

The faithful old hero died on a Sabbath morning, May 31st,

His Demise 1846, near the end of his ninety-first year, and was buried the next day in the family burying ground, near the public road, leading from Union to Cook's Bridge, on Tyger River.

The Life of Major Thomas Young

IN HIS invaluable writings published about seventy-five years ago that eminent Presbyterian divine and noted local historian, Rev. James H. Saye, says: "Persons in the habit of attending Union on public days within the last twenty years have hardly failed to notice an old gentleman, moving about in the crowd, of rather a thick make, broad shoulders and brawny arms. Among his gray locks several deep scars may be traced across his head. If his right arm was made bare, similar evidences of violent dealing would be manifest. This gentleman was familiarly known as Major Tom Young."

Mr. David Anderson Thomas, a soldier of the Confederacy, and direct descendant of a Revolutionary hero, Colonel William Farr, tells the writer that he remembers Major Young well, and more than once has seen him lift his hat and exhibit those scars. When we think that at this day (June, 1924), we have among us those who have looked upon the person of real soldiers, and beheld the scars that were inflicted by Britons in the contest for Independence, the time of that momentous event is not very far back after all.

Having before us a copy of Major Young's reminiscences, related by himself, we can assure our readers that the following events narrated are authentic.

Thomas Young was born in Laurens District, January 17th, 1764. He was the son of Thomas Young, Sr., and Katherine, his wife, whose maiden name was Brandon, a sister of Colonel Thomas Brandon, who played such a conspicuous part in the drama of the Revolution. As to church relations, his father was an Episcopalian, and his mother a Presbyterian. The elder Young moved from Laurens to Brown's Creek, some miles below the present town of Union, to use the Major's own expression, "when a sucking child."

In the spring of 1789, his uncle, Colonel Thomas Brandon, was encamped with a party of seventy or eighty Whigs, about five miles below Union, to collect forces for the summer campaigns and to keep a check upon the Tories. In the meantime, they had taken prisoner one Adam Steedham, a vile and unscrupulous Tory. By some means,

Begins His Military Career

Steedham escaped during the night and notified the Tories of Brandon's position. He was attacked by a large party of the enemy before day, and completely routed. On that occasion John Young, a brother of Thomas, was murdered. "I shall never forget my feelings," says the Major, when told of his death. "I do not believe I had ever used an oath before that day, but then I tore open my bosom and swore that I would never rest until I had avenged his death. Subsequently a hundred Tories felt the weight of my arm for the deed, and around Steedham's neck I fastened the rope as a reward for his cruelties. On the next day I left home in my shirt sleeves and joined Brandon's party." Thomas Young was only sixteen years old when he joined the army, enlisting in Captain Jolly's company, under Colonel Brandon. Being defeated and scattered by the Tories, Brandon's party dodged around in squads for some time.

Hearing that there was a body of Tories assembled at the house of a Loyalist named Stallions (probably Stallings), in York District, Colonel Brandon took a detachment of about fifty Whigs to attack them. The youthful Thomas Young was one of the number, for he says· "Before we arrived at the house in which they were fortified we were divided into two parties. Captain Love—with a party of sixteen, of which I was one—marched to attack the front, while Colonel Brandon, with the remainder, made a circuit to intercept those who should attempt to escape, and also to attack the rear. Mrs. Stallions was a sister of Captain Love, and on the approach of her brother, she ran out and begged him not to fire upon the house He told her it was too late now, and that their only chance for safety was to surrender. She ran back to the house and sprang upon the doorstep, which was pretty high. At this moment the house was attacked in the rear by Colonel Brandon's party, and Mrs. Stallions was killed by a ball shot through the opposite door. At the same moment with Brandon's attack, our party raised a shout and rushed forward. We fired several rounds, which were briskly returned. It was not long, however, before the Tories ran up a flag, first upon the end of a gun, but as that did not look exactly peaceful, a ball was put through the fellow's arm, and in a few moments it was raised on a ramrod, and we ceased firing While we were fighting, a man was seen running through an open field near us, I raised my gun

His First Engagement

to shoot him, when someone of the party exclaimed: 'Don't fire; he is one of our men.' I drew down my gun, and in a moment he halted, wheeled around and fired at us. Old Squire Kennedy, who was an excellent marksman, raised his rifle and brought him down. We had but one wounded, William Kennedy, who was shot by my side. I was attempting to fire in at the door of the house, when I saw two Tories in the act of shooting at myself and Kennedy. I sprang aside and escaped, calling at the same time to my companion, but while moving he was shot through the wrist and thigh."

The Tory loss was two killed, four wounded and twenty-eight prisoners. The prisoners were sent to Charlotte, N. C. After the fight Love and Stallions met and shed bitter tears over the dead body of the wife and sister. Stallions was dismissed on parole that he might bury his wife and arrange his affairs. Brandon and his party then retreated to North Carolina.

Soon after the affair at Stallions, a most pathetic incident occurred, which Major Young relates as follows: "One Captain Reid was at a neighbor's house, in York District, on a visit. The landlady saw two men approaching the house whom she knew to be Tories, and told Captain Reid he had better escape, for they would kill him. He replied, No; they had been his neighbors; he had known Love and Saddler all his life, and had nothing to fear from them. He walked out into the yard, offered them his hand, and they killed him. His mother, a very old woman, came to where we were encamped in North Carolina. One morning we were called out on parade and this old woman came before us, leaning on the arms of two officers. She drew from her bosom the bloody pocketbook of her son, and three times attempted to go to her knees, but was prevented by the officers who supported her."

A Pathetic Incident

"Colonel Brandon stepped out and asked if there were any here willing to volunteer to avenge her wrongs. Twenty-five stepped out at once. I was one of the number. We started, rode all night, halted in the day, kept watch in the woods, but slept not; the next night we arrived at old Love's. One part of our company was to attack the house, the other the barn. The house was attacked, and the door broken down by a powerful man by the name of Maddox, who was afterwards killed at Kings Mountain.* In staving open the door, he floored old Love and knocked some of his teeth out. At this moment a cry was raised that they were in the barn, and to the barn we all rushed. One of our men fired through the door and killed one of the murderers; the other was killed in the skirmish. What is most strange about the matter is that another man was sleeping with them, and in the melee he escaped unhurt."

Their guns were taken, and those of all the other Tories they found on their return. Says Young: "By the time we got back every man of us had two guns apiece. We now felt that we had done all that was required of us." The dastardly and cowardly murder of Captain Reid was thus avenged

In these "sketches" we have given several partial accounts of this most momentous battle, but in this case we will let Major Thomas Young tell the story in his own language:

At Kings Mountain

"The next engagement I was in was at Kings Mountain, S. C., I believe, on the 7th of October, 1780. I was under the command of Colonel Brandon. Late in the evening preceding the battle, we met Colonels Campbell, Shelby, Cleveland and Sevier, with their respective regiments, at The Cowpens, where they had been killing some beeves. As soon as we got something to eat (for we were very hungry) we retired, to sleep at random through the woods. When I awoke in the morning, Joseph Williams, the little son of Colonel Williams, was lying at my back. In the morning we received intelligence that Major Ferguson was encamped somewhere near the Cherokee Ford, on Broad River. We pushed forward, but heard no tidings of the enemy. At a meeting house, on the eastern side of the river, we discovered some signs (the enemy had cut off the tops of the chestnut trees to get the fruit), and continued our pursuit for some distance, when a halt was ordered, and we were on the point of sending out for some beeves when we met George Watkins, a Whig, who had been taken prisoner and was on his way home on parole. He gave us information of the position of the enemy."

"A consultation of the officers was then held, and the command was given to Colonel Campbell. Watkins had informed us that we were within a mile of the enemy. We were then formed into four

---

*No doubt but that this was Captain John Mattocks, who was among the first to fall at Kings Mountain, his grave being marked by the old monument at the branch —J D B

divisions; who commanded each division I cannot now say. I think Colonel Roebuck commanded the one I was in."

"Major Ferguson had taken a very strong position upon the summit of the mountain, and it appeared like an impossibility to dislodge him, but we had come there to do it, and we were determined, one and all, to do it or die trying. The attack was begun on the north side of the mountain. The orders were at the firing of the first gun for every man to raise a whoop, rush forward, and fight his way as he best could. When our division came up to the northern base of the mountain we dismounted, and Colonel Roebuck drew us a little to the left, and commenced the attack. I well remember how I behaved. Ben Hollingsworth and myself took right up the side of the mountain, and fought from tree to tree, our way to the summit I recollect I stood behind one tree and fired until the bark was nearly all knocked off and my eyes pretty well filled with it. One fellow shaved me pretty close, for his bullet took a piece out of my gun-stock. Before I was aware of it, I found myself apparently between my own regiment and the enemy, as I judged, from seeing the paper which the Whigs wore in their hats and the pine tops the Tories wore in theirs, these being the badges of distinction. I heard our regiment halloa, and looked around and saw our men; about a dozen of them shook hands with me A little fellow by the name of Clerry gave me a round scolding for my conduct, and told me to stick to him, or I should be killed. I did stay with him for some time."

"On the top of the mountain, in the thickest of the fight, I saw Colonel Williams fall, and a braver or better man never died upon the field of battle. I had seen him but once before that day—it was in the beginning of the action, as he charged by me at full speed around the mountain. Toward the summit a ball struck his horse under the jaw, when he commenced stamping as if he were in a nest of yellowjackets. Colonel Williams threw the reins over the animal's neck, sprang to the ground, and dashed onward."

"The moment I heard the cry that Colonel Williams was shot I ran to his assistance, for I loved him as a father. He had ever been so kind to me, and almost always carried a cake in his pocket for me and his little son Joseph. They carried him into a tent and sprinkled some water in his face. He revived, and his first words were, 'For God's sake, boys, don't give up the hill.' I remember it as well as if it had occurred yesterday. I left him in the arms of his son Daniel, and returned to the field to avenge his fall."

"We now had the enemy huddled up on the top of the mountain; they wheeled to fire a platoon upon us. Some of our men ran back, but I was too much fatigued to run. They fired, but without effect. They soon hoisted two flags and surrendered. I had no shoes, and, of course, fought in this battle barefoot. When it was over my feet were much torn, and bleeding all over. The next morning we were ordered to fire a round. I fired my large, old musket, charged in the time of the battle with two musket bullets, as I had done every time. The recoil in this case was dreadful I had two cousins in this battle on the Tory side—Colonel Young and Matthew McCreary, whose father was a prisoner with the British, on Edisto Island. His mother made Matthew turn out with Ferguson's army, for fear his father would be hung. Just after we had reached the top of the hill, Matthew saw me, ran and threw his arms around me I told him to get a gun and fight. He said he could not. I told him to let me go that I might "

"Our loss at Kings Mountain was about twenty-five killed and wounded. The enemy lost above three hundred, who were left on the ground, among them Major Ferguson. We took, moreover, seven or eight hundred prisoners Awful indeed was the scene of the wounded, the dying and the dead, on the field after the carnage of that dreadful day."

"After this battle, we went on with the Virginians and North Carolinians to help guard the prisoners for a considerable distance through the mountains of North Carolina. A few days after the battle a courtmartial was held to try some of the Tories, who were known to be of the most outrageous and blood-thirsty characters. About twenty were found guilty, but ten received a pardon or respite. Nine were hung and the tenth was pinioned, awaiting his fate. It was now nearly dark. His brother, a mere lad, threw his arms around him and set up a most piteous criying and screaming, as if he would go into convulsions. While the soldiers were attracted by his behavior, he managed to cut the cords and his brother escaped."

"We then marched upon the headwaters of Cane Creek, in North Carolina, with our prisoners, where we all came very near starving to death. The country was very thinly settled, and provisions could not be had for love or money. I thought green pumpkins, sliced and fried, about the sweetest eating I ever had in my life. When I got home to my mother, I buried the few rags I had left in consequence of the abundance of lice with which they were infested. From that point we marched over into the Dutch settlement, in the fork of the Catawba, and remained until we joined General Morgan, at Grindal Shoals."

Although Major Patrick Ferguson and his devastating army had been destroyed at Kings Mountain, the outlook for the patriotic cause in upper South Carolina was far from bright, and the sufferings of the Whig families were very great. In order to relieve this situation, soon after General Nathaniel Greene superceded Gates in command of the Southern army, he ordered General Morgan to march into that section. Morgan's detachment numbered five hundred men. Colonels John Eager Howard, William Washington, and Major Triplett were his subordinate officers.

Leaving Charlotte, December 16, 1780, Morgan advanced into South Carolina and took post at Grindal Shoals, on the east bank of the Pacolet River, on Christmas Day.*

Soon after his arrival at the Grindal Shoals, Morgan was joined by small parties, under Major Joseph McDowell, of North Carolina; Colonels Thomas Brandon, John Thomas and McCall, of South Carolina, and Majors Jackson and Cunningham, of Georgia.

Hearing that a body of about two hundred Tories, from the Laurens District, had approached as near as Fairforest Creek, **At Hammond's Store** where they were committing their usual depredations, Morgan immediately detached Colonel Washington, with two hundred mounted militia and seventy-five cavalrymen, to drive these Loyalists from the country. Major Thomas Young was one of Washington's number, and we will let him describe the contest:

"The next engagement I was in was at Hammond's Store, on Bush River, somewhere near Ninety-Six. General Morgan was encamped at Grindal Shoals to keep the Tories in check. He dispatched Colonel Washington, with a detachment of militia and about seventy dragoons, to attack a body of Tories who had been plundering the Whigs. We came up with them at Hammond's Store—

---
*For a full description of this place, see the writer's "History of Grindal Shoals and Some Early Adjacent Families."

in fact, we picked up several scattering ones within about three miles of the place, from whom we learned all about their position."

"When we came in sight, we perceived that the Tories had formed a line on the brow of the hill opposite to us. We had a long hill to descend and another to rise. Colonel Washington and his dragoons gave a shout, drew swords, and charged down the hill like mad men. The Tories fled in every direction without firing a gun. We took a great many prisoners and killed a few. Here I must relate an incident which occurred on this occasion. In Washington's corps there was a boy of fourteen or fifteen, a mere lad, who, in crossing Tyger River, was ducked by a blunder of his horse. The men laughed and jeered at him very much, at which he got very mad, and swore that boy or no boy, he would kill a man that day or die. He accomplished the former. I remember very well being highly amused at the little fellow, charging around a crib after a Tory, cutting and slashing away with his puny arm till he brought him down."

"We then returned to Morgan's encampment at Grindal Shoals, on the Pacolet, and there remained, eating beef and scouting through the neighborhood until we heard of Tarleton's approach."

"Having received intelligence that Colonel Tarleton designed to cross the Pacolet at Easterwood Shoals, above us, General Morgan broke up his encampment early on the morning of the 16th and retreated up the mountain road by Hancocksville, taking the left hand road not far above, in the direction toward the head of Thickety Creek. We arrived at the field of The Cowpens about sundown, and were then told that there we would meet the enemy. The news was received with great joy by the army. We were very anxious for battle, and many a hearty curse had been vented against General Morgan during that day's march for retreating, as we thought to avoid a fight."

Morgan Falls Back to Cowpens

"Night came upon us, yet much remained to be done. It was all important to strengthen the cavalry. General Morgan knew well the power of Tarleton's legion, and he was too wily an officer not to prepare himself as well as circumstances would permit. Two companies of volunteers were called for. One was raised by Major Jolly, of Union District, and the other, I think, by Major McCall. I attached myself to Major Jolly's company. We drew swords that night, and were informed

At The Cowpens

we had authority to press any horse, not belonging to a dragoon or an officer, into our service for the day."

"It was upon this occasion I was more perfectly convinced of General Morgan's qualifications to command the militia than ever before. He went among the volunteers, helped them fix their swords, joked with them about their sweethearts, told them to keep in good spirits, and the day would be ours. And long after I had lain down he was going about among the soldiers, encouraging them and telling them that the 'Old Wagoner' would crack his whip over Ben Tarleton in the morning as sure as they lived."

"'Just hold up your heads, boys, three fires,' he would say, 'and you are free. And when you return to your homes, how the old folks will bless you and the girls kiss you for your gallant conduct.' I don't believe that he slept a wink that night."

"Our pickets were stationed three miles in advance Samuel Clowney was one of the picket guards, and I often heard him afterwards laugh at his narrow escape. Three of Washington's dragoons were out on a scout when they came almost in contact with the advance guard of the British army. They wheeled, and were pursued almost into camp. Two got in safely, but one poor fellow, whose horse fell down, was taken prisoner. It was about day that the pickets were driven in."

Major Young's Description of the Battle

"The morning of the 17th of January, 1781, was bitterly cold. We were formed in order of battle and the men were slapping their hands together to keep warm—an exertion not long necessary."

"The battlefield was almost a plain, with a ravine on both hands, and very little undergrowth in front or near us. The regulars, under command of Colonel Howard, a very brave man, were formed in two ranks, their right flank resting upon the head of the ravine on the right. The militia was formed on the left of the regulars, under the command of Colonel Pickens, their left flank resting near the head of the ravine on the left. The cavalry formed in the rear of the center, or rather in rear of the left of the regulars. About sunrise, the British line advanced at a sort of trot, with a loud halloo. It was the most beautiful line I ever saw. When they shouted I heard Morgan say, 'They give us the British halloo, by G—,' and he galloped along the lines, cheering the men, and telling them not to fire until they could see the whites of their eyes. Every officer was crying, 'Don't fire,' for it was a hard matter for us to keep from it."

"I should have said the British line advanced under cover of their artillery, for it opened so fiercely upon the center that Colonel Washington moved his cavalry from the center toward the right wing."

"The militia fired first. It was pop, pop, pop, and then a whole volley. But when the regulars fired it seemed like one sheet of flame from right to left. Oh, it was beautiful! I have heard old Colonel Farr say often that he believed John Savage fired the first gun in this battle. He was riding to and fro along the lines when he saw Savage fix his eye upon a British officer. He stepped out of the ranks, raised his gun, fired, and he saw the officer fall."

"After the first fire, the militia retreated and the cavalry covered their retreat. They were again formed and renewed the attack, and we retired to the rear. They fought for some time and retreated again, and there formed a second time. In this I can hardly be mistaken, for I recollect well that the cavalry was twice during the action between our army and the enemy. I have understood that one of the retreats was ordered by mistake by one of Morgan's officers. How true this is, I cannot say."

"After the second forming, the fight became general and unintermitting. In the hottest of it I saw Colonel Brandon coming at full speed to the rear, and waving his sword to Colonel Washington. In a moment the command to charge was given, and I soon found that the British cavalry had charged the American right. I fell in with Colonel Brandon, who accompanied Washington in the charge. I was just about engaging a British dragoon, when Colonel Brandon darted between us and killed him, and told me to follow him. I did till he killed two more. We made a most furious charge, and cutting through the cavalry, wheeled and charged them in the rear. In this charge I exchanged my tackey for the finest horse I ever rode. It was the quickest swap I ever made in my life."

"At this moment the bugle sounded. We, about half formed and making a short circuit at full speed, came up in the rear of the British line, shouting and charging like mad men. At this moment, Colonel Howard gave the word, 'Charge bayonets,' and the day was ours. The British broke, and throwing down their guns and cartridge boxes, made for the wagon road, and did the prettiest sort of running."

The battle of Cowpens was fought on Major Young's birthday. He was just seventeen years old.

"After this (*i. e.*, the surrender), Major Jolly and seven or eight of us resolved upon an excursion to capture some of the baggage.

How Major Young Got His Scars

We went about twelve miles and captured two British soldiers, two negroes, and two horses laden with portmanteaus. One of the portmanteaus belonged to the paymaster in the British service and contained gold. Jolly insisted upon my returning with the prize to camp, while he pursued a little further. I did so. Jolly's party dashed onward and soon captured an armorer's wagon, with which they became so much engaged that they forgot all about me. I rode along for some miles at my leisure, on my fine gray charger, talking to my prisoners, when, all at once, I saw coming in advance a party which I soon discovered to be British. I knew it was no time to consider, so I wheeled, put spurs to my horse, and made down the road, in the hopes of meeting Jolly and his party. My horse was stiff, however, from the severe exercise given him that morning, and I soon found that they were gaining on me. I wheeled abruptly to the right into a crossroad, but a party of three or four dashed through the woods and intercepted me. It was now a plain case, and I could hope no longer to engage one at a time. My pistol was empty, so I drew my sword and made battle. I never fought so hard in my life. I knew it was death anyhow, and I resolved to sell my life as dearly as possible. In a few minutes one finger on my left hand was split open. Then I received a cut on my sword arm by a parry that disabled it. In the next instant, a cut from a sabre across my forehead (the scar of which I shall carry to my grave), the skin slipped down over my eyes and the blood blinded me so that I could see nothing. Then came a thrust in the right shoulder, then a cut upon the left shoulder, then a last cut (which you can feel for yourself) on the back of my head, and I fell upon my horse's neck. They took me down, bound up my wounds, and placed me again on my horse, a prisoner of war."

"When they joined the party in the main road there were two Tories who knew me well—Littlefield and Kelly. Littlefield cocked his gun and swore he would kill me. In a moment nearly twenty

British soldiers drew their swords, and cursing him for a d—d coward for wanting to kill a boy without arms and a prisoner, ran him off. Littlefield did not like me, and for a very good reason. While we were at Grindal Shoals with Morgan, he once caught me out and tried to take my gun from me. I knocked him down with it, and as he arose I clicked it and told him if he didn't run I'd blow him through. He did not hesitate long which of the two to choose."

"I was then accused of robbing the women at the British camp and searched for proof of the fact, but nothing was found in my pockets but about seventy-five cents in cash. This was given back. Tarleton's party went on and overtook Jolly and his party. These made their escape, but two—Deshazer and McJilton—had been taken by Tarleton before I was. McJilton was slightly wounded in the head, fainted, and was left near a house and taken care of by a woman. This lady gave Washington information of McJilton being there, and McJilton told them that I was a prisoner with Colonel Tarleton, and cut all to pieces. I asked Kelly not to tell the British who I was, and I do not think the fellow did."

"Colonel Tarleton sent for me on the march and I rode by his side for several miles. He was a very fine looking man, with rather a proud bearing, but very gentlemanly in his manners. He asked me a great many questions, and I told one lie, which I have often thought of since. In reply to his inquiry as to whether Morgan was reinforced before the battle, I told him he was not, but that he expected reinforcements every minute. He asked me how many dragoons Washington had. I replied that he had seventy, and two volunteer companies of mounted militia, but you know they won't fight. 'By God, they did today, though.' I begged him to parole me, but he said if he did I would go right off and turn fighting again. I then told him he could get three men in exchange for me, and he replied: 'Very well, when we get to Cornwallis' army you shall be paroled or exchanged, and meanwhile I will see that your wounds are taken care of.'"

"We got to Hamilton's Ford, on Broad River, about dark. Just before we came to the river, a British dragoon came up at full speed and told Colonel Tarleton that Washington was close behind in pursuit. This caused some confusion. It was now very dark, and the river was said to be swimming. The British were not willing to take the water. Colonel Tarleton flew into a terrible passion, and drawing his sword swore he would cut down the first man who hesitated. They knew him too well to hesitate longer. During the confusion, a young Virginian by the name of Deshazer, also a prisoner, and myself, managed to get into the woods. In truth, a British soldier had agreed to let us escape, and to desert if we would assist him in securing the plunder he had taken."

"We slipped away, one at a time, up the river—Deshazer first, then myself. I waited, what I thought a very long time, for the British soldier, and he came not. At last I began to think the British were across, and I gave a low whistle. Deshazer answered me and we met. I was almost dead with thirst, having drank nothing that day but some vinegar given me by a British soldier. Deshazer lifted a little water in his hands and held it to my mouth. We left the river and proceeded toward a ford, on Pacolet River, with which I was acquainted. It was now very dark, and raining when we came to the Pacolet. But, providentially, I was unable to find the way to the ford, as I have reason to believe the river was swimming there from its depths where we did cross. We passed through a plantation, by a barn. It had a light in it, and I heard a cough. We halted and reconnoitered, and finding it occupied by some British soldiers, we passed on silently by the dwelling house, crossed Pacolet by another ford, and soon arrived at old Captain Grant's, where we passed the night. The old man and his lovely daughter washed and dressed my wounds, and in looking over the bag of plunder which the soldier had given us they found a fine ruffled shirt, which I put on and went to bed. I shall never forget that girl or the old man for their kindnesses."

Major Young Escapes

"On the next day, I left with Deshazer and reached my mother's residence, though very feeble through fatigue, the loss of blood, and the soreness of my head and arm. I was confined by a violent fever for eight or ten days, but thanks to the kind nursing and attention of old Mrs. Brandon, I recovered. I now slept in the woods for about three weeks, waiting for some of the Whigs to come in and commence operations. I was concerned about a horse. The British soldiers, when they took me, dismounted me from the fine charger I captured at The Cowpens, and put me on a prancing pony. One day I met old Molly Willard, riding a very fine sorrel horse, and told her we must swap. She wouldn't listen to it, but I replied that there was no use in talking,

At Home Again

the horse I would have, and the exchange was made, not much to the old woman's satisfaction, for she didn't love the Whigs. I don't believe the Willards have forgiven me for that horse swap to this day."

After recovering somewhat from his wounds, Thomas Young again joined his uncle, Colonel Thomas Brandon, and party, which amounted to fifty or sixty men. Among these were Captain Ben Jolly and William Giles, who was afterwards captain. They proceeded down the Broad and Congaree rivers, leaving Granby on their right, and reached Fort Motte after the siege of that place had commenced Remaining there for a few days, Young joined a detachment, under Colonel Wade Hampton, who was sent to aid in reducing Orangeburg. Says Young: "The State troops outmarched us, for we had a piece of artillery to manage. The siege was commenced by a party at night. In the morning, the rest of us reached the place with a three pounder. The main body of us marched down the road and drew the whole attention of those engaged in the defense of the house. The house was a two-story brick building, and the Tories, who defended it, were in the second story. They shot at us and hallooed furiously as we passed on. When we were beyond the reach of their balls, we waited till our cannon had got near enough at another point to play upon the house. It was discharged three times, a breach was made through the gable end, then another a little lower, then about the center, and they surrendered."

Takes the Field Again

"Here we found a quantity of rum and sugar, but the common soldier received none of it, but a gill of rum to a man. One man, who was set to guard the sugar, filled his pockets with it, and this was all of that article that was of any benefit to us, and we at that time needed that article very much, as we were in pressing need of provisions. Colonel Wade Hampton was the commander, who is said to have made private property of the spoils on this occasion."

This accusation against Colonel Wade Hampton will be news to most of us.

"I then joined a party of dragoons under Captain Boykin, at the solicitation of Captain Giles, to capture some horses we heard

Joins a Party Under Captain Boykin were billeted out by the British, near Bacon's Bridge, in the low country. It was a most hazardous expedition, and required great courage and prudence. Captain Boykin had both. We went to the hotel and called for the hostler. Captain Boykin drew his pistol, cocked it, and told him if he did not open the stable doors he would shoot him dead. You may rest assured he did not long consider about it. They got three very fine animals, two stallions and a gelding. Neither Giles nor I got a horse, and we were in no very good humor, as we knew that we should have to go back at so rapid a pace that our nags could not stand it. Sure enough, after one day and night's travel our horses began to fail, and we resolved to take the woods, but Boykin begged us to try to keep up, and as we soon should come to another billet of horses, we should have the first choice. Well, next day we did come upon a fine lot of horses, wild as devils. Giles and I went in and I soon caught a yellow sorrel mare. Giles, who was an excellent judge of horse flesh, was struck with her form, and said to me, 'Young, if you will let me have that mare, I will help you catch any horse in the lot.' I gave her to him, and picked me out a bay mare. Time proved that Giles was correct in his judgment, as the yellow mare was never caught in a chase, or beaten in a race afterwards. We were all now well mounted, and pushed off to join our detachment above."

Arriving at Granby, the Boykin party was dismissed, and nearly all returned home. Says Major Young: "Colonel Brandon, Major **Takes Part in the Siege of Ninety-Six** Jolly and myself resolved to make an excursion to Ninety-Six, where the siege was going on. Here I remained during the siege. As we every day got our parallels nearer the garrison, we could see them very plain when they went out to a brook or spring for water. The Americans had constructed a sort of moving battery, but as the cannon of the fort were brought to bear upon it, they were forced to abandon the use of it. It had not been used for some time, when an idea struck old Squire Kennedy, who was an excellent marksman, that he could pick off a man now and then as they went to the spring. He and I took our rifles and went into the woods to practice at two hundred yards. We were arrested and taken before an officer, to whom we gave our excuse and design. He laughed, and told us to practice no more, but to try our luck from the battery if we wanted to. So we took our position, and as a fellow came down to the spring, Kennedy fired and he fell; several ran out and gathered round him, and among them I noticed one man raise his head and look around as if he wondered where the shot could have come from. I touched my trigger and he fell, and we made off, for fear it might be our time to fall next."

After the siege of Ninety-Six, Major Young returned to his old neighborhood, in Union District, and was engaged in scouting expeditions until peace was declared.

Says he, "I was taken prisoner in company with the McJilton previously mentioned. We were engaged in hauling corn at the

Again Captured

time. Our captors were a parcel of Tories, who lived on Fairforest, above McBeth's Mill. They were a set of outlaws, who murdered a great many Whigs, but did us no injury. Their names were Jess Gray, Sam Gray, and a little fellow by the name of Morgan. On account of the kindness I had once shown to one of them while a prisoner in my charge, I was set at liberty without being hurt.

"Some time before the battle of Cowpens, a party of the Moores and others, who lived on Sandy River, in Chester District, had erected

Some Other Expeditions

a large tent in a thicket, in which they had deposited a great amount of plunder and some negroes. A party, of which I recollect Colonel Brandon, Colonel Casey, Colonel Hughes, and Major Jolly were members, went to attack them. We got there early in the day, and it was not long before we had possession of the place. In the fight, I took a little fellow by the name of Tom Moore prisoner. I ran him for some distance, shot at him and broke his arm. When I took him back Tom Salter wanted to kill him, because Moore had once had him prisoner and would, in all probability, have killed him if he had not escaped I cocked my gun and told him no; he was my man, and I would shoot the first one who harmed him. In this excursion we got a good deal of plunder, which had been concealed by the Tories."

"It was on a scouting expedition to Mud Lick, under Colonel Brandon. We were all mounted. We saw two spies before we came

The Affair at Mud Lick

upon the Tories, and pursued them to the creek. Colonel Brandon sent out Major Jolly, with a flank guard, to prevent their outflanking us. They were on the opposite side of the creek and commanded the ford, so that we could not cross. Jolly and I approached very near, so that a cousin of mine, William Young, hailed us, and inquired who commanded. A good deal was said to keep us engaged. Young waved his sword to me several times, and halloed to me to go away; a moment after we were fired upon by a party who had crept up the creek through the bushes. A shot went under Jolly's horse's belly, and another shaved my horse's forelegs. We returned the fire, but did no damage, save putting a ball through Young's horse's nose. We then retreated under the hope that they would pursue us, but they did not. This same cousin of mine had offered a hundred guineas to any man who would bring me into Ninety-Six."

Major Young says: "The first personal acquaintance I ever had with Colonel James Williams occurred under the following circumstances: Some two hundred of us were in North Carolina, probably in Lincoln County. The first time I was ever on guard I heard a horse walking I hailed, but the beast walked on. I fired, and the horse fell. The picket guard were greatly alarmed, and one of them fired in the air. An examination was had and the horse was found dead. I was greatly troubled at the occurrence. The next day Colonel Williams sent for me and inquired if I was the little lad that killed the horse last night. I answered in the affirmative. 'Well,' said he, 'my little son, you did right,' and from that time to the time of his death he treated me with great kindness. His conduct towards the soldiers was always kind and parental, and he was greatly beloved by them. He had two of his sons with him—Daniel, hardly grown, and Joseph, about thirteen."

An Incident and a Tribute

Peace, the boon for which Thomas Young fought so long, and for which he suffered so severely, having been won, he married and settled not far from Union, where he brought up a large family. An admirer said of him: "He is beloved by his neighbors for his kindness, and respected by all for the scars he received in the cause of liberty."

After the War

The venerable hero passed away from all earthly scenes, November 7, 1848, at the advanced age of eighty-three years, nine months and twenty days. He is buried in the old Union cemetery, about two miles east of Union, not far from the present Monarch Cotton Mill. His grave is only marked by a government marker, placed by the Daughters of the American Revolution.

A chapter of men in Union have recently honored him and honored themselves by the name—Thomas Young Chapter, Sons of the Revolution.

Some Other Heroic Personages and Thrilling Incidents of the Revolution

ANNE KENNEDY

AMONG THE CHAMPIONS of liberty, there were none that surpassed the Kennedy family, who resided in the old Union District. Some of them are described as "the bravest of the brave," and what was true of the males was equally true of some of the females; for among the heroines of Independence none were more daring and fearless than Anne Kennedy.

When General Morgan came to South Carolina, previous to the battle of Cowpens, there were Tories and Loyalists lurking in every quarter. This greatly increased Morgan's perils when he was pursued by the "Bloody Scout." None were more apprehensive of this than the Kennedys. The situation was desperate, and for the Americans to be surprised and defeated was more than they could think of. But few, if any, trusted messengers were available for the grave undertaking; but Morgan must be apprised, at all hazards, of the latest movements of the enemy. Anne Kennedy, though a fair young maiden, was equal to the emergency. Saddling the best horse on the premises and concealing a pistol in her bosom, she kissed the family good-bye and set out alone on her perilous journey.

Crossing Pacolet River at the Grindal Ford, she hastened on to overtake Morgan and inform him of his danger. She had not gone very far when she came upon a batch of the enemy halted for the night. They were mostly Tories, and some of them her neighbors, whom she knew. Concealing her face with a veil, she rode by them They had killed a wild turkey and were so busy quarreling over it that they paid little or no attention to her. She rode on quietly until she got out of sight, when she put the lash to her horse and was soon out of their reach.

Stopping at the house of a man by the name of Bryant, somewhere near Goucher Creek, she learned from a sick American soldier the whereabouts of General Morgan After getting the necessary directions, she proceeded on her journey Night soon came on, and it was intensely dark; but her faithful steed shot through the gloom like a well-directed arrow. She came to a creek—most probably Thickety—of which she had not been told, and her hopes came near being crushed; but to be lost and fail in her mission was too much for our heroine to contemplate. Riding back a short distance, she noticed another road turning to the right. This revived her hopes. She dismounted and examined the ground the best she could in the darkness; feeling for the horse tracks, she satisfied herself that that was the road over which the army had gone. She then remounted and pressed on with all possible speed. She knew that she must be near the American camp, and that by the help of God her mission would be accomplished. She was in a strange country and knew nothing of where the enemy was encamped, or upon what roads their pickets and spies were posted, nor what would be her fate if detected. But animated by love of country, and with an undaunted spirit, she pushed on. As her noble horse leaped forward, carrying his load of precious freight, the clattering of his hoofs aroused the faithful watch-dogs as they kept vigil over the homes of their masters. Turning her horse aside, and halting before the door of a backwoodsman, she inquired after General Morgan and his army. The response came from the trembling voice of an excited woman on the inside of the cabin, that the encampment was about two miles from there in the direction of the North Carolina line.

She turned her horse into the road again, and with head erect, nostrils dilated, and eyes flashing fire, as though the beast understood the importance of the mission, he dashed on over hill and dale, knocking the fire from the rocks as he crushed them beneath his iron heels or sent them whizzing to the roadside. She passed the first line of pickets, only to be halted by a cordon of American bayonets at the second post.

Without disclosing the object of her visit, Miss Kennedy asked to be conducted to General Morgan's headquarters, where she made known to him her mission, which, it is said, was largely instrumental in his winning the victory at Cowpens.

Morgan received his fair visitor with all the gallantry and etiquette that a distinguished American soldier and gentleman could command. As soon as our brave heroine had warmed herself and been refreshed with the rude fare of the Whig soldier, her horse fed with his scanty feed, General Morgan sent a small escort of cavalry under Lieutenant Patterson to pilot her across the country to Pacolet River, to see her safely on its western bank. This crossing took place at the present Clifton Cotton Mills.

The remainder of her journey was uneventful, having passed quietly through the country without attracting attention. Late in the evening she arrived at home in safety, where the open arms of the family were in readiness to receive her. After relating the incidents of her trip, she was informed that there was great activity among the British sympathizers in trying to find out the cause of her sudden disappearance from the neighborhood.

The next morning, after Miss Kennedy's night visit, was clear and cold. The sun having risen, the tall and outstanding form of Thickety Mountain threw its long shadows across the field of The Cowpens, where the patriot army was drawn up in battle array. The bright uniforms, the shining guns and bayonets of the bombastic, conceited and over-confident Tarleton glistened in the rays of the early morning sun, as they haughtily marched to their doom; for soon the two armies grappled in the deadly contest. Sheets of flame flashed like the lightnings, the guns roared like the thunders, while the smoke arose like that of a furnace. In a little more than an hour's time the flower of the British army was killed and captured, and the leader and a few of his henchmen were fleeing like fugitives from justice. One of the most brilliant of victories had been won, and thrills of joy and gladness filled to the overflowing every liberty-loving heart. A writer has said: "The home and family circle of every patroit, in which the family altar was a part of the furniture, besought at the throne of God that the god of battles would give them the victory, and the result was that the sun, which rose that morning upon a ghastly field, went down upon a free and independent nation. The news of the battle was received the next day with acclamations of great joy by the patriots, and none felt more fully compensated for their trouble and the danger to which they had been exposed than our heroine, Anne Kennedy."

Just what particular information this fair maiden conveyed to General Morgan, we shall never know; but when we think of those who shared in the Cowpens' victory, the name of Anne Kennedy should not be forgotten.*

---

*We are indebted for the information contained in the above narrative to an article written by J L Strain and published in the Union Times many years ago.

DICEY LANGSTON

There was a black-eyed girl baby, born on a South Carolina plantation in the year 1760, who was to grow up with far more of guile than the fear of man in her heart, and who was to do deeds of daring during the war for independence that would send her name down in history along with those of Sumter and Marion, Pickens and Moultrie and other chivalrous souls of the Southland.

The little maid, Dicey Langston, was the daughter of Solomon Langston, an elderly planter living in the Laurens District, on the Enoree River, a section overrun with British soldiers, Tories and outlaws, who trained with the Tories during the latter days of the Revolution. Her mother died during her childhood, a period of which we have little record except that she grew up with her brothers, learning their lessons and playing her part in their boyish sports Naturally she became a bold and reckless rider and an expert shot, along with her more lady-like accomplishments, and was a proud, imperious, high-spirited young woman, rather below the medium height, but graceful and attractive in face and manner. Of course, she became a fearless and out-spoken patriot, as were her brothers, though they had relatives in their own neighborhood who were strong sympathizers with the policy of King George.

Old Solomon Langston was an ardent Whig, and though incapacitated by age and infirmities from active participation in the struggle, he was always ready with purse and influence to aid the cause of independence. Both the sons were in the field and had been since the breaking out of hostilities, in some capacity or other. In order to save the family from annoyance, they did not live at home nor visit the home except surreptitiously at rare intervals, but were in constant communication with their sister.

Living as she did in a community where she was surrounded by Royalists, some of whom were her own relatives, the girl found it easy to learn what was going on, the movements and plans of the enemy and how it was likely to affect their friends, and she did not hesitate to secure and use this information by communicating with her brother, who was encamped with a little band of Whigs along the opposite shore of the river, some miles away. After a time there began to arise questions as to how certain information could have come to the ears of the rebels, and the suspicions of their Tory neighbors were turned toward Solomon Langston and his spirited and outspoken daughter. The old gentleman was waited upon by some of these same Tories and told that if there was any more information carried he would be held personally responsible for his daughter's conduct. Mr. Langston was an old man, and not only his own safety but that of his daughter and his property depended upon these same neighbors, so he administered a stern rebuke to Miss Dicey, and warned her of the danger in which they stood. The meekness with which the young woman received the admonitions of her esteemed parent may be imagined, also the mental reservations with which she promised to carry no more news to the Whig camps.

For a time she obeyed the commands of her father, but the probabilities are that it was because she had nothing worth telling. A few weeks later, however, it came to her ears accidentally that a band of Tory outlaws called the "Bloody Scouts" because of their ruthless cruelty in wantonly killing and plundering many defenseless families known to be sympathizers with the patroit cause, were next day to attack Little Eden settlement, where her brother and his little band lay in hiding. She knew that the band were especially incensed at her brother, and that if captured he and all his band would be put to death. Orders or no orders, she determined to warn her brother and the people of Little Eden settlement. Yet how, was the question. The slightest suspicion falling on her father's family would bring down on their heads the wrath of the "Bloody Scouts," already looking for an excuse to harry the old man and plunder his property. She had no one to seek, no one to whom she could trust even to take with her. No, she must go alone at night and on foot if she would avoid suspicion.

That was a journey long to be remembered. Starting late at night, after the family and servants had all gone to bed, she walked many miles through the woods, across marshes and creeks, over which there were no bridges and often no foot-logs, and finally came to the Tyger, a stream where the only chance of crossing lay in wading a ford. It had rained and the stream was swollen. Yet there was no other way than wading through, and she waded. Deeper and deeper the water became, and stronger and stronger grew the current with each forward step. Near the middle of the stream, in fighting to retain her footing against the current, with the rushing waters up to her shoulders, she fell and becoming bewildered, "turned around," as she expressed it in later years, and could not tell for the life of her from which bank she had come and toward which bank she wanted to go. For some time—how long she never could tell—she plunged and struggled out in the stream, falling and regaining her footing, only to fall again, until finally she dragged herself out on the bank and lay, half-drowned and water-soaked, until she had recovered. She found the path again, decided that she was on the right side, and after a short time she was with her brother and his little party.

In a few words she told of the coming attack and of the peril of the little settlement, and urged that no delay be made in sending the warning to every settler. The soldiers had just returned from a long and tiresome excursion and were worn out, wet and hungry. There came complaint that the men were faint for lack of food, and though tired, wet and shivering herself, the girl at once said:

"Build me a fire and get me some cornmeal or flour."

It was short work to pull down a few boards from the roof of their hovel and start fire, and in a few minutes a hoecake was baking in the embers. This, done, and broken into pieces, was thrust into the shot pouches of the men so that they could eat as they ran on their messages of warning. So well did young Langston and his party do their work that when morning came and the "Bloody Scouts" descended on the settlement at Little Eden it was as empty of human occupation as was that other Eden after the angel of the Lord had driven out Adam and Eve. And the demure Miss Dicey, fresh and dainty, sat with her family at their breakfast and made irrelevant replies to the conversation until they rallied her upon her absent-mindedness. And it was many weeks before they knew of that twenty and more miles tramp through the woods and morasses in the darkness of the night.

The failure of the "Bloody Scouts" to find the settlers of Little Eden only added to the enmity of the band toward the few patriots in Laurens District, and though they could not trace the carrying of any warning to the Langston family, the growing hate and suspicion toward the old man marked him for a victim. After a sortie with a party of Whigs, of which his son was a member, made on the Tories it was decided that the old man must die, and the band went to his house to kill him and plunder his belongings. Mr. Langston, too infirm to escape or even to attempt to hide, and too proud to ask for mercy, faced them boldly and denied that he was in any way taking part in the struggle.

"You lie, you old rebel!" angrily shouted the leader, pointing a pistol at the old man's breast. The girl sprang between her father and the maddened Tory.

"You get out of the way, or I'll put a bullet through your heart."

"He's an old man, you coward," said the girl, almost beside herself with terror, but only clasping her father the closer and still keeping herself between him and his would-be assassin. Her fearless devotion must have touched another of the "Bloody Scouts," for he interfered and the old man was spared.

At another time, when coming home from a Whig settlement, Miss Langston was met by a company of Loyalists, who ordered her to tell them the news among the rebels.

"I have seen no rebels, and I know of no news," she said, trying to evade further parley, as the leader was a lawless character who had been a renegade from justice before he won the protection of the British by taking up arms against his neighbors.

"Yes, you have, too. Now, tell, or I'll shoot you," at the same time drawing his pistol.

"I'll tell you nothing," was her spirited reply.

"Tell, d—n you, or you'll die in your tracks."

"Shoot if you dare. I have nothing to tell."

The outlaw would have carried out his threat had not a young man of the company struck up the barrel of his pistol, and the bullet was wasted in the air. In the altercation that ensued between the guerrillas, the girl, who was mounted on a fleet young horse, made her escape.

It is told of her that at one time her brother, James Langston, had left a rifle in her keeping with the understanding that he would send a man for it who would give a certain countersign for it. A company of men came to the house one day, and one of them said that her brother had told him to bring his gun back with them. Miss Dicey went after the gun, and then at once chanced to think that she did not know but that they might be Tories. So she refused to give up the gun until they had given her the countersign.

"You're too late, Mistress Langston," said the leader, a big, handsome, happy-go-lucky sort of fellow, "both you and the gun are now in our possession."

"Oh, we are," she said, quick as a flash turning the gun point blank at his head and cocking it, "then come and get us."

She was so deeply in earnest that the young man lost no time in giving the countersign, and that very respectfully, while his companions laughed louder and louder. This was the young man, it is said, who came back after the war was over, and then kept on coming until one day he carried her away with him for better or worse.

On one occasion Miss Dicey came near getting into trouble from trying to carry water on both shoulders. A party of Whigs stopped at her father's house for refreshments, and in the conversation said that they were on their way to visit a Tory neighbor of the Langstons and take away his horses. As the neighbor was, in the main, a peaceful citizen and a good neighbor, the girl determined to save him his horses. She slipped out and going to the neighbor's house warned him that the horses had been marked for a change of ownership without his leave. What was her consternation to hear, accidentally, just before leaving for home, that the neighbor had sent a message to a band of Tories which he knew was in the neighborhood to capture the unsuspecting Whigs. She hurried back in time to warn the Whigs, and so in one day had saved the property of a Tory neighbor and probably the lives of several Whig friends.

Dicey Langston was married shortly after the war to Thomas Springfield, of Greenville, S. C., where she lived until her death, at a very old age, surrounded by a large and prosperous family. She was wont to boast in her last days that she had 32 sons and grandsons able to vote or fight in defense of their liberty. She sleeps in the old graveyard in Greenville, and her State is still proud to do her honor.*

Mrs. Springfield, *nee* Dicey Langston, is buried near Traveler's Rest, and about 1907 the D. A. R's. of Greenville placed a marker at her grave.

A REMARKABLE ADVENTURE OF SAMUEL CLOWNEY

Samuel Clowney was a native of Ireland and first settled on the Catawba River, in North Carolina, but finally located in South Carolina. He was an ardent Whig, and joined Colonel John Thomas' regiment at the Cedar Spring in July, 1780. With several

---
*This story of Dicey Langston is the reprint of an article published in the Greenville Mountaineer many years ago, and is supposed to have been written by Governor B. F Perry

others, Clowney obtained a short leave of absence to visit their friends and procure a change of raiment. They set off for the settlement on Fairforest, known as Ireland, or the Irish settlement, on account of the large number of settlers from the Emerald Isle. On their way they left with a Mrs. Foster some garments to be washed, and appointed a certain hour and an out-of-the-way place where they would meet her and get them on their return to the camp. In accordance with this arrangement, when the party reached Kelso's Creek, about five miles from Cedar Spring, they dismounted and left the road, going through the woods to the appointed place to get their washing. Clowney and a negro named Paul were left to take charge of the horses until they should return. While Clowney's comrades were absent, he saw five Tories ride down to the creek. Clowney at once conceived an idea. In low tones he directed the negro Paul how he should act the part of a company while he went forward. He then yelled out in a commanding tone to his imaginary party: "Cock your guns, boys, and fire at the word;" and then advancing to the banks of the stream, just as the Tories were passing through it, demanded who they were? They answered, "Friends of the King" Not dreaming of a Whig party in the country, great was their astonishment when Clowney peremptorily ordered them to come upon the bank, lay down their arms and surrender, or "every bugger of them would be instantly cut to pieces." Being somewhat slow in yielding, Clowney sternly repeated his demand, and threatening them with his well-directed rifle of the fatal consequences of disobedience. The terror-stricken Tories, believing that a large force was upon them, quietly surrendered without uttering a word.

Paul took charge of their guns, and Clowney gave some orders to his imaginary soldiers to follow at some distance in the rear, and commanded the prisoners to "right about wheel," when he marched them across the creek, directly before him, till he at length reached the rest of the party at Mrs. Foster's washing camp. They were then conducted to Colonel Thomas' quarters at the Cedar Spring. The prisoners were much chagrined when they learned that their captors consisted of only two men, one of whom was an unarmed negro. When Colonel Thomas was told that Clowney and the negro alone had captured the whole party, he seemed at first to be a little incredulous that they could accomplish such a feat.

"Why, Paddy," said the Colonel, "how did you take all these men?"

"May it plase yer honor," he replied exultantly, "by me faith, I *surrounded* them."

It is said that Clowney's achievement at Kelso's Creek was well attested by many who knew him, and reveals the fact that he was a real hero.

One of his acquaintances, in his terse way, described him as "a little dry Irishman," and though he belonged to the Presbyterian Church, like all of his Celtic race of that day, while not intemperate, he could not refrain from getting *dry* once in a while, and dearly loved "a wee bit of the crathure" occasionally.

A writer says: "He possessed a remarkable talent for sarcasm and invective; but he was, nevertheless, a most kind-hearted, benevolent man, greatly beloved by all who knew him. His brogue was quite rich, and this, combined with a fund of genial Irish wit, made him a fascinating companion."

He lived until September the 27th, 1824, when he passed away in his eighty-second year.

He had a son, William K. Clowney, who was a graduate of the South Carolina College; became a prominent lawyer and represented his native district for four years in Congress. General James K. Means married a daughter of Samuel Clowney.*

WILLIAM SHARP'S ADVENTURES AT GRINDAL'S AND LOVE'S FORD

William Sharp was a brave and fearless hero, who lived on Brown's Creek, a few miles northeast of the present town of Union. A party of British and Tory raiders were passing through the country, committing their usual depredations, and coming to the Grindal Ford, on Pacolet River, they encamped for the night. Without the least suspicion on their part, Sharp and two of his associates were close on their trail. The night being very dark, their first intimation of danger was Sharp's bold demand for their immediate surrender, or they would be blown into that region which is reputed to be pretty hot. In the surprise and consternation of the moment, they begged for quarter, and twenty men laid down their arms. The victors threw the enemy's guns into the river before they dis-

*Draper's "Kings Mountain and Its Heroes," pages 127-128

covered the fewness of their captors, and the captives were driven into the nearest Whig encampment.

Love's Ford is on Broad River, a few miles below its confluence with the Pacolet. In time of the Revolution, crossing at that place was difficult and not without danger to persons unacquainted with it. In addition to these perils, the country around was in a wild and unsettled state. The low ground was covered with dense canebrakes, and the hills, which were many, were clad with vines and other undergrowth. Hence, this vicinity offered excellent shelter for fugitives during the period of Tory ascendency in South Carolina. At this time the ford was rarely passed, except by armed bands and the more adventurous persons in the vicinity. The Whigs of the neighborhood were accustomed to frequent the locality for the double purpose of concealment and to embarrass the movements of the enemy. On the evening of the next day after the battle of Cowpens, a party of some fifty or sixty British troops, who had succeeded in making a safe retreat that far, were moving on towards Love's Ford. Their object was to reach Cornwallis' camp, in York District. Some distance from the river their leader turned off the road to the house of a Mr. Palmer to get directions. Here he met Sharp. The latter immediately presented his rifle and ordered him to surrender. The officer obeyed, and Sharp then learned his purposes as quickly as possible. Having secured the commander, he determined to lose no time in pursuing his party. He went to his hiding place in the woods to rally his little force, which consisted of James Savage, Richard Hughes, and perhaps a few others. About the time the men were gotten together, a Mrs. Hall, a resident in the vicinity, came up in great haste. She had seen the British on their way, and ran to give the Whigs notice. Sharp and his party pursued and, when a half mile from the ford, they met a man running as for life. He reported that on crossing the river he encountered a party of British soldiers; that they had stopped on the top of a hill, apparently with a view of spending the night; that their armor and uniforms glistened in the sun, and though they took no notice of him, he was greatly alarmed. Sharp led his men on and suddenly they presented themselves before the enemy and ordered them to surrender. The summons was obeyed by some thirty or forty men. The balance ran off down the river, and some threw their guns into it and leaped in themselves. Sharp led his prisoners to Morgan's army and delivered them up as prisoners of war.*

Among the "bravest of the brave" who fought under Colonels Williams and Brandon at Kings Mountain were those daring heroes **Sharp at Kings Mountain** —William Sharp and William Giles. This battlefield was a suitable arena for the exploits of such brave and fearless spirits. Giles entered the contest with his accustomed zeal and, while fighting, he received a ball which passed through the back of his neck, and he fell as if dead. Sharp, who was his fellow-hero, his neighbor, his friend and relation, stopped for a moment, and as he viewed him, he brushed a tear from his eye, saying: "Poor fellow, he is dead; but if I am spared a little longer, I will avenge his fall." Sharp passed on with greater determination than ever, and after firing his rifle several times, to his great astonishment, he saw Giles raise himself up, rest on his elbow, and commence loading his gun. In the olden time, when horses ran at large and were difficult to catch, they were sometimes *creased;* i. e., they were shot through the upper part of the neck, when they would fall helpless to the ground, but after a little while would recover. Giles got *creased* and was soon upon his feet again, fought through the remainder of the battle, and lived to a good old age.†

MAJOR SAMUEL OTTERSON

The adventure of Sharp at Love's Ford has its counterpart in the following, which is taken from Mills' "Statistics of South Carolina":

Major Samuel Otterson, being on his way to join Morgan at Cowpens, was followed by a few badly-mounted volunteers. Finding on his approach that the battle was begun, he determined to halt his men near a cross-road, which he knew the enemy would take on their return, and wait either to make some prisoners in case of their defeat, or to attempt the rescue of the prisoners who might be in their hands. It was not long before a considerable body of British horsemen were discovered coming down the road in full speed. They appeared to have been defeated. Otterson now proposed to his men to follow the enemy and, if possible, make some prisoners;

---
*Saye's "Memoirs of McJunkin"
†Draper's "Kings Mountain and Its Heroes"

but only one man was willing to go with him. Mounting that man on the best horse in the company, and arming themselves in the best manner possible, they pushed on after the flying enemy. In the pursuit Major Otterson prudently determined to keep some distance in the rear until dark. He occasionally stopped at some house along the road, ascertained the situation, number and distance of the enemy, and found his suspicions verified, that they had been defeated and that these horsemen were a part of Tarleton's cavalry. Towards dusk, Otterson and his companion pushed their horses nearer the enemy, and when it was dark, dashed in among them with a shout, fired their guns and ordered them to surrender. The darkness prevented the enemy from knowing the number of those by whom they were surprised, and they surrendered at once. They were required to dismount, come forward and deliver up their arms, which they did. They all being secured, a light was struck, and nothing could have exceeded the mortification of the British officer when he found that he had surrendered to two men.

But this was not the end of this gallant affair. The prisoners, thirty in number, were all conducted safely by their captors into North Carolina, and delivered to Morgan as prisoners of war. Several days had to elapse before this was done, during which time these brave men never closed their eyes in sleep.

Major Otterson resided on Tyger River, in the vicinity of Hamilton's Ford. He distinguished himself on several occasions during the war, and proved to be a highly respectable and useful citizen after its close. He finally removed to Alabama.

THE NARROW ESCAPE OF CAPTAIN JAMES CALDWELL

James Caldwell was born July 8th, 1755. With his mother, he came to South Carolina and settled in Newberry District about 1770. He was a Revolutionary patriot and commanded a company at Cowpens. He belonged to Pickens' Brigade, and was in a position that exposed him to the charge of Tarleton's cavalry. When the second line under Pickens was attacked, Tarleton was cutting down the militia, but not until they had delivered a most effective fire, when the advancing British column was only thirty or forty yards away. It was there that Captain James Caldwell was cut down by a dragoon. His hands were severely mutilated in the attempt to protect his head, which received many sabre cuts, and one blow was delivered below his right eye on the cheek bone, which left a scar and a lump which disfigured his face as long as he lived. He was supposed to be dead, and after the action was over he was sought for by his brother William among the slain. He was found still alive and suffering more for water than from his many wounds. This his brother brought to him in his hat. His wounds were bound up with strips torn from his brother's shirt. He was then removed to a neighbor's house, and after many weeks of suffering recovered. He was thus incapacitated for further service during the war. He died in 1813.*

THE RUGGED HONESTY OF ADAM SKAIN

Three brothers, Adam, Peter and John Skain, resided in the Santuc section of Union District and belonged to the command of Colonel Thomas Brandon. All three were in the battle of Cowpens, and John fell mortally wounded. After the fight was over, Adam was carrying some water to his brother John, and passing a wounded British officer, he asked him for a drink, Skain promised that when he waited on his brother, who was in the same fix, he would return and give him some water, which he did. So great was the gratitude of this wounded officer for this kindness that he told Skain that he had a gold watch in his pocket, and that he wanted him to take it out, that he might have it. Skain thanked him, but declined, saying: "It never shall be said that Adam Skain plundered a fallen enemy." The Briton then asked a by-stander to take the watch out and present it to Skain for him, and then he accepted it with appropriate thanks. John Skain died and was buried on the battlefield.

"LONG SAM" ABNEY

Samuel Abney—better known as "Long Sam" Abney, to distinguish him from others of that name—was a resident of Edgefield County, South Carolina, and a good Whig both in principle and practice. When Charlestown fell, in May, 1780, and Ninety-Six and Augusta were occupied by large British forces, many loyal patriots, including several distinguished officers, felt well-nigh forced to take British protection, which they understood to mean that their lives and property were to be safe-guarded; but they soon

*O'Neal's "Annals of Newberry"

found that the British leaders construed it quite differently. They were treated as conquered Rebels, and in many instances compelled to take up arms and fight against the freedom of their country. Such was Abney's situation. He was forced into Ferguson's Loyalists corps, and was marched to Kings Mountain.

At the commencement of the battle, he stationed himself behind a rock, where he would be secure from the bullets of either side, for he resolved that he could not, and would not, take part in shooting his friends, and thereby array himself against the cause that he loved. But amid the shower of missiles that were soon flying in every direction, he found that he was not so safe as he supposed himself to be; for while leaning on his rifle, probably anxious to see the progress of the contest, he unintentionally exposed his person more than he had designed, when a ball penetrated the fleshy part of his arm. This made him "a little mad," as he expressed it; still he had, as yet, no thought of taking part in the fray. A few moments later he was struck with another ball, which made him "mighty mad," and he then turned in and fought with the bravery of the boldest of Ferguson's troops. Before the action was over, he was riddled with bullets, seven having taken effect on his person. He was left in a helpless, unconscious condition, lying among the slain and wounded on the battlefield; but fortunately the cool dews and frost of the ensuing night revived him, and he crawled to a nearby branch and slacked his burning thirst. He was subsequently found by a resident in that vicinity, who compassionately carried him to his home, bound up his wounds and nursed him for many days, when he recovered and returned to his home and friends. He lived to a good old age, and used to relate with much merriment how he was shot and how he was provoked to shoot back again at Kings Mountain.*

"OLD" ARTHUR PATTERSON

On Kings Creek, in the neighborhood of Kings Mountain, resided Arthur Patterson, an Irishman, who was devoted to the Whig cause, and with him were his several sons, who were settled around him. On the morning preceding the battle, a party of Ferguson's foragers, who were ranging along the creek, came across three of the young Pattersons, Arthur, Jr., Thomas and William, together

---
*Draper's "King Mountain and Its Heroes," pp 310-312

with James Lindsay. They were arrested by Ferguson's party and marched to his camp, where they were put under guard to await trial. The same day, learning of the capture of his sons, "Old" Arthur, the father of the Pattersons, started for the camp, to see if he could do anything towards securing their release. Just before his arrival, the Whigs suddenly made their appearance, encircled the mountain and began their attack. During the progress of the action, while the Americans were pressing the enemy, the guards were ordered to take their places in the line of defense and aid, if possible, in checking the mountaineers. The prisoners, being left to themselves amid the confusion of the battle, they resolved to make a break for liberty. Lindsay, with William and Arthur Patterson, Jr., ran through an opening in the British lines and escaped unhurt—Arthur with a portion of the rope with which he had been fastened still dangling from his neck. Thomas Patterson, who seemed to have been of a more belligerent nature, watched his opportunity and, between fires, he made a bold dash for the Whig lines. When he reached Shelby's corps, he picked up the gun of a wounded soldier and fought bravely until victory was proclaimed. His aged father was not so fortunate. As he came in view of the noble army of patriots, his old Irish blood was stirred within him, and hoping that he might be of some help in liberating both his sons and his country, he warmly joined in the fray and was killed.*

One of the twenty-three who laid down their lives at Kings Mountain in the defense of American liberty was "Old" Arthur Patterson, a man long past the age when they are supposed to fight in war. Some of his descendants are living in the vicinity of that noted battlefield until this day.

THE GOFORTH BROTHERS

Wilkinson, in his "Memoirs," states that Colonel Shelby related to him that at Kings Mountain, *"two brothers, expert riflemen, were seen to present at each other, to fire and fall at the same instant.* Their names were given to me, but they have escaped my memory."

Draper thinks it not improbable that these two brothers who confronted and killed each other, as related by Colonel Shelby, were of the Goforth family, of Rutherford County, North Carolina. At least four brothers—Preston Goforth, on the Whig side; John Go-

*Draper's "King Mountains and Its Heroes."

forth and two other brothers, on the Tory side—all participated in the battle and were all killed. It was a most remarkable fatality.

ANOTHER WHIG SOLDIER KILLS HIS BROTHER

Draper relates another instance of brother killing brother, as follows: "A Whig soldier noticed a good deal of execution in a particular part of his line from a certain direction on the other side. On close observation, he discovered that the fatal firing on the part of Ferguson's men proceeded from behind a hollow chestnut tree, and *through a hole in it*. He concluded to make an effort to silence that battery, and aimed his rifle shots repeatedly at the aperture. At length, the firing from that quarter ceased. After the battle, his curiosity prompted him to examine the place, and he discovered that he had killed one of his own brothers and wounded another, who had joined the Loyalist forces and had concealed themselves in the rear of this tree. So much did the patriot brother take the circumstances to heart that he became almost deranged in consequence."

THE FOUR LOGAN BROTHERS

There were four brothers, all of Lincoln County, North Carolina, who took part in the battle of Kings Mountain, viz.: William and Joseph Logan, on the Whig side, and John and Thomas Logan, among Ferguson's forces. William Logan belonged to Captain John Mattock's company, and was close by his captain when he fell at the northeast end of the mountain—the fatal ball having been fired when Ferguson's men made their first charge down the hill. Joseph Logan, the other Whig brother, was a Baptist preacher, and during the engagement he, with a Presbyterian minister, wrestled with the Lord in prayer, as in the olden time, to stay up their hands and give them the victory. Thomas Logan, one of the Tory brothers, had his thigh badly shattered and was left on the field of battle. John Logan, the other Tory brother, was taken among the prisoners, and afterwards died a pauper.*

The above incidents serve to show how the country was divided, and the awful conditions that existed in time of the Revolution— neighbor against neighbor, friend against friend, family against family, brother against brother, father against son, and son against

---

*Draper's "Kings Mountain and Its Heroes"

father, the one grappling at the throat of the other for the supremacy.

THE AFFAIR AT GRAHAM'S FORT

William Graham was born in Augusta County, Virginia, in 1742, emigrated to North Carolina before the Revolution, and settled on the north bank of Buffalo Creek, in what is now Cleveland County, only a short distance from the South Carolina line, and about eight miles northwest from Kings Mountain and about seven miles southeast from the present town of Shelby. He was a member of the Provincial Congress in 1775, and was appointed Colonel of Tryon County, serving on the snow campaign and Rutherford's Cherokee expedition. In the summer of 1780, he took part in the capture of Thickety Fort and the second battle of Cedar Spring, or Wofford's Iron Works.

Colonel Graham's residence on Buffalo was a large hewn-log house, weather-boarded, and to some extent fortified, and was well fitted for a successful defense against any party with small arms alone, when not prepared to prosecute a regular siege. It was called *Graham's Fort*.

Some time in 1780, a Tory marauding party, consisting of about twenty-three in number, suddenly made their appearance before Graham's Fort. There were many people, old and young, congregated there, but the only ones capable of using arms in the defense were Colonel Graham, David Dickey and William Twitty, the Colonel's step-son—a brave youth of nineteen summers. These three were fearless and determined to make the strongest resistance possible. The Tory party demanded admittance, but Colonel Graham and his associates promptly and positively refused. A vigorous assault was begun, the Tories firing several volleys without doing much damage, yelling at the top of their voices, after each discharge, "D—n you, won't you surrender now?"

One fellow, John Burke, who was more venturesome than the rest, ran up to the house, thrust his gun through a crack and aimed at young Twitty, when Susan, the sister of the young soldier, seeing his danger, jerked her brother down just as the gun fired, the ball embedding itself in the opposite wall. She then looked out through the aperture and saw Burke, not far off, on his knees, re-loading for another fire; and quickly comprehending the situation, exclaimed: "Brother William, now's your chance—shoot the rascal!" In a moment, young Twitty's gun fired and the impudent Tory tumbled over, shot through the head. Miss Twitty then performed a most daring and dangerous feat. Desirous of rendering the patriot cause any service in her power, she at once unbarred the door, darted out and brought in, amid a shower of Tory bullets, Burke's gun and ammunition as trophies of victory. Fortunately, she escaped unhurt. This was a brave act for a girl of seventeen, and Susan Twitty deserves to be classed among the heroines of the Revolution. She subsequently married John Miller and died April the 14th, 1825, at the age of sixty-two years.

Losing one of their number killed and three wounded, the Tories gave up the assault and at length beat a retreat. Anticipating that the enemy, smarting under their repulse, would return with reinforcements, Colonel Graham and his friends retired to a more distant place of safety, when, sure enough, a large Tory party did return, and finding no opposition, they plundered the house of clothing, valuables, etc., and carried off six of the Colonel's negroes

William Twitty, the youth, who aided so gallantly in the defense of Graham's Fort, was born in South Carolina, July 13th, 1761; he fought at Kings Mountain, and subsequent to the war lived at Twitty's Ford, on Broad River, where he died February 2nd, 1816, in his fifty-fifth year. He had many worthy descendants, among whom were William L. and Dr. T. B. Twitty, grandsons, the latter living at the old homestead.*

A TORY'S SAD EXPERIENCE AT KINGS MOUNTAIN

The following is taken from Draper's "Kings Mountain and Its Heroes," page 313:

"Drury Mathis, who resided at Saluda Old Town, on the Saluda River, in South Carolina, some two and a half miles above the mouth of Little River, had united his fortunes with Ferguson. In the third charge which was made against Campbell's men, Mathis was badly wounded and fell to the ground. The spot where he had fallen was half way down the mountain, where the balls from the Virginians fell around him almost as thick as hail. He used to relate that as the mountaineers passed over him, he would play 'possum, but he could plainly observe their faces and eyes, and to him

*Draper's "Kings Mountain and Its Heroes," pp 145-146

those bold, brave riflemen appeared like so many devils from the infernal regions, so full of excitement were they as they darted like enraged lions up the mountain. He said they were the most powerful looking men he ever beheld; not over-burdened with fat, but tall, raw-boned, and sinewy, with long matted hair—such men, as a body, as were never before seen in the Carolinas. With his feet down the declivity, he said he could not but observe that his Loyalist friends were very generally over-shooting the Americans, and that if ever a poor fellow hugged mother earth closely, he did on that trying occasion. After the battle—the next day, probably—he was kindly taken to a house in that region and nursed till his wound had healed, when he returned to Ninety-Six an humbled, if not a wiser man. He lived to enjoy a good old age, but used to stoutly swear that he never desired to see Kings Mountain again."

THE ORIGIN OF THE NAME FAIRFOREST

As Fairforest is the most historic stream in the up-country, and reference to it having been far more frequent than that of any other, it is fit to conclude this work with the origin of the name.

The most trustworthy and reliable authority is James H. Saye. The following is from his "Memoirs of McJunkin": About twenty-four years before the United States became a nation, the first party of white men found a home in this vicinity (*i. e.*, of the old Fairforest Presbyterian Church). Among them was George Story and James McIlwain. They encamped upon an eminence (said to be about two miles east from Glenn Springs), commanding a beautiful prospect. A valley stretched far in the distance. A grove of lofty trees concealed the meanderings of the stream that fertilized the extended plain. The rays of the declining sun lit up the vast amphitheatre of tree tops waving gently in the beeze, overlooked now for the first time by the eyes of white men. One of the party, believed to have been James McIlwain, looked abroad for a time over the rich scenery of the place and exclaimed, *"What a fair forest!"* The party immediately gave the name to the place, and it soon fastened upon the principal stream in the vicinity; hence, the northeastern branch of Tyger River has been called, since those days, Fairforest Creek, a bold and beautiful stream, which rising in the vicinity of the mountains, sweeps through the central parts of the present districts of Spartanburg and Union.

Some Other Heroic Personages

This story is doubted by some because, they say, that these early settler were rugged, uneducated, and had none of the finer poetic perceptions or imaginations. We believe that Mr. Saye's narrative is true, for two reasons: First, That these pioneers were not roughnecks nor ignoramuses. Listen to him again: "It may not, however, be improper to remark that the men who composed the congregation—the early Fairforest—were not an ignorant rabble, though their homes had been recently a wilderness. They were a body of citizens collected from various parts, and had, generally, come from communities enjoying high privileges of a social and religious nature." Second, That Mr. Saye was for a long time pastor of the immediate descendants of these first settlers, and, no doubt, heard the story repeated many times, as told to them by their fathers and mothers.

In some way, it has gone out that Lord Cornwallis gave Fairforest its name. Even so eminent an historian as Dr. Landrum gives Cornwallis the credit. We regret this exceedingly, for it cannot be true. The name was a fixture long before Cornwallis ever set foot on American soil. The Presbyterian Church composed of these pioneers took the name—Fairforest—as early as 1762.

Morgan Edwards, a distinguished Baptist preacher and historian, visited the Fairforest Baptist Church in 1772. The house of worship then stood near the east bank of the stream, a few miles west of Union. Hear Mr. Edwards: "Fairforest (1760). So distinguished from a tract of land where the meeting house stands in the County of Craven and Parish of St. Marks, about two hundred miles N.W. from Charlestown, and seven hundred and fifty S.W. from Philadelphia. The land is formed into an angle by the running of *Fairforest* River into the Tyger, etc."

The above is a part of a certified copy of the original Edward's manuscript; hence it is unquestionably correct. The proof is, therefore, conclusive that Cornwallis had nothing to do with it; that the very first settlers did name it, and why not give the credit to James McIlwain. Anyone wishing to look on the grave of McIlwain and read the epitaph on his tombstone can do so by visiting the old Fairforest cemetery, eleven miles from Union, on the Meansville road.